PEOPLE OF COLOR
Black Genealogical Records and Abstracts from Missouri Sources

Volume 2

Teresa Blattner

HERITAGE BOOKS
2010

HERITAGE BOOKS
AN IMPRINT OF HERITAGE BOOKS, INC.

Books, CDs, and more—Worldwide

For our listing of thousands of titles see our website at
www.HeritageBooks.com

Published 2010 by
HERITAGE BOOKS, INC.
Publishing Division
100 Railroad Ave. #104
Westminster, Maryland 21157

Copyright © 1998 Teresa Blattner

Other Heritage Books by the author:

Divorces, Separations and Annulments in Missouri, 1769 to 1850

Gasconade County, Missouri Marriage Records: Books A-C, 1821–1873

People of Color: Black Genealogical Records and Abstracts from Missouri Sources, Volumes 1 and 2

CD: People of Color: Black Genealogical Records and Abstracts from Missouri Sources, Volumes 1 and 2

All rights reserved. No part of this book may be reproduced or transmitted in any form or by any means, electronic or mechanical, including photocopying, recording or by any information storage and retrieval system without written permission from the author, except for the inclusion of brief quotations in a review.

International Standard Book Numbers
Paperbound: 978-0-7884-0927-1
Clothbound: 978-0-7884-8369-1

ACKNOWLEDGEMENTS

I would like to thank the staffs of the Missouri State Archives, the Western Historical Manuscript Collection-Columbia, and the Callaway County Public Library. A very special thanks to all the individuals who helped me locate cemeteries in their areas.

PREFACE

After much controversy, the 1820 Missouri Compromise was passed. Missouri became a state on August 21, 1821, with the stipulation free blacks could not be prevented from entering or remaining in that state. Since many of the other slave states forbade manumitted slaves and free blacks from remaining within their borders, they migrated to Missouri.

This volume presents the first transcription of free black households extracted from the 1830 and 1840 census, plus many other records pertaining to free blacks in Missouri. On the early censuses, only the head of each household was named. All others were categorized by sex, with males listed first, then by age groups. Age categories are: those under ten, ten to twenty-three, twenty-four to thirty-five, thirty-six to fifty-four, fifty-five to ninety-nine, and those one hundred years of age and older.

Other information in this volume has been extracted from territorial, county, state, federal, and religious records. I hope this work will be of use to those researching their own ancestry. Good luck!

TABLE OF CONTENTS

60th Regiment U. S. C. T. Infantry............1

Marriage Records............................25
   Nodaway, Jefferson, Miller, Dade, Cooper, and Audrain Counties.

Cemeteries..................................45
   Johnson, Boone, Callaway, Newton, Greene, Harrison, Lincoln, Howard, Saline, Lafayette, Moniteau, Livingston, Pike, Cooper, Montgomery, and Chariton Counties.

Slave Schedules.............................83
   Cole and Osage Counties.

Burial Records..............................95
   Greene, Oregon, Livingston, Callaway, and Barton Counties.

Free Blacks................................107

Church Records.............................121

Territorial Records........................135

Transfers, Sales, and Hires................145

Claims for Compensation of Enlisted Slaves..161

Resolution by the First Session of the tenth
   General Assembly........................169

60th REGIMENT
U.S.C.T. INFANTRY

After each enlistees name is their rank, company, age, date and location at the time of enlistment, and other relevant information.

Smith ADAMS, Pvt, Co. K, 12/3/1863, Benton Barracks.
Calvin ALLEN, Pvt, Co. K, 23, 11/26/1863, Mexico.
Henry ALLEN, Corp, Co. G, 26, 10/1/1863, St. Louis.
John H. ALLEN, Pvt, Co. D, 18, 9/6/1863, Canton.
Reuben ALLEN, Pvt, Co. K, 20, 11/23/1863, Macon.
Thomas ALLEN, Pvt, Co. G, ?, 10.1.1863, St. Louis, died 5/29/1864 at the regimental hospital at Helena, Ark..
Thomas ALLISON, Pvt, Co. K, 23, 11/24/1863, Washington.
George ANDERSON, Pvt, Co. G, 17, 10/1/1863, St. Louis.
Francis A. ANDERSON, Pvt, Co. I, 18, 11/18/1863, St. Louis.
Lindsey ANDERSON, Pvt, Co. I, 20, 11/20/1863, Macon.
Charles ANTHONY, Corp, Co. I, 24, 11/18/1863, Chillicothe.
Richard ATWELL, Pvt, Co. G, 26, 11/17/1864, St. Charles.
James AUSTEN, Pvt, Co. G, 22, 10/1/1863, St. Louis.
Peter BAILEY, Pvt, Co. H, 28, 10/21/1863, St. Louis.
Nelson BAILEY, Pvt, Co. K, 18, 11/25/1863, Warrensburg.
Wm. BANION, Pvt, Co. H, 28, 10/27/1863, St. Louis.
Edward BANKS, Corp, Co. G, 26, 10/1/1863, St. Louis.
Thornton BANKS, Pvt, Co. K, 18, 11/23/1863, Warrensburg.
Samuel BARBOUR, Pvt, Co. I, 23, 10/10/1863, Paris.
Jacob BARNES, Pvt, Co. K, ?, 11/29/1863, Mexico, died 1/14/1864 at Helena, Ark..

Rufus BASKET, Pvt, Co. G, ?, 10/1/1863, St. Louis, died 7/19/1865 at Little Rock, Ark. of consumption.
Henry BASS, Corp, Co. G, 28, 10/1/1863, St. Louis.
Wm. BATES, Pvt, Co. H, ?, 12/5/1863, St. Louis, died 12/30/1863.
Wm. BATES, Pvt, Co. H, 18, 11/13/1863, St. Louis.
Wm. BAYMONT, Pvt, Co. H, ?, 11/1/1863, St. Louis, died 11/19/1864 at Helena, Ark. of chronic bronchitus.
Frank BECKET, Pvt, Co. F, ?, 11/26/1863, St. Louis, transfered from the company on 12/9/1863.
Charles BELL, Pvt, Co. H, 22, 10/28/1863, St. Louis.
Henry BELL, Pvt, Co. G, 21, 10/1/1863, St. Louis.
George BENJAMIN, Pvt, Co. G, 22, 10/1/1863, St. Louis.
Albert BENNETT, Pvt, Co. G, 22, 10/1/1863, St. Louis.
Thomas BENTON, Pvt, Co. A, ?, 9/4/1863, Monticello, died 12/24/1863, at Helena, Ark. of pneumonia.
Isaac BERNARD, Pvt, Co. H, ?, 10/13/1863, St. Louis, died 1/18/1864.
John BERNARD, Pvt, Co. H, ?, 10/13/1863, St. Louis, died 12/27/1863.
Henry BERRY, Pvt, Co. A, ?, 9/4/1863, Monticello, died 12/26/1863 at Benton Barracks.
Peter BERRY, Pvt, Co. A, ?, 9/4/1863, Monticello, died 2/13/1864 at Helena, Ark.. diarrhea.
Peter M. BERRY, Pvt, Co. E, drafted, mustered in on 11/17/1864 at Jefferson City.
Robert BEAS, Pvt, 38, Co. I, 10/28/1863, Shelbyville.
Jackson BIGGS, Pvt, Co. B, 20, 8/29/1863, Lagrange.
Redman BIGSBY, Pvt, Co. B, ?, 8/29/1863, Lagrange.
Joseph BINGHAM, Pvt, Co. K, ?, 11/25/1863, Sedalia, died 5/8/1864 at Helena, Ark. of typhus malarial fever.

Wm. BLATTNER, Corp, Co. G, 19, 10/1/1863, St. Louis.
David BLUE, Pvt, Co. I, ?, 11/18/1863, Chillicothe.
Moses BOHANNON, Pvt, Co. G, 19, 10/1/1863, St. Louis.
Napoleon BONAPARTE, Pvt, Co. I, 45, 10/1/1863, Brunswick.
John BOOKER, Pvt, Co. A, 19, substitute, mustered in on 12/14/1864.
George W. BOOSIER, Sgt, Co. B, 23, 8/18/1863, Lagrange.
Albert BOWLER, Pvt, Co. H, 22, 9/27/1863, St. Louis.
Edward BOYD, Sgt, Co. A, 23, 9/9/1863, Edina.
James BRAWLEY, Pvt, Co. F, ?, 9/28/1863, Liberty.
Lawson BROWN, Pvt, Co. G, ?, 10/1/1863, St. Louis, died 8/29/1864.
Thomas BROWN, Pvt, Co. A, 9/9/1863, Edina, died 12/5/1864.
Foster BROWN, Pvt, Co. A, 44, 9/9/1863, Edina.
George BROWN, Pvt, Co. I, ?, 11/20/1863, Macon.
John BROWN, Wagoner, Co. B, ?, 8/29/1863, Lagrange, died 3/22/1864.
John BROWN, Pvt, Co. G, 22, 10/1/1863, St. Louis.
Samuel BROWN, Pvt, Co. A, 22, 9/9/1863, Edina.
Samuel BROWN, Co. G, 18, 10/1/1863, St. Louis.
Wright BROWN, Pvt, Co. E, 18, substitute, mustered in on 11/17/1864 at Jefferson City.
Silas BROWNING, Pvt, Co. D, ?, 9/10/1863, New Ark.
Alfred BRYANT, Pvt, Co. E, ?, 9/28/1863, Edina.
George BRYANT, Pvt, Co. B, 25, substitute, mustered in 12/30/1864 at St. Louis.
Walter BUCKLIN, Pvt, Co. E, 18, substitute, mustered in 11/17/1864 at Jefferson City.
Wm. BUCKNER, Pvt, Co. E, ?, 9/29/1863, Canton, died 3/27/1864.
Alfred BURDERS, Pvt, Co. H, ?, 10/27/1863, St. Louis, died 3/23/1864.
Francis BURROWS, Pvt, Co. A, ?, substitute, mustered in on 12/13/1864, St. Louis.
Jefferson BUTLER, Pvt, Co. F, ?, 9/20/1863, Chillicothe, died 8/14/1865 at Little Rock,

Ark. of interment fever.
Edward CAMP, Pvt, Co. G, 10/12/1863, St. Louis, died 7/2/1864.
Mark CAMP, Pvt, Co. G, 10/12/1863, St. Louis, died 2/22/1864 at Helena, Ark. of pneumonia.
Lewis O. CARROLL, Pvt, Co. F, 24, 10/2/1863, Brunswick.
Frank CARSON, Pvt, Co. E, 18, substitute, mustered in on 11/16/1864 at Jefferson City.
Allen CARTER, Pvt, Co. E, 20, 12/16/1864, St. Louis.
Ballet CARTER, Pvt, Co. H, 21, 10/25/1863, St. Louis.
Thornton CARTER, Pvt, Co. B, ?, 8/29/1863, Brunswick, died 7/3/1864.
Frank CHAMBERS, Pvt, Co. B, 25, 8/29/1863, Brunswick.
Wm. CHAMBERS, Pvt, Co. B, 18, 8/29/1863, Lagrange.
Albert CHANDLER, Pvt, Co. I, ?, 10/10/1863, Paris.
Richard CHAPMAN, Corp, Co. G, ?, 10/1/1863, St. Louis.
Alex CHASSEAN, Pvt, Co. G, 18, 10/12/1863, St. Louis.
Hampton CHASSEAN, Pvt, Co. G, 21, 10/1/1863, St. Louis.
Harry CHEEK, Pvt, Co. F, 18, 11/16/1863, St. Louis, tranfered from Co. I, on 12/9/1863.
Aaron CLARK, Pvt, Co. K, ?, 11/29/1863, Mexico, died 7/22/1865 at Little Rock, Ark. from typhus malarial fever.
Clemens CLARK, Pvt, Co. K, 43, 11/27/1863, Sedalia.
Alfred CLAY, Pvt, Co. G, 28, 10/21/1863, St. Louis.
Charles CLAY, Pvt, Co. G, 21, 10/12/1863, St. Louis.
John H. CLAY, Corp, Co. G, 22, 10/12/1863, St. Louis.
Thomas CLAY, Pvt, Co. A, 44, 9/9/1863, Edina.
Lewis COCK, Wagoneer, Co. I, ?, 10/2/1863, Keytesville.
Henderson COLLINS, Pvt, Co. K, 22, 11/28/1863, Jefferson City.
Isaac COLUMBUS, Pvt, Co. G, ?, 10/1/1863, St.

Louis.
George COMBS, Pvt, Co. F, 18, 9/20/1863, Chillicothe.
Wm. J. COOPER, Pvt, Co. G, 21, 10/1/1863, St. Louis.
Henry COUTON, Pvt, Co. K, 21, 10/28/1863, Sedalia.
Scott COVER, Pvt, Co. H, ?, 10/25/1863, St. Louis.
Edmund COX, Pvt, Co. I, ?, 11/18/1863, Chillicothe, died 8/14/1865 at Little Rock, Ark. from inflammation of the stomach.
Archie CRAMER, Pvt, Co. H, 22, 10/30/1863, St. Louis, died 9/16/1865 at Powhatton, Ark. of pneumonia.
Felix CROCKET, Pvt, Co. K, 18, 11/27/1863, Sedalia.
Charles F. CUMMINGS, Corp Sgt, Co. F, ?, 10/6/1864, Helena, Ark..
Charles CUNNINGHAM, Corp, Co. K, 22, 11/26/1863, Sedalia.
George W. CUNNINGHAM, Pvt, Co. K, 20, 11/29/1863, Mexico.
Samuel CUNNINGHAM, Pvt, Co. K, 18, 11/28/1863, Mexico.
Polk DALLAS, Pvt, Co. G, ?, 10/1/1863, St. Louis, died 12/1/1863 at Benton Barracks from typhoid fever.
John DANIELS, Pvt, Co. k, 20, 11/28/1863, Sedalia.
Robert DANIELS, Pvt, Co. G, 31, 3/1/1865, Jefferson City.
Elijah DATSON, Pvt, Co. C, ?, 9/2/1863, Brunswick, died 11/11/1863, Keokuk, Iowa of pneumonia.
Charles DAVIS, Corp, Co. B, 19, 9/22/1863, Chillicothe.
Frank DAVIS, Pvt, Co. H, 19, 10/13/1863, St. Louis.
Henry DAVIS, Pvt, Co. H, ?, 10/20/1863, St. Louis.
Henry DAVIS, Pvt, Co. K, ?, 12/15/1864, St. Louis, died 2/11/1863 of bronchitus.
Joseph DAVIS, Sgt, Co. G, 24, 10/1/1863, St. Louis.
Frank DAY, Pvt, Co. B, ?, substitute, mustered

in on 12/6/1864 at Ironton.
Isaac DAYD, Pvt, Co., D, ?, 9/11/1863, New Ark.
Sampson DECATUR, Pvt, Co. G, 24, 10/1/1863, St. Louis.
John F. DEMAR, Pvt, Co. B, 18, 8/23/1863, Lagrange.
Isaac DIXON, Pvt, Co. I, 18, 10/25/1863, Shelbyville.
Edward A. DOCKINS, Pvt, Co. I, ?, 10/19/1863, Hannibal, died 4/13/1864.
Thomas DORSEY, Pvt, Co. K, 22, 11/30/1863, Benton Barracks.
Mason DOUGLAS, Pvt, Co. I, ?, 9/19/1863, Hannibal.
Wm. DOUGLAS, Pvt, Co. E, 40, substitute, mustered in on 12/15/1864, St. Louis.
Wm. DOWNER, Pvt, Co. B, 22, 8/29/1863, Lagrange.
Andrew DOXIE, Pvt, Co. F, ?, 10/2/1863, Bowling Green, died 2/18/1864 at Helena, Ark. of disease.
Peter DUNN, Pvt, Co. H, 18, 9/23/1863, St. Louis.
John EBERT, Pvt, Co. A, 29, substitute, mustered in 12/14/1864, St. Louis.
Thomas EDWARDS, Pvt, Co. K, 19, 11/24/1863, Jefferson City.
Branch ELLINGTON, Pvt, Co. F, 21, 10/2/1863, Keytesville.
Jacob ELLINGTON, Pvt, Co. I, 18, 10/19/1863, Hannibal.
Alfred ELLIS, Pvt, Co. A, 37, 9/4/1863, Monticello.
Wm. ELWOOD, Pvt, Co. I, ?, 10/25/1863, Shelbyville, died 9/30/1864.
Edward ENGLISH, Pvt, Co. G, 32, 10/12/1863, St. Louis.
Joseph ENGLISH, Pvt, Co. K, ?, 11/19/1864, died 1/11/1865 of pneumonia.
Andy EUBANKS, Pvt, Co. G, ?, 1/1/1863, St. Louis, died 1/2/1865.
John EVANS, Pvt, Co. A, ?, 9/9/1863, Edina.
David EWING, Pvt, Co. H, 25, 10/28/1863, Keytesville.
Thomas EWING, Sgt, Co. H, 23, 10/28/1863, Keytesville.
Wm. EWING, Pvt, Co. H, 19, 10/2/1863, Keytes-

ville.
James FERGUSON, Pv, Co. E, ?, 9/29/1863, Ravanna, discharged 2/5/1865 at Benton Barracks because of disability.
Jack FIGGINS, Pvt, Co. K, 18, 11/23/1863, Warrensburg.
Levi FILPOT, Pvt, Co. I, 18, 10/19/1863, Hannibal.
Charles FISHER, Pvt, Co. I, ?, 10/25/1863, Shelbyville, died 4/1/1864.
John FLEMING, Pvt, Co. E, ?, substitute, mustered in 12/9/1864, St. Louis, deserted on 1/5/1865.
Joseph FLOOD, Pvt, Co. H, 10/25/1863, St. Louis, died 4/16/1864.
Daniel FLOYD, Musician, Co. A, ?, 9/9/1863, Edina, died 1/26/1864 at Helena, Ark. of pneumonia.
Wm. FORT, Pvt, Co. E, 9/8/1863, New Ark.
Absolam FOREMAN, Pvt, Co. E, 18, substitute, mustered in 11/16/1864, St. Louis.
Joshua FOSEY, Pvt, Co. I, 43, 10/25/1863, Shelbyville.
John FOSTER, Corp, Co. K, ?, 11/24/1863, Sedalia, died 2/15/1864 at Helena, Ark, of pneumonia.
Benjamin FRANKLIN, Pvt, Co. E, 25, substitute, mustered in 12/15/1864, St. Louis.
Benjamin FRANKLIN, Pvt, Co. K, ?, 11/23/1863, Jefferson City, died 12/26/1863 at Helena, Ark..
Thomas FRANKLIN, Pvt, Co. I, ?, 10/25/1863, Shelbyville.
George GAMBLE, Pvt, Co. K, 18, 11/23/1863, Mexico.
Archie GANNAWAY, Pvt, Co. G, ?, 10/1/1863, St. Louis.
Jason GARDNER, Pvt, Co. D, 19, 7/7/1864, High Hill.
Richard GARNER, Pvt, Co. I, 26, 10/25/1863, Shelbyville.
Alexander GARNETT, Pvt, Co. G, 19, 10/1/1863, St. Louis.
Charles GIBSON, Pvt, Co. E, 23, drafted, mustered in 11/17/1864, Jefferson City.
Wm. GOODWIN, Pvt, Co. G, ?, 10/1/1863, St.

Louis, died 1/1/1864 at Helena, Ark, of diarrhea.
Washington GRAHAM, Pvt, Co. C, 11/23/1863, Jefferson City, transfered from Co. K.
Peter GRAY, Pvt, Co. G, ?, 10/12/1863, St. Louis, died 11/11/1863 at Fort No. 8, St. Louis of gunshot wounds accidentally received.
John GREY, Pvt, Co. I, 28, 10/1/1863, Randolph county.
Joackson HAGGINS, Musician, Co. B, 19, 8/29/1863, Lagrange.
John HAINES, Pvt, Co. A, 18, 11/23/1863, Warrensburg.
James HALE, Pvt, Co. D, ?, 9/9/1863, New Ark, died 6/26/1865, Little Rock, Ark. of diarrhea.
Frederick HALL, Corp, Co. E, ?, 9/25/1863, Ravanna.
Richard HALL, Pvt, Co. K, ?, 12/4/1863, Benton Barracks, died 1/20/1864 at Helena, Ark. of pneumonia.
Wm. HALL, Pvt, Co. H, 26, 10/20/1863, St. Louis.
John HAMMOND, Pvt, Co. G, 20, 10/1/1863, St. Louis.
Anderson HANNAH, Pvt, Co. K, 25, 11/23/1863, Macon.
Smith HANNAN, Pvt, Co. I, ?, 11/23/1863, Chillicothe.
James HARRIS, Pvt, Co. K, 23, 11/23/1863, Warrensburg.
Jasper HARRIS, Pvt, Co. G, 18, 10/1/1863, St. Louis.
Joseph HARRIS, Pvt, Co. G, 18, 10/1/1863, St. Louis.
Robert HARRIS, Pvt, Co. K, ?, 11/29/1863, Mexico.
Samuel HARRIS, Pvt, Co. A, ?, 9/9/1863, Edina, died 2/8/1864 at Helena, Ark. of typhoid fever.
Thomas HARRIS, Pvt, Co. G, 18, 11/1/1863, St. Louis.
Henry HARRISON, Pvt, Co. G, 18, 11/24/1863, Warrensburg.
John HARRISON, Pvt, Co. K, 21, 11/29/1863, Mexico.
Wm. HARRISON, Pvt, Co. D, 18, 9/5/1863, New Ark.
Wm. H. HARRISON, Pvt, Co. B, ?, substitute,

mustered in on 12/6/1864, St. Louis, deserted 1/13/1865, Helena, Ark..
Samuel HART, Pvt, Co. E, ?, substitute, mustered in on 12/15/1864, St. Louis, discharged by Order of the War Department dated 8/15/1865.
Jacob HARVEY, Pvt, Co. G, 31, 10/1/1863, St. Louis.
Mark HARVEY, Pvt, Co. K, ?, 11/23/1863, Macon, died 1/27/1864, Helena, Ark..
John HATTON, Corp, Co. A, 32, 9/4/1863, Monticello.
Henry HAWKINS, Pvt, Co. K, ?, substitute, mustered in on 11/3/1864, Benton Barracks.
John HAYES, Pvt, Co. F, ?, 9/20/1863, Chillicothe.
George HEIGHT, Pvt, Co. I, 25, 10/19/1863, Hannibal.
David HENDERSON, Pvt, Co. G, 27, 10/1/1863, St. Louis.
James HENNASON, Pvt, Co. G, ?, 10/1/1863, St. Louis.
George HENRY, Pvt, Co. G, 18, 10/1/1863, St. Louis.
James HENRY (no. 2), Pvt, Co. I, ?, substitute, mustered in on 11/16/1864, Cooper County.
John HENRY, Pvt, Co. K, ?, 12/15/1864, St. Louis, deserted on 6/3/1865.
John HENRY, Pvt, Co. H, 24, 12/17/1864, St. Louis.
John HENRY (no. 2), Pvt, Co. H, 31, substitute, mustered in 12/19/1864, Benton Barracks.
Anderson HENSLEY, Pvt, Co. H, 19, 10/23/1863, St. Louis.
Henry HERRIFORD, Pvt, Co. B, ?, 9/22/1863, Chillicothe, died 1/14/1865 at Helena, Ark. of pneumonia.
John HERRIFORD, Corp, Co. B, 26, 9/20/1863, Chillicothe.
Joseph HIGGINS, Pvt, Co. A, 28, substitute, mustered in on 12/14/1864, St. Louis.
John HIPKINS, Pvt, Co. K, ?, 11/23/1863, Jefferson City, died at Helena, Ark. on 8/7/1864.
George HOLDER, Musician, Co. D, 18, 8/17/1863, New Ark.
Felix HOWARD, Pvt, Co. G, 19, 10/1/1863, St.

John HOWARD, Corp, Co. I, 28, 10/25/1863, Louis.
Shelbyville.
Thomas HOWARD, Pvt, Co. G, ?, 10/1/1863, St. Louis, died 6/15/1864 at Helena, Ark. of consumption.
Henry HOWELL, Pvt, Co. I, 23, 10/10/1863, Paris, died 8/19/1865 at Little Rock, Ark. of dropsy.
James HUBBARD, Pvt, Co. B, ?, 10/2/1863, Linn County, died at Keokuk, Iowa on 10/23/1863.
Esse HUGHES, Pvt, Co. C, ?, 9/2/1863, Brunswick, died 11/2/1863 at Keokuk, Iowa from pneumonia.
David HUNT, Pvt, Co. H, 19, 11/17/1864, Jefferson City.
Preston HUTCHINSON, Sgt, Co. K, 30, 11/28/1863, Sedalia.
Robert HUTCHINSON, Wagoneer, Co. D, ?, 9/25/1863, Ravanna, died 12/22/1863.
Frank IRWIN, Pvt, Co. H, 20, 10/26/1863, St. Louis.
Andrew JACKSON, Pvt, Co. H, ?, 10/28/1863, St. Louis, died 5/10/1864 at Helena, Ark. of typhoid malarial fever.
Andy JACKSON, Pvt, Co. G, ?, 10/1/1863, St. Louis, died of typhoid fever.
Benjamin JACKSON, Pvt, Co. F, ?, 10/2/1863, Chariton County.
Charles JACKSON, Corp, Co. D, 18, 9/19/1863, Canton.
Charles H. JACKSON, Pvt, Co. B, ?, 8/29/1863, Brunswick, died 1/8/1864 at Helena, Ark. of pneumonia.
Henry JACKSON, Pvt, Co. K, ?, 11/25/1863, Sedalia, died 1/18/1864 at Helena, Ark..
Jacob JACKSON, Pvt, Co. A, ?, 9/9/1863, Edina, died 1/27/1864 at Helena, Ark. of congestion of the spinal chord.
Jerry JACKSON, Pvt, Co. A, 9/9/1863, Edina.
John JACKSON, Corp, Co. C, 22, 9/2/1863, Brunswick.
Lewis JACKSON, Pvt, Co. K, 22, 11/10/1864, St. Charles.
Louis JACKSON, Corp, Co. G, ?, 10/1/1863, St. Louis, died 2/24/1864 at Helena, Ark..

Perry JACKSON, Pvt, Co. D, 38, 7/2/1864, Fulton.
Peter JACKSON, Pvt, Co. A, 21, 9/9/1863, Edina.
Preston JACKSON, Corp, Co. K, 35, 11/23/1863, Mexico.
John JAMES, Pvt, Co. C, ?, 9/30/1863, Brunswick, died 6/26/1864 at Helena, Ark. of dropsy.
Bias A. JOHNSON, Pvt, Co. A, ?, 9/9/1863, Edina.
Charles JOHNSON, Pvt, Co. G, ?, 10/1/1863, St. Louis.
Harry JOHNSON, Pvt, Co. A, ?, substitute, mustered in on 12/14/1864, St. Louis, died at Little Rock, Ark. on 7/8/1865 from disease.
Henry JOHNSON, Pvt, Co. A, ?, substitute, mustered in on 12/14/1864, St. Louis, deserted at Helena, Ark. on 1/1/1865.
Henry JOHNSON (no. 2), Pvt, Co. K, 21, substitute, mustered in on 12/14/1864, Benton Barracks.
Isaac JOHNSON, Pvt, Co. A, ?, 9/4/1863, Monticello.
Jacob JOHNSON, Pvt, Pvt, Co. K, 11/23/1863, Macon, died 6/23/1864 at Helena, Ark. of dysentery.
John JOHNSON, Pvt, Co. E, 20, substitute, mustered in on 12/16/1864, St. Louis.
Joseph JOHNSON, Pvt, Co. I, 18, 11/20/1863, Macon.
Lewis JOHNSON, Pvt, Co. H, 23, 2/3/1865, Hannibal.
Moses JOHNSON, Pvt, Co. A, ?, 10/2/1863, Brunswick, died 1/14/1864, Benton Barracks.
Robert JOHNSON, Pvt, Co. K, 24, 11/24/1863, Jefferson City.
Samuel JOHNSON, Pvt, Co. K, /, 11/24/1863, Warrensburg.
Wm. JOHNSON, Pvt, Co. E, 26, 9/25/1863, Ravanna.
Harrison JONES, Pvt, Co. I, 19, 11/23/1863, Benton Barracks.
Henry JONES, Pvt, Co. D, 25, 9/8/1863, New Ark.
Henry JONES, Pvt, Co. B, 19, substitute, mustered in on 12/16/1864, St. Louis.
Henry JONES, Pvt, Co. I, 42, drafted, mustered in on 11/18/1864, Benton Barracks.
John JONES, Pvt, Co. H, 20, 11/17/1863, St. Louis.
Thomas JONES, Pvt, Co. K, 35, 11/23/1863, Macon.

Wm. JONES, Corp, Co. A, 18, 9/9/1863, Edina.
Thomas JORDAN, Pvt, Co. A, 21, substitute, mustered in on 12/14/1864.
George KEIBO, Sgt, Co. I, 37, 10/25/1863, Shelbyville.
Wm. KEMP, Pvt, Co. I, ?, 11/21/1863, Callaway County, died 12/23/1863 at Benton Barracks.
John KIRTLEY, Corp, Co. K, 47, 11/3/1863, Mexico.
Augustus KURTS, Pvt, Co. D, 18, 7/2/1864, Macon.
James LAMAR, Corp, Co. H, 19, 10/28/1863, St. Louis.
Henry LANGFORD, Pvt, Co. D. ?, 11/24/1863, Warrensburg.
Perry LAWRENCE, Pvt, Co. H, ?, 10/30/1863, St. Louis, died 6/2/1864 of dysentery.
Wm. LEGAN, Pvt, Co. D, 20, 9/5/1863, New Ark.
Willis LEGAN, Pvt, Co. D, 18, 9/4/1863, New Ark.
Boyd LENA, Pvt, Co. A, 30, 9/9/1863, Edina.
Samuel B. LEVI, Pvt, Co. B, 18, 9/29/1863, Legrange.
Clay LEWIS, Pvt, Co. I, 18, 10/25/1863, Shelbyville.
James LEWIS, Pvt, Co. K, 19, 12/4/1863, Benton Barracks.
John LEWIS, Musician, Co. I, 19, 11/25/1863, Shelbyville.
Mason LEWIS, Pvt, Co. I, 21, 11/25/1863, Shelbyville.
Robert LEWIS, Pvt, Co. K, ?, 12/4/1863, Benton Barracks.
George LINCOLN, Pvt, Co. K, 21, 11/20/1863, Benton Barracks.
Pinckney LINN, Pvt, Co. G, 21, 10/1/1863, St. Louis.
Edward LIVENS, Pvt, Co. G, 22, 10/1/1863, St. Louis.
Gabrial LONG, Pvt, Co. I, ?, 11/5/1863, St. Louis, died 2/8/1864 at Helena, Ark. of chronic diarrhea.
Richard McCLURE, Pvt, Co. H, ?, 10/18/1863, St. Louis, died 12/14/1864.
Jerry McCOY, Pvt, Co. H, ?, 10/10/1863, St. Louis, drowned 8/21/1865, after falling from a boat near Devall's Bluff, Ark..
Henry McCRACKEN, Pvt, Co. H, 21, 10/30/1863,

St. Louis.
Henry McCULLOCH, Pvt, Co. D, ?, 6/27/1864, Warrenton, died 3/15/1865.
Scott McKINNEY, Pvt, Co. I, 35, 10/2/1863, Platsada (sic).
Charles McPIKE, Pvt, Co. H, ?, 10/17/1863, St. Louis, died 10/2/1864.
Richard McPIKE, Pvt, Co. H, 24, 9/21/1863, St. Louis.
Wm. McQUIDDY, Pvt, Co. H, 19, 10/30/1863, St. Louis.
Wm. MACK, Pvt, Co. G, 32, 10/1/1863, St. Louis.
James MADISON, Corp, Co. B, 21, 8/29/1863, Brunswick.
James MAGRUDER, Musician, Co. B, 19, 8/28/1863, Legrange.
Albert MALONE, Pvt, Co. I, ?, 10/6/1863, Randolph County.
Lewis N, MANSFIELD, Pvt, Co. K, 18, 10/1/1863, Macon.
Frank MARION, Pvt, Co. G, 18, 10/1/1863, St. Louis.
Frank MARTIN, Pvt, Co. E, 36, substitute, mustered in on 12/9/1864, St. Louis.
Hiram MARTIN, Pvt, Co. G, 18, 10/1/1863, St. Louis.
Isaac MARTIN, Pvt, Co. G, 18, 10/1/1863, St. Louis.
John MARTIN, Pvt, Co. D, ?, 6/26/1864, Fulton, died 7/3/1865 at Little Rock, Ark. of interment fever.
Robert MARTIN, Pvt, Co. K, ?, 11/23/1863, Macon.
Wm. MARTIN, Pvt, Co. K, 22, 11/21/1863, Jefferson City.
Fort MASON, Pvt, Co. I, 22, 11/19/1863, St. Louis.
George MASON, Pvt, Co. A, ?, substitute, mustered in on 12/14/1864, St. Louis, deserted from Helena, Ark. on 1/27/1865.
John MASON, Pvt, Co. G, 18, 10/1/1863, St. Louis.
Henry MATHEWS, Pvt, Co. B, 22, 9/28/1863, Randolph County.
Alexander MAY, Pvt, Co. G, ?, 10/12/1863, St. Louis.

Willie MIDDLETON, Pvt, Co. A, ?, 9/9/1863, Edina, died 8/6/1864.
David MILLBURN, Pvt, Co. G, 18, 10/1/1863, St. Louis.
James MILTON, Pvt, Co. ;A, ?, 9/6/1863, Monticello, died 11/8/1863, Keokuk, Iowa of congestion of the brain.
Scipis MINOR, Pvt, Co. G, 23, 10/1/1863, St. Louis.
James MOFFIT, Sgt, Co. G, 21, 10/12, 1963, St. Louis.
Horace MONROW, Pvt, Co. A, ?, 9/7/1863, Monticello, died 12/27/1863, Benton Barracks.
Sipsy A. MONROW, Pvt, Co. I, ?, 10/19/1863, Hannibal, died 3/24/1864.
Washington MONTGOMERY, Pvt, Co. G, ?, 10/1/1863, St. Louis.
Alexander MOORE, Pvt, Co. I, ?, 11/18/1863, Chillicothe.
Andy MOORE, Corp, Co. K, ?, 11/29/1863, Sedalia.
Edward MOORE, Pvt, Co. K, ?, 11/26/1863, Benton Barracks, died at Helena, Ark. on 12/27/1863.
Charles MORGAN, Pvt, jCo. C, ?, 4/2/1863, Brunswick, died 3/8/1864.
George MORRIS, Pvt, Co. B, 18, 8/29/1863, Brunswick.
Wm. MORRIS, Sgt, Co. I, 19, 10/10/1863, Paris.
Merideth MORTON, Pvt, Co. K, ?, 11/25/1863, Sedalia, died 3/7/1864.
Joseph MOURNIN, Pvt, Co. K, ?, 11/30/1863, Mexico.
Irvin MULDRON, Pvt, Co. K, 42, 11/30/1863, Mexico.
Anderson MURPHY, Pvt, Co. K, ?, 12/3/1863, Benton Barracks.
George MYERS, Pvt, Co. K, 20, 11/25/1863, Mexico.
Richard NEAL, Pvt, Co. A, 27, 9/7/1863, Monticello.
Vert NEAL, Pvt, Co. A, ?, 9/7/1863, Monticello, died 3/8/1864.
George NELSON, Pvt, Co. A, ?, 9/9/1863, Edina, died 4/16/1864.
George NELSON, Pvt, Co. A, 12/4/1863, Benton Barracks, died 1/16/1864 at Helena, Ark. of meningitis.

Henry NELSON, Pvt, Co. K, ?, 11/25/1863, St. Louis, died 7/28/1864.
Henry NELSON, Pvt, Co. G, 36, 10/1/1863, St. Louis.
Austin NICHOLAS, Pvt, Co. A, ?, 9/9/1863, Edina, died 1/27/1864 at Helena, Ark. of pneumonia.
James NICHOLAS, Pvt, Co. G, 19, 10/1/1863, St. Louis.
John NUNN, Pvt, Co. B, 31, 9/31/1863, Legrange.
Alfred OWENS, Pvt, Co. G, 18, 10/1/1863, St. Louis.
Ned OWENS, Pvt, Co. I, 30, substitute, mustered in on 12/17/1864, Benton Barracks.
Calvin PAINE, Pvt, Co. A, ?, substitute, mustered in on 12/14/1864, St. Louis, deserted from Helena, Ark. on 1/27/1865.
James PAINE, Pvt, Co. I, 21, 11/17/1863, St. Louis.
Armstead PALMER, Pvt, Co. A, 22, 12/14/1863, St. Louis.
James W. PARE, Pvt, Co. H, 22, 3/30/1865, Jefferson City.
Charles H. PARKER, Pvt, Co. K, 18, 11/24/1863, Sedalia.
Henry PARKER, Pvt, Co. A, ?, substitute, mustered in on 12/14/1864, St. Louis, deserted from Helena, Ark. on 2/4/1865.
Anderson PARSONS, Pvt, Co. B, ?, 8/29/1863, Legrange, died 6/5/1864 at Helena, Ark. of hepatitis.
Charles PATTON, Corp, Co. I, ?, 10/19/1863, Hannibal, died 3/6/1864.
Benjamin PATTERSON, Pvt, Co. G, 18, 10/15/1863, St. Louis.
Walter PEACH, Pvt, Co. A, ?, 9/4/1863, Monticello, died 3/6/1864.
Charles PERKINS, Pvt, Co. G, ?, 10/1/1863, St. Louis, died 4/6/1865 at Helena, Ark..
Jenkins PERNELL, Pvt, Co. I, 28, 10/28/1863, Shelbyville.
John PETERS, Pvt, Co. A, 25, substitute, mustered in on 12/14/1864, St. Louis.
Thomas PETTUS, Pvt, Co. K, ?, 11/24/1863, Mexico, died 12/18/1863, Benton Barracks.
Anderson PHILLIPS, Pvt, Co. I, 19, 11/18/1863, Chillicothe.

John P. PHILLIPS, Pvt, Co. C, ?, 9/2/1863, Brunswick, died 7/24/1864.
Logan PHILLIPS, Pvt, Co. K, ?, 11/28/1863, Mexico, died 12/14/1863, Benton Barracks.
Franklin PURSON, Musician, Co. G, 18, 10/1/1863, St. Louis.
Joseph PITTS, Pvt, Co. I, ?, 10/25/1863, died 2/3/1864 at Helena, Ark. of typhoid fever.
Linsey PITTS, Pvt, Co. I, 18, 11/20/1863, Macon.
Frank POLK, Pvt, Co. D, 17, 7/7/1864.
George W. POLK, Sgt, Co. A, ?, 9/9/1863, Edina, died 3/22/1864.
Sanford PORTER, Pvt, Co. B, 18, 8/29/1863, Legrange.
Wm. PORTER, Pvt, Co. I, 31, 10/25/1863, Shelbyville.
Cyrus PORTER, Pvt, Co. G, 19, 10/1/1863, St. Louis.
Richard POWELL, Pvt, Co. K, 21, 11/30/1863, Mexico.
Dallas PRICE, Pct, Co. I, ?, 10/2/1863, Keytesville, died 7/16/1865 at Little Rock, Ark. of congestive chills.
Franklin PRICE, Pvt, Co. K, 25, 11/23/1863, Jefferson City.
Lewis PRICE, Pvt, Co. K, ?, 11/24/1863, Mexico, died 4/25/1865.
George P. PROPHET, Pvt, Co. D, ?, 10/3/1863, Keytesville, died 2/28/1864 at Helena, Ark. of pneumonia.
Rolin PROPHETT, Pvt, Co. D, 26, 10/2/1863, Keytesville, transfered from Co. I on 12/9/1863.
Archie PULLEN, Pvt, Co. C, 18, 9/2/1863, Brunswick.
Lewis PULLEN, Fifer, Co. K, ?, 11/25/1863, Benton Barracks. died 3/1/1865.
Robert RAY, Pvt, Co. I, 21, 11/18/1863, Chillicothe.
David C. READING, Pvt, Co. H, 21, 9/28/1863, Keytesville.
Monroe READING, Pvt, Co. H, 21, 10/2/1863, Keytesville.
Wm. READING, Pvt, Co. H, 20, 10/2/1863, Keytesville.

Charles REDDEN, Pvt, Co. I, 18, 9/28/1863, Keytesville.
George REES, Pvt, Co. B, 39, 8/29/1863, Brunswick.
Solmon REYNOLD, Pvt, Co. G, 18, 10/1/1863, St. Louis, committed suicide in Sep, or Oct, 1865 at Jacksonport, Ark..
Samuel RICHARDS, Pvt, Co. B, ?, substitute, mustered in on 12/13/1864, Benton Barracks, deserted immediately.
Henry RICHARDSON, Pvt, Co. K, 18, 11/24/1863, Sedalia.
Wm. RICHARDSON, Pvt, Co. B, 18, 8/29/1863, Legrange.
George W. RICKS, Pvt, Co. G, 18, 10/12/1863, St. Louis, died 5/24/1865.
James T. RICKS. Sgt, Co. G, 18, 10/12/1863, St. Louis.
Wm. RICKS, Sgt, Co. G, 21, 11/10/1863, St. Louis.
Franklin RIDDLE, Pvt, Co. D, 18, 7/5/1864, Warrenton.
John RILEY, Pvt, Co. K, 20, substitute, mustered in on 12/15/1864, Benton Barracks.
David ROAD, Pvt, Co. G, ?, 10/12/1863, St. Louis.
George ROBERTS, Pvt, Co. B, ?, 8/29/1863, Brunswick, died 6/15/1864 at Helena, Ark. of pneumonia.
James ROBERTS, Pvt, Co. H, 18, 10/28/1863, St. Louis.
Lucken ROBERTS, Pvt, Co. K, ?, 11/25/1863, Sedalia, died 12/28/1863 at Helena, Ark..
Daniel ROBINSON, Pvt, Co. K, 22, 11/30/1863, Sedalia.
George ROBINSON, Pvt, Co. H, 26, substitute, mustered in on 12/19/1864, St. Louis.
Joseph ROBINSON, Pvt, Co. I, 22, 10/10/1863, Paris.
Morton ROBINSON, Pvt, Co. G, 19, 10/1/1863, St. Louis.
Carey RODGERS, Pvt, Co. K, 45, 11/23/1863, Sedalia.
Jesse RODGERS, Pvt, Co. C, 21, 11/30/1863, Chillicothe.
Moses RODGERS, Pvt, Co. C, ?, 11/23/1863,

Sedalia, died 1/15/1864 at Helena, Ark. of pneumonia.
John ROLER, Pvt, Co. B, 32, substitute, mustered in on 12/15/1864, St. Louis.
John ROAL, Pvt, Co. A, ?, 9/9/1863, Wentzville, died 1/24/1865 at Helena, Ark. of chronic diarrhea.
Henry M. ROWE, Pvt, Co. I, 19, substitute, mustered in on 12/17/1864, Benton Barracks.
John RUCKER, Pvt, Co. B, ?, 9/22/1863, Chillicothe, died 12/27/1863 on board the steamer "W. L. Ewing".
James RUSH, Pvt, Co. I, ?, 11/18/1863, Chillicothe, d. 12/27/1863.
James RUSSELL, Pvt, Co. C, ?, 9/23/1863, Chillicothe, died 1/28/1864 at Helena, Ark. of consumption.
Irvin P. RUSSELL, Corp, Co. I, 22, 10/25/1863, Shelbyville.
George RUTHERFORD, Corp, Co. G, 19, 10/1/1863, St. Louis.
Lorenzo RUTHERFORD, Pvt, Co. I, ?, 11/20/1863, Macon, died 1/24/1864 at Helena, Ark. of diarrhea.
Isaac RYAN, Pvt, Co. I, 18, 11/18/1863, Chillicothe.
Henry SAMUELS, Pvt, Co. I, ?, 11/20/1863, Macon, died 12/30/1863.
Henry SAMUELS, Pvt, Co. K, 46, 11/24/1863, Sedalia.
Silas SAMUELS, Pvt, Co. I, 19, 11/20/1863, Macon.
Silas SAXON, Pvt, Co. A, 19, 9/9/1863, Edina.
Burrell SCOTT, Pvt, Co. I, ?, drafted on 12/25/1864, Ironton, died 8/15/1865 at Little Rock, Ark. of consumption chills.
George SCOTT, Pvt, Co. H, 37, substitute, mustered in on 12/19/1864, St. Louis.
Samuel SCOTT, Pvt, Co. K, 22, 11/25/1863, Jefferson City.
Wm. SCOTT, Musician, Co. E, 20, substitute, mustered in on 12/12/1864, St. Louis.
Wm. SCOTT, Pvt, Co. K, 24, 11/24/1863, Benton Barracks.
Stephen SCRUGGS, Sgt, Co. K, 43, 11/22/1863, Jefferson City.

Samuel L. SHARP, Sgt, Co. G, ?, 10, 1, 1863, St. Louis, died 2/6/1864 at Helena, Ark. of pneumonia.
Allen SHAW, Pvt, Co. G, 25, 3/21/1865, Jefferson City.
Leander SHAW, Pvt, Co. H, 21, 10/28/1863, St. Louis.
Robert SHELTON, Pvt, Co. D, 22, 7/5/1864, Warrenton.
Thomas SHELTON, Pvt, Co. F, 18, 9/28/1864, Moniteau County.
Frank SHEPHERD, Pvt, Co. D, ?, 10/2/1863, Keytesville, died 12/24/1863, Benton Barracks.
Enoch SIMCOE, Pvt, Co. I, 25, substitute, mustered in on 12/19/1864, Benton Barracks.
Henry SIMPSON, Pvt, Co. a, ?, 9/9/1863, Edina, died 6/25/1864 at Helena, Ark, of hepatitus.
Albert SIMS, Pvt, Co. C, ?, 11/25/1863, Warrensburg, died 1/5/1864 at Camp Pile, Helena, Ark. of pneumonia.
Samuel SKINNER, Pvt, Co. H, ?, 11/28/1863, St. Louis, discharged 6/14/1865 as a corporal.
Sandy A. SMALLEY, Corp, Co. I, 38, 11/20/1863, St. Louis.
Evans SMALLWOOD, Pvt, Co. G, 30, 10/1/1863, St. Louis.
Charles SMITH, Pvt, Co. G, 18, 10/1/1863, St. Louis.
David SMITH, Pvt, Co. H, 25, 10/13/1863, St. Louis.
Doctor SMITH, Corp, Co. K, 21, 11/30/1863, Jefferson City.
George SMITH, Pvt, Co. D, ?, 11/23/1863, Warrensburg, died 3/4/1864.
Henry SMITH, Pvt, Co. I, ?, 10/2/1863, Keytesville, died 3/5/1864.
Huson SMITH, Pvt, Co. K, 18, 11/25/1863, Mexico.
Troop SMITH, Pvt, Co. A, 18, 11/2/1863, Warrensburg.
Turner SMITH, Pvt, Co. B, ?, 8/29/1863, Brunswick, died 4/1/1864.
Wm. SMITH, Pvt, Co. F, ?, 11/22/1863, Macon, transferred from Co. I on 12/9/1863.
John SNELL, Pvt, Co. I, ?, 10/19/1863, Hannibal, died 1/15/1864, Benton Barracks.
Albert SNOWDON, Pvt, Co. I, ?, 11/18/1863,

Chillicothe, died 12/25/1863.
Harrison SPOTZER, Pvt, Co. G, 20, 10/1/1863, St. Louis.
Joseph SPOTZER, Corp, Co. G, 19, 10/1/1863, St. Louis.
Frank STALEY, Pvt, Co. F. ?, substitute, mustered in on 11/16/1864, Moniteau County.
John STANFORD, Musician, Co. H, 19, 11/20/1863, St. Louis.
Preston STANFORD, Corp, Co. H, 27, 10/28/1863, St. Louis.
Mingo STANLEY, Wagoneer, Co. K, ?, 11/22/1863, Jefferson City, died 4/16/1864.
Henry STANLEY, Pvt, Co. C, 17, 11/23/1863, Jefferson City, transferred from Co. K on 12/9/1863.
Henry STAPLETON, Pvt, Co. G, 35, 10/1/1863, St. Louis.
Leroy STEVENS, Pvt, Co. E, 25, 9/20/1863, Chillicothe.
Wm. STEVENS, Pvt, Co. F, 18, 9/20/1863, Chillicothe.
Dennis STEWART, Pvt, Co. B, ?, 8/29/1863, Lagrange, died 2/13/1864 at Helena, Ark..
Harrison STEWART, Pvt, Co. I, 21, 10/25/1863, Shelbyville.
Wm. STEWART, Pvt, Co. B, ?, 11/27/1863, Sedalia, died 8/12/1864.
Wm. B. STONE, Pvt, Co. K, ?, 11/23/1863, Jefferson City, died 12/26/1863 at Helena, Ark..
Preston SURBER, Pvt, Co. K, ?, 11/30/1863, Mexico, died 11/15/1864.
Joseph SUTHERLAND, Pvt, Co. C, ?, 11/27/1863, Sedalia, transferred from Co. K on 12/9/1863, died 1/5/1864 at Helena, Ark. of pneumonia.
Albert SWITZER, Pvt, Co. F, 25, 9/20/1863, Chillicothe.
John SWITZLER, Pvt, Co. I, 23, 11/20/1863, Macon.
Burrill TAITS, Pvt, Co. B. 8/29/1863, Lagrange, died 7/27/1864 at Benton Barracks of disease.
Wm. T. TALBOT, Corp, Co. B, 21, 8/29/1863, Lagrange.
Daniel TATE, Pvt, Co. K, 21, 11/23/1863, Mason (sic).
Conrad TAYLOR, Pvt, Co. H, 27, 10/9/1863, St.

Claiborne TAYLOR, Pvt, Co. I, ?, 11/20/1863, Mason (sic), died 1/5/1864, Benton Barracks.
James TAYLOR, Pvt, Co. G, ?, 10/1/1863, St. Louis, died 11/23/1863 at Fort No. 6, St. Louis.
John TAYLOR, Pvt, Co. G, 20, 10/1/1863, St. Louis.
George THOMAS, Pvt, Co. D, 44, 9/27/1863, Hannibal.
Henry THOMAS, Pvt, Co. K, 34, 11/29/1863, Mexico.
Robert THOMAS, Pvt, Co. B. 20. 8/29/1863. Lagrange, he last reported for roll call on Aug 31, 1865. He was later found murdered at Searcy, Ark..
Samuel THOMPSON, Pvt, Co. G, 20, 10/1/1863, St. Louis.
Wm. THOMPSON, Pvt, Co. A, ?, substitute, mustered in on 12/14/1864, St. Louis, deserted from Helena, Ark. on 1/27/1865.
Henry THORNE, Pvt, Co. A, ?, 9/9/1863, Edina, died 11/6/1863 at Keokuk, IA, of pneumonia.
Samuel THURMAN, Corp, Co. K, 21, 11/28/1863, Mexico.
Robert TILISON, Pvt, Co. I, ?, 10/19/1863, Hannibal, died 1/6/1864.
James TINSLEY, Pvt, Co. C, 33, 11/27/1863, Mexico, transferred from Co. K on 12/9/1863.
Levi TODD, Pvt, Co. B, ?, 8/29/1863, Lagrange.
Henry TOLSON, Pvt, Co. K, 18, 11/23/1863, Jefferson City.
James TURNER, Pvt, Co. K, 32, substitute, mustered in on 12/15/1864, St. Louis.
John TURNER, Pvt, Co. B, 23, substitute, mustered in on 12/15/1864, St. Louis.
John VALLE, Pvt, Co. I, 23, drafted on 11/18/1864, mustered in at Benton Barracks.
Wm. VENABLE, Pvt, Co. I, ?, 10/2/1863, Hannibal, died 1/1/1864 at Benton Barracks.
John VANCE, Corp, Co. H, 29, 10/30/1863, St. Louis.
Charles WALES, Pvt, Co. H, ?, 10/30/1863, St. Louis.
George WALKER, Pvt, Co. K, 21, substitute, mustered in on 12/18/1864, St. Louis.

Louis.
Arpe (sic) WASHINGTON, Pvt, Co. I, 32, 10/25/1863, Shelbyville.
George WASHINGTON, Pvt, Co. B, 19, substitute, mustered in on 12/30/1864, St. Louis.
George WASHINGTON, Pvt, Co. C, ?, 9/2/1863, Chillicothe, died 11/1/1863 at Keokuk, IA, of pneumonia.
George WASHINGTON #1, Pvt, Co. I, ?, 10/25/1863, Shelbyville.
George WAHINGTON #2, Pvt, Co. I, ?, 11/18/1863, Chillicothe.
George WAHINGTON #3, Pvt, Co. I, 26, drafted, mustered in on 11/18/1864.
Henry WASHINGTON, Pvt, Co. I, 29, 11/18/1863, Chillicothe.
James WASHINGTON, Pvt, Co. D, 17, 9/11/1863, Canton.
Riley WASHINGTON, Pvt, Co. I, 29, 11/18/1863, Chillicothe.
Spriggs WASHINGTON, Pvt, Co. G, 27, 10/1/1863, St. Louis.
Benjamin WATSON, Pvt, Co. C, 18, 12/1/1863, Benton Barracks.
Henry WATTS, Pvt, Co. C, 21, 9/3/1863, Brunswick.
Theophilus WATTS, Sgt, Co. K, ?, 11/30/1863, Mexico.
Daniel WEBSTER, Corp, Co. K, 18, 11/29/1863, Mexico.
John WESLEY, Pvt, Co. K, ?, 11/25/1863, Sedalia.
Joshua WHALEY (spelled WALEY on another record), Pvt, Co. D, ?, 9/25/1863, Sedalia, died 8/12/1864.
Peter WHALEY (spelled WALEY on another record), Pvt, Co. D, ?, 9/27/1863, Edina, died 8/23/1864.
Henry WHEELER, Pvt, Coo. G, 20, 10/1/1863, St. Louis.
Jackson WHEELER, Pvt, Co. A, ?, 9/28/1863, Edina.
Stephen WHEELER, Pvt, Co. D, 18, 8/31/1863, Brunswick.
Griffen WHITE, Pvt, Co. D, ?, 9/4/1863, New Ark, died 12/14/1863.
Horace WHITE, Pvt, Co. B. 8/29/1863, Brunswick,

died 8/11/1865, at Little Rock, Ark. of typhoid fever.
Moses A. WHITE, Pvt, D, ?, 9/4/1863, New Ark, died 12/15/1863 at Benton Barracks.
Wm. WHITE, Pvt, Co. B. 28, 8/29/1863, Brunswick.
Benjamin WHITESIDE, Pvt, Co. E, ?, 10/2/1863, Keytesville.
Benjamin WHITESIDE, Pvt, Co. I, 25, 10/2/1863, Keytesville.
John WHITNEY, Pvt, Co. H, 25, 10/20/1863, St. Louis.
Sidney WIGGS, Pvt, Co. H, 20, 10/22/1963, St. Louis.
Adam WILLIAMS, Pvt, Co. D, ?, 12/3/1863, Benton Barracks, died 6/2/1864 at Helena, Ark..
Albert WILLIAMS, Corp, Co. K, 19, 11/27/1863, Warrensburg.
Fleur WILLIAMS, Pvt, Co. F, 19, 9/3/1863, Brunswick.
Frederick, WILLIAMS, Pvt, Co. G, ?, 10/1/1863, St. Louis, died 1/28/1864 at Benton Barracks.
George WILLIAMS, Pvt, Co. A, 25, 9/9/1863, Edina.
George WILLIAMS, Pvt, Co. E, 19, substitute, 12/16/1864, St. Louis.
George W. WILLIAMS, Pvt, Co. K, 18, 11/23/1863, Mason (sic).
Hanson WILLIAMS, Pvt, Co. F, 19, substitute, mustered in on 11/17/1864, Cooper County.
Jake WILLIAMS, Pvt, Co. B, ?, substitute, St. Louis, deserted 1/13/1865 at Helena, Ark..
John WILLIAMS, Pvt, Co. K, 29, substitute, mustered in on 12/15/1864, Benton Barracks.
Lewis WILLIAMS, Pvt, Co. I, 18, 10/2/1863, Keytesville.
Richard WILLIAMS, Pvt, Co. A, 23, substitute, mustered in on 12/14/1864, St. Louis.
SAMUEL WILLIAMS, Pvt, Co. G, ?, 10/1/1863, St. Louis, died 2/8/1864 of pneumonia.
Wm. WILLIAMS, Pvt, Co. H, ?, substitute, 12/13/1864, St. Louis.
Ellis WILLIS, Pvt, Co. B, ?, 10/30/1863. St. Louis, died 8/10/1864.
Henry WILLIS, Pvt, Co. K, 26, 11/24/1863, Sedalia.

Esau WILSON, Pvt, Co. H, ?, 11/11/1863, St. Louis.
Henry WILSON, Pvt, Co. G, ?, 11/1/1863, St. Louis.
Lindsey WILSON, Pvt, Co. G, ?, 11/1/1863, St. Louis.
Robert WILSON, Pvt, Co. I, 33, 10/25/1863, Shelbyville.
Wesley WILSON, Sgt, Co. K, 22, 11/22/1863, Mexico.
Wm. WILSON, Corp, Co. B, ?, 8/29/1863, Lagrange, died 1/9/1864 at Helena, Ark. of epilepsy.
Allen WINN, Corp, Co. D, 21, 9/28/1863, Ravanna.
Alexander WINSTON, Pvt, Co. B, 21, substitute, mustered in on 12/13/1864, St. Louis.
Elijah WITTLE, Pvt, Co. K, 18, 11/28/1863, Mexico.
Isaac WOODS, Pvt, Co. B, ?, substitute, mustered in on 12/13/1864, St. Louis, died 7/29/1865 at Little Rock, Ark. of typhoid fever.
Moses WOODSON, Pvt, Co. B, 20, 11/28/1863, Warrensburg.
David WRIGHT, Pvt, Co. D, 48, 7/2/1864, High Hill.
Henry WRIGHT, Pvt, Co. H, ?, 10/13/1863, St. Louis, died 4/2/1864.
Wm. WRIGHT, Pvt, Co. H, 19, 10/2/1863, Keytesville.
Jacob YATES, Pvt, Co. A, ?, 9/9/1863, Edina, died 6/8/1865.
Henry YOUNG, Pvt, Co. K, 18, substitute, mustered in on 12/15/1864, St. Louis.

MARRIAGE RECORDS

Nodaway County. There may be more black marriages, but only those where the race was stated have been included.
Benjamin LANERE to Sarah PRATHER - Jan 21, 1866.
Wyatt GUNN to Violetta Ann KEYES - Feb 4, 1866.
McDonald SMART to Mary Alice JOHNSON - Jan 25, 1866.
Cezar SMART to Jane MILLER - Aug 18, 1866.
Winders PETERS to Josephine INLOW, both mulattoes - Nov 25, 1868.
Sam GUNN to Susan KEES - July 19, 1869.
Stephen MARTIN to Dolly HOOKER - Sep 4, 1870.
John H. cramer to Angeline JONES - Mar 3, 1871.
Lindsey GRAVES to Mariah VANCE - Oct 10, 1871.
Henry BOLDEN to Mary A. JONES - Aug 31, 1872.
Grandville FLEENOR to Harriet TURNER - Oct 20, 1872.
Frank AUSTIN to Eliza J. HOOKER - Oct 4, 1873.
Winslow PETERS to Katy BELL - Oct 8, 1873.
Robert STEWART to Emma PORTER - Nov 3, 1880.
Mack SMART to May WILLS - Nov 19, 1880.
Frank SMART, by consent of Mack SMART to Henrietta PALMER - Oct 5, 1881.
Albert WHITE to Letha ANTHONY - Nov 5, 1881.
William CAMPBELL to Mamie WILLIAMS - Dec 1, 1881. Bride of St. Louis.
Will CLAYTON to Henrietta DAVID - Dec 1, 1881. Both of St. Louis.
Winslow PETERS to Sarah HILLMAN - Mar 30, 1882.
Grandville FLEENER to Katie BELL - Aug 15, 1882.
Frank AUSTIN - Amanda BOLDEN - Sep 4, 1882.
Simon WILLS to Sylvia LATTIMORE - July 15, 1886.
Charles B. BAKER to Fannie COLLIER - Dec 24, 1886.
Frank SHERMAN to Dora MARTIN - June 7, 1888. Dora was the daughter of Stephen MARTIN.
George PALMER to Eliza ANDERSON - Nov 9, 1888.
Winslow PETERS to Amanda MATLAND KING - Dec 3, 1890.

Jefferson County, 1867 - 1874.

Deamer HAWKINS to Jane CHAMBERLAIN - Nov 14, 1866.
HARVARD ANDERSON to MeLinda SHORES - Dec 26, 1866.
Alexander BARRICK to Rebecca LEWIS - Nov 27, 1866.
Mack McPHEARSON to Lucy Anner OLLEVILLE - Dec 30, 1866.
Edward THOMPSON to Anna TURNER - Apr 3, 1867.
George Washington WILLIAMS to Rosanna CLAY - Apr 30, 1867.
Pohn POSTON to Josephine BECKET - Dec 26, 1866. Child: Lucy, age 11.
Giles MOORE to Ellen SANGIUNETTE - June 20, 1867.
Gabriel BOYD to Ellen Minerva COLE - Feb 6, 1868.
Thomas WEBB to Margaret BURRIS - May 17, 1868.
Francis HANKY to Fanny LAMBERT - June 25, 1868.
John PETTETT to Ellen McFARLAND - Nov 13, 1867.
Isaac KELLY to Ann PETTETT - Nov 13, 1867.
Kelso PERRY to Emiline BOSIER - Dec 12, 1867.
Antona SANGANET to Sarah LYEES - Sep 6, 1867.
William ELWOOD to Anna CANE - June 25, 1868.
Nelson DORNAN to Charlotte JONES - Oct 28, 1868.
Christopher HAYS to Lucinda GILES - Oct 28, 1868.
Rufus JACKSON to Alsie STRICKLAND - Dec 15, 1868.
James GILES to Midona DARLY - Dec 31, 1868.
Antaven GREEN to Julia Elwood - Dec 24, 1868.
William RAMEY to Roseller WEASE - Feb 7, 1869.
Jesse WAIR to Lenda NULL - Apr 18, 1869.
John BATES to Hettie HARNESS - Mar 19, 1869.
George BRUCE to Aggie BRUCE - Mar 7, 1869. Children: Emily, Margaret, Robert, and Samuel.
Richard COLLIER to Sara B. E. COLLIER - Mar 7, 1869. Children: Charles, Sarah, Mary, Malinda, Giddy Ann.
William JAMES to Nancy JOHNSTON to Apr 11, 1869.
George WILLIAMS to Isabella BLACKWELL - Mar 24, 1869.
Edward KEE to Eliza Clementine - Sep 1, 1869.

Robert WILLIAMS to Harriet WINES - Oct 29, 1869.
Frank MARSHALL to Louisa RENO - Dec 27, 1869.
Wilson HARRIS to Annie JACKSON - Mar 14, 1870.
Jeremiah McMEAN to Harriet Ann BINUM - Feb 24, 1870.
James KELLY to Lavinia CHEATUM - Jan 19, 1869.
Charles O'NEAL to Mary WINES - May 26, 1870.
William ROBINSON to Allen ALEXANDER Sep 18, 1870.
Richard JACKSON to Jane FARRIS - Mar 27, 1871.
Anderson BOIS to Jane BLACKWELL - Jan 22, 1873.
Thomas SIMPSON to Lucy McCARTY - Feb 14, 1873.
Antony BARNES to Amanda BOYCE - Mar 13, 1873.
James ABERNATHY to Cynthia COLE - Sep 20, 1873.
Vick NULL to Sarah VAUGHN - Apr 20, 1873.
Charles CASLY to Jane CUNNINGHAM - Aug 24, 1875.
Louis KEY to Sarah BILLINGS - Mar 11, 1875.
Henry HENDERSON to Charlotte BOYCE - Sep 17, 1875.
Washington MARTIN to Adaline GILL - Oct 24, 1875.
Abraham BOICE to Millie Ann BOLLINGER - Jan 4, 1876.
Charley LEE - Adaline CORMAN - Aug 27, 1876.
Henry SMITH to Sarah COLE - Mar 22, 1877.
Benjamin McSPADIN to Martha CARR - Mar 31, 1877.
Giles MOORE to Emily SANGUINETT to Nov 29, 1878.

Miller County, negro marriages extracted from Book A.
Willis PROCTOR to Mary E. WALKER to Sep 11, 1865.
Thomas PROCTOR to Caroline ETTER - Sep 11, 1865.
Anderson DOOLEY to Harriet DOOLEY - Jan 30, 1866.
William LAWLESS to Manda LAWLESS - Feb 3, 1866.
Henry LAWLESS to Violet LAWLESS - Mar 14, 1866.
Wm. LOUSE to Eliza WILLSON - Apr 26, 1866.
George LENOX to Jenny ALLEN - Nov 4, 1866.
Josephus ALLEN to Stephen Ann ALLEN - Dec 2,

1866.
Alexander PRIDEMORE to ___?___ POPPLEWELL - Jan 31, 1867.
Henry HAWKIN to Margaret ALLEN - Mar 1, 1868.

Dade County, extracted from Book 1, 1863 - 1867.
Henderson CARLOCK to Dorcas S. M. PEMBERTON - June 18, 1865. Child: L. CARLOCK.
Emanuel U. DICUS to M_____ SLOAN - June 18, 1865. Children: George Albert, Malinda Emiline, Albert Newton, and Betty Frances.
Anderson McGEE to Susan Rean McCONNELL - July 9, 1865.

Cooper County, 1865 - 1866
Luke WILLIAMS to Levona DOWNING - May 26, 1865.
Burrill PAGE to Ester BANKS - July 14, 1865.
Robert MOORE to Mary BRIEN - July 23, 1865. Children: Angeline, Lizzie, Landon, Henry, Patty, Hetty, Fannie, Frank, Lucinda, and Eliza.
Randall CARTER to Barbary ALLEN - July 23, 1865. Children: Harriett, Lilea, Polly, James, and Eliza.
Leo BRASIER to Jane FRANKLIN - july 15, 1865.
Charles LOUIS to Lizza PRESTON - July 9, 1865. Child: James Franklin.
Edward WILSON to Elizabeth SCOTT - Aug 27, 1865. Children: Lucinda Ann, age 11; Delia Ann, age 9; Martha Ann, age 5; Frank Blair, age 4; and James F. age 3.
Nathan WILLIAMS to Eveline RENLAS - Aug 27, 1865, Children: Julia Ann, age 3; Jeyse, age 2; and Patsy, 1 .
Peter WILLIAMS to Angeline TATE - Aug 27, 1865.
James BROWN to Martha ADAMS - Aug 27, 1865. Children: Baswell, age 20; Wright Roman, born Dec 1847; Violet, born 1856; Jane, born 1854; Miles, born 1856; and Edward, born Feb 1863.
Gerand FOULER to Amanda PIERCE - Aug 6, 1865. Child: Jimmie, born Dec 1, 1863.
Jack WILEY to Nancy GARF - Aug 13, 1865. Children: Delia Ann, born Jan 9, 1843; Henry,

born Mar 27, 1847; George Jr., born Feb, 22, 1856; and Tabby, born Jan 13, 1863.
Isac BIRGE to Lucinda WOOD - Aug 13, 1865.
Joseph ONURY to Ella BARRETT - Aug 13, 1865.
Nelson PORTER to Liza Jane CHILDS - Aug 13, 1865. Children: George, age 30; Morris, age 25; Henry, age 22; and Laura, age 16.
Edward HERMAN to Mary CREPPER - Aug 13, 1865. Children: Sarah E., born Nov 21, 1854; Joseph P., born Jan 9, 1853; John W., born Sep 2, 1858; and Henry, born Oct 31, 1865.
George BROWN to Sarah PHILLIPS _ Aug 13, 1865. Children: Henry, age 20; Allen, age 18; George Fred, born Apr 14, 1857; and Samuel, born Jan 2, 1859.
Noble CROSS to Ellen WILLIAMS - Aug 18, 1865. Child: Ellen, age 23.
Jacob CREATH to Lucinda TAYLOR - Aug 13, 1865.
Pail DONNAL to Mina STEPHENS - Aug 13, 1865. Children: Green, age 30, and Nellie, age 18.
Harrison PRESTON to Sarah Ann SHY - Aug 13, 1865. Children: Liza, age 20, Effalinda, age 18, Isabelle, age 14; Isaac, age ;9; Emma, age 7; Sally, age 5; and Andrew, age 1.
William DOUGLASS to Angeline HENDERSON - Aug 13, 1865. Children: Alexander, age 20; Henry, age 15; Jane, age 8; and Mahalie, age 14.
Henry PRESTON to Charlotte CEOSTON - Aug 13, 1865. Children: Mary, age 23; James, age 20; Daniel, age 18; and Sarah, age 13.
Henry BREASETON to Millie WATSON - Aug 13, 1865. Children: Hannah, age 23; Delcia, age 25; ___?___, age 16; Lewis, age 15; Watson, age 14; and Hugh, age 9.
Preston JOHNSON to Jessie WAIL - Aug 13, 1865. Children: Fannie, age 20; Hettie, age 11; Dick, age 7; Susia, age 5; and Mary, age 3.
Patrick SMITH to Abbie CARPENTER - Aug 13, 1865. Children: Greer, age 16; Barney, age 13; Abbot, age 13; Catherine, age 11; Liza, age 11; and Caroline, age 4.
John MARTIN to Lina WOODSON - Aug 13, 1865. Children: Mary, age 21, and Sarah, age 18.
Daniel WATSON to Irena SYMPSON - Aug 13, 1865.

Children: Anna, age 18, and Elijah, age 16.
Thomas JONES to Leoli ASLIMAN - Aug 12, 1865. Children: Manda, age 21; Mary, age 20; William, age 18; Nimrod, age 15; Andrew, age 13; Peggie Ann, age 11; Alice, age 9; Sarah, age 7; Nanny, age 5; Belle, age 3; and Thomas, age 1.
James LAWRENCE to Winney FRANKLIN - Aug 13, 1865.
Thomas WILSON to Harriett WILITE - Aug 13, 1865. Children: Emily, age 5; Lewis, age 2; and John W., age 8 months.
Peter WATKINS to Eliza SAMUELS - Aug 13, 1865. Children: Mary E., age 17; Abram, age 14; and Andrew, age 5.
Peter TAYLOR to Harriett MARSHALL - Aug 24, 1865. Children: Abraham, age 24; Mary, age 22; Ann, age 21; Amanda, age 19; Permelia, age 17; David W., age 14; Martilda, age 8; and John W., age 4.
Henry FISHER to Lucy HULL - Aug 24, 1865. Son: George Henry, age 25.
Joseph CLAY to Mary GREY - Aug 27, 1865. Children: Watson Isac, age 13; Jannie Eliza, age 7; and Louis, age 3.
James SHOEMAKER to Martha WASHINGTON - Aug 27, 1865. Children: Mollie, age 12; Harriett, age 10; Tom Thompson, age 8; Phil Thompson, age 5; and Anna, age 4.
Jasper HERRON to Amanda Jane GLASGOW - Aug 13, 1865. Children: Mary F., age 15; Charity A., age 13; and Alen Jasper, age 5.
Anthony CARR to Ellen ELLIS - Sep 3, 1865.
John WASHINGTON to Celia HOBBS - Oct 15, 1865.
Lewis STANFORD to Marthey BLAKEY - Oct 7, 1865.
Jack GARRETT to Kisah WING - Oct 18, 1865. Child: Robert B..
Taylor GALES to Louisa SLAUGHTER - Oct 19, 1865. Child: Eunice.
Robert GARRETT to Emily TIPTON - Oct 19, 1865. Child: Cassandra.
Manuel POINDEXTER to Mary STAPLES - Oct 23, 1865. Children: Jane, Bruce, and Susan Emily.
Benjamin HERGAN to Salley WILLIAMS - Nov 2, 1865. Children: Alsey Ann, Benjamin S.,

Alexander, Amanda J., Sarah M., Salley Ann, Cintha Ann, William S., Nancy Mary, Catherine George.
Sampson WILLS to Matilda POINDEXTER - Nov 5, 1865. Children: Mary A., George W., William Harrison, Sarah J., Isaac, Robert, Caroline, and James F..
Richard FINDLEY to Sarah THORNTON - Oct 8, 1865.
John SMITH to Henrietta SMITH - Nov 13, 1865. Children: Manda, age 20; Irena, age 18; Charles, age 11; and Minnie, age 5.
Granderson ROBERTS to Marry Ann ROBERTS - Nov 13, 1865. Children: Edward, John, Charles, and Margaret.
Peter WILSON to Jane WILSON - Nov 14, 1865. Child: Ellen, age 2.
Lewis Henry BRADFORD to Miamid BRADFORD - Nov 14, 1865. Children: Maria, age 19; Lucy, age 18; Robert, age 14; Thomas, age 13; Eliza, age 10; John, age 6; and Sally, age 4.
George W. WHILTON to Sarah WITTON - Nov 20, 1965. Children: Mary, age 7; Albert, age 4; and Maria, age 2.
Richard TAYLOR to Mary TAYLOR - Nov 14, 1865. Children: Jane, age 21; Ellen, age 18; Henry, age 13; Richard, age 10; James, age 8; ? , age 6; Sally and Charles, age 1.
Osher TAYLOR to Maria TAYLOR - Nov 19, 1865. Children: Cora, age 16; Richard, age 14; Geels, age 10; Howard, age 8; Alica, age 7; Jane, age 5; and Milton, age 2.
Shelby WILLIAMS to Fanny JONES - Oct 22, 1865.
Ransom BILLS to Peggy BRISCOE - Nov 11, 1865. Children: Alfred, age 25; Clara, age 23; Filda, age 18; Jack, age 16; Franklin, age 13; Rhoda, age 11; Emery, age 6; and Fanny, age 2.
Major NASLY to Louisa ADAMS - Nov 11, 1865. Children: Thom, age 18; Mary, bor Dec 1850; Job, born Dec 1852; Ellen, born Dec 1854; Alfred, born Mar 1859; Millie, born Dec 1860; and Matilda, born in 1865.
Stephen ADAMS to Fannie ? - Nov 25, 1865. Children: John, age 25; William, age 21; Ellis, age 20; Ann, age 19; Harriett, age 16;

Stephen, age 14; Mary, age 13; Lizza, age 12; Margaret, age 11; Amy, age 8; Julia, age 6; Michael, age 3; and Benjamin, born Nov, 1865.

Andrew BROWN to Caroline SIMMONS - Nov 13, 1865. Children: Shelby, Willis, Lucia, Allice, and Mary.

Anthony PHILLIPS to Caroline GLASCO - Oct 29, 1865.

July TAYLOR to Sarah TAYLOR - Nov 13, 1865. Children: Agnes, George, and Henry Lee.

James LUCINE to America JONES - Nov 12, 1865. Children: Lonny and Kitty.

George WASHINGTON to Ray GUYER - Oct 22, 1865. Children: Charles, Columbus, Mary, Hester, and Elaney.

Frank JONES to Celia SAPPINGTON - Oct 29, 1865. Children: Mary, William, Catherine, and Joe.

Henry TERRELL to Ellen WEARFIELD - Oct 29, 1865.

Albert GLASGO to Elizabeth DUNCAN - Oct 29, 1865. Child: William C..

Spencer JOHNSON to Ann FIELDING - Nov 4, 1865.

Austin LUDDINGTON to Cate LINDSEY - Dec 9, 1865.

Edward WATSON to Charlotte CLYNE - Dec 19, 1865. Children: Aron, age 37; Robert, age 26; Margaret, age 22; Fannie, age 15; Ella, age 13; Joseph, age 8.

Robert TAYLOR to Manda CREATH - Dec 17, 1865. Child: Alexander.

Jordan TAYLOR to Patsy O'Brien - Nov 25, 1865. Children: Louisa, born in 1848; Henry in 1852; Lucy in 1854; Eliza, in 1856; Delia in 1855; John in 1860, Maria in 1862, and James born in 1864.

Andrew FINLEY to Ellen HENDERSON _ Dec 25, 1865.

Robert MALORY to Martha ELIOTT - Nov 25, 1865. Children: Eliza, age 15; Alexander, age 13; James, age 11; Joseph, age 10; Millie, age 8; David, age 7; and Charles, age 6.

Jesse HENDERSON to Lucy HENDERSON - Dec 25, 1865.

Archie MILLER to Amanda - Oct 22, 1865.

Thomas WILSON to Mary E. SIMPSON - Dec 30, 1865. Children: Celia Ann, age 6; Francis, age 4; and George Washington, age 2.

Charles MONROE to Malinda MONROE - Dec 29, 1865. Children: Catherine, age 5; Wm. Henry, age 2; and David, age 7 months.
John MARSHALL to Isabella SUNDERLAND - Dec 31, 1865.
Reuben Milton THORNTON to Virginia STAPLES - Dec 31, 1865.
Samuel CONNER to Nancy TRIGG - Dec 31, 1865.
Boral RICHARD to Caroline STEPHENS - Jan, 1866.
Henson WILLIAMS to Martha SMITH - Dec 31, 1865. Children: Elizabeth Anna and Francis.
Phillips WRIGHT to Sarah H. BANKS - Dec 24, 1865. Children: Mary Matilda and John.
Luke JOHNSON to Zilla HEART - Dec 24, 1865. Child: Mary.
Calep WRIGHT to Elizabeth MURPHY - Dec 10, 1865.
Tom Lowrey BABS to Clarrisy GREEN - Jan 18, 1866.
Bird BATY to Lucinda JOHNSON - Jan 14, 1866.
Andrew HANES to Margaret HOW - Dec 3, 1865.
Calvin CANON to Jenny BENCI - Jan 1, 1866. Children: Lewis, age 30; Charles, age 28; George, age 18; and Harriett, age 15.
Jesse MANN to Francis NEAL - Jan 14, 1866.
Joseph SMITH to Ann MILLS - Nov 12, 1865. Two children, not named.
Abraham NAPFIELD to Minda POINDEXTER - Nov 12, 1865. Child: Fanny.
George N. POINDEXTER to Lilly NAPFIELD - Nov 12, 1865. Children: Joshua, Moses, Sampson, Susan, and David.
Joseph SIMPSON to Celey HENDERSON - Nov 12, 1865. Children: Henrietta, Mary Ann, Margaret, Jennes, Martha C., Levisa E., Laten E., James S., and Richard Y.
Amstead GREEN to Ellen WEST - Nov 17, 1865. One adopted child, Fanny.
Pleasant HILL to Hetta FANIS - Nov 17, 1865. Children: Catherine, Josepha Ella, John B., Docie, Robert, and William H.
Augustus DAVIS to America McMAHAN - Nov 17, 1865.
Jesse H. DAVIS to George A. POSE - Dec 24, 1865. Children: America, Susan, and Kitty.
Dennis JACKSON to Louisa HERNDON - Dec 24,

1865. Children: ? and Thomas.
Isaac WARD to Dorcus SOUTHERLAND - Dec 31, 1865. Child: James.
Marton WASHINGTON to Matilda HARRISON - Jan 6, 1866.
George W. MILLS to Nancy Jane POINDEXTER - Dec 31, 1865.
James LEWIS to Martha ROBINSON - Jan 30, 1866. Children: Caroline, Sally A., Florada, Mary, Carto, Hannah, Mattie, and Hetta.
George GATES to Harriett THOMPSON - Jan 30, 1866.
John STEWART to Agnes STEWART - Jan 23, 1866. Children: Charlotte, age 14; Ellen, age 10; Cealy, age 9; and Mary, age 6.
Peter GIBSON to Lucy GIBSON - Jan 29, 1866. Children: Amanda, age 14 and Martha Ann, age 3.
John JACKSON to Betty JACKSON - Feb 4, 1866.
Henry KINEY to Patsy LEWIS - Feb 6, 1866, Children: James, age 18; George, age 11; Peter, age 9; and Charles, age 7.
Samuel BROWN to Lucy BROWN - Jan 30, 1866.
Albert FRISLY to Catherine BROWN - Jan 30, 1866. Children: Henry, age 3.
Benjamin HULL to Fanny HULL - Jan 25, 1866. Children: Lucy, age 47; Nancy, age 45; Diana, age 43; Maria, age 41; Marri, age 21.
Samuel CARTER to Levinia Ann JONES - Feb 4, 1866. Children: Virginia, age 6 and Sarah, age 3.
Aron LABO to Millie LABO - Jan 21, 1866. Child: Paul.
Newton BORAS to Margaret BORAS - Feb 4, 1866. Children: Margaret, age 11, and William, age 9.
John BUTLER to Lucy Ann SMITH - Feb 6, 1866.
William GREEN to Mrs. Louisa GREEN - Feb 6, 1866. Children: William, age 5, and Pheba, age 3.
Robert REVIS to Lucinda ASHCROFT - Jan 31, 1866. Children: Freeman, age 27, and Charles, age 26.
Green ROBERTSON to Mariah McCULLOCK - Jan 31, 1866. Child: Charles Lee, age 4 months.
Thomas WILSON to Mary Eliza SIMPSON - Feb 24,

1866. Children: Celia Ann, age 6; Francis, age 4; and George Washington, age 2.
John WILSON to Polly Ann WILLIAMS - Feb 2, 1866. Children: Catherine, age 5; William Henry, age 2; and David, age 7 weeks.
Thomas GENTRY to Phebe CHURCHWELL - Jan 6, 1866. Child: Isam, age 25.
Green WILSON to Mary Frances COBLER - Feb 2, 1866. Children: John Walker, age 14; Anna, age 8; and Josephine, age 4.
Abram MARTIN to Hannah HENDERSON - Feb 4, 1866. Children: Missouri, age 20; Allen, age 19; Lucretia, age 17; Isaac, age 15; Hiram, age 15; Anna Elizabeth, age 14; Daniel Webster, age 11; Melia, age 10; Dolly, age 8; and Wesly, age 6.
James SHIPLEY to Emma Juda - Feb 10, 1866. Children: Rebecca Jane, age 9 and James Thomas, age 1.
Gilbert DIXON to Leanna DIXON - Feb 14, 1866.
Adam J. DANFORD to Harriett PONTON - Feb 4, 1866.
Daniel CROW to Gerimy EUBANKS - Feb 4, 1866. Children: Clarsa, Francis, and John.
James BATY to Leah BANTON - Feb 4, 1866. Children: David, Fanny, Martha, Mary, Harriet, Lewisa, Henry, John, Ann, Medre, and Lucinda.
Rueben NELSON to Dicey NELSON - Sep 25, 1866. Children: Calip, Calvin, Sarah Jane, John, and Parker.
Jack MILLS to Dorcas Ann JOHNSON - Feb 24, 1866.
James WOODS to Ellen TAYLOR - Dec 28, 1865.
William NELSON to Jensthy NELSON - Feb 24, 1866. Children: Margaret Elizabeth, age 17, and Emily Catherine, age 16.
Alfred H. HAYTON to Martha ANN HAYTON - Feb 25, 1866. Children: Sura Ann, age 16; Armstead, age 13; Mary Elizey, age 10; Emily Williams, age 8; and Thomas Barton, age 2.
Allen GORDEN to Eliza GORDEN - Feb 29, 1866. Children: Jackson, age 18; Robert, age 16; Walter, age 15; and Franklin, age 12.
John WARREN to Hannah WILEY - Feb 28, 1866.
B. F. BARGER to Margaret ROBINSON - Feb 17,

1866. Children: Polly, Ann, and Louisa.
Addison DIGGS to Emily THOMAS - Feb 18, 1866.
Spencer BROWN to Juda REED - Feb 28, 1866.
Nimrod JONES to Lucretia COLKINS - Feb 28, 1866.
Robert ROBERTSON to Phebe Adlaida - Feb 5, 1866.
Abraham FRY to Jane BOWLER - Feb 4, 1866.
Addison LACY to Davy DOUGLASS - Feb 4, 1866.
Thomas A. SIMMS to Margaret M. TUT - Feb 4, 1866.
Chapeman COMMADORE to Elizabeth TAILOR - Feb 4, 1866.
William GLASGOW to Huldah JOHNSON - Mar 11, 1866.
David CLARK to Amy CLARK - Feb 28, 1866.
 Children: Cynthia Jane, age 12; Harriet, age 9; Ellin, age 6; and Loghly, age 3. David's age was given as 43, and Amy's as 32.
Moses BELL to Alley Wood - Feb 26, 1866.
 Children: Ann, Mary, George, and Moses.
Thomason HENDERSON, age 25, to Louisa WILLSON, age 22 - Feb 28, 1866. Child: Margaret Jane.
Warner TAYLOR to Pokehontus BOONE - Feb 4, 1866. Child: Mary Ann, age 11 months.
George MARTIN to Mary TAYLOR - Feb 8, 1866.
 Children: Jimmy, age 4; Walter and George, age 2.
Daniel BROWN to Silvia BROMLER - Feb 9, 1866. Their license noted all the children were grown.
Goin FAIRFAX to Carrey JACKSON - Feb 9, 1866.
 Children: Martha, born May of 1847; Darson, born Dec 1843; Hannah, born June, 1840; Daniel, born in Apr, 1838; and Jane, born Aug, 1836.
Henry VAUGHN to Susan E. JONES - Feb 4, 1866.
 Children: Smith, age 8; Thomas, age 5; Ellen, age 4; and Bill, age 14 months.
Aron JACKSON to Mary ESTIS - Feb 16, 1866.
 Children: Ellen, age 3, and Thomas, age 1.
Nathan BAKER to Sally HOUF - Feb 16, 1866. One child, age 2, not named.
Henry CURTIS to Matilda SMITH - Feb 9, 1866.
 Children: Charles, age 25; Henrietta, age 23; Lora, age 21, and Martha, age 19.

John PERRY to Ann JOHNSON - Feb 4, 1866. Children: Winny, age 3, and Squire age 18 months.
Nelson WIMBLE to Susan HOWARD - Feb 8, 1866. Children: Allin, age 5; William, age 10; Samuel, age 4; and Martha, age 2.
Harrison SATTON to Samaria COLLINS - Feb 16, 1866. Children: Austin, age 21; Morris, age 20; Rebecca, age 10; Joseph, age 12; Green, age 8; and Harrison, age 13.
Edward GATEWOOD to Caroline GATEWOOD - Feb 18, 1866. Children: Lousandra, Sarah, Eda, David, Faret, Davis, Margaret, Louellar, and Louis,
Willis JONES to Rebecca Jane TURPIN - Jan 21, 1866. Child: Mathew.
Henry TAYLOR to Sima MAYHAN - Jan 22, 1866. Children: George, Susan, Phillis, Lydia, Mary, Sophia, Ellen, Elizabeth, Finis, Duncan, and Ann.
Stephen TAYLOR to Madalin TAYLOR - Jan 22, 1866. Children: Rebecca and Julia,
Joseph JOHNSON to Kitty YOUNG - Feb 3, 1866. Child: Betsy.
James CAMPBELL to Jully Ann BOWERS - Feb 4, 1866.
George TAYLOR to Clara TITSWORTH - Feb 4, 1866. Children: Bill, Ellen, Jacob, and Littey.
Frank HOPSON to Eliza Ann SMITH - Feb 4, 1866. Children: Daniel, Luthar, Ann, Martha, Jane, Julius, Franklin, John, Allen, Calvin, Cutterdon, Marian, and Walker.
Michael ANDERSON to Elisa BOILER - Feb 4, 1866. Children: Judy, Salley, Francis, James Richard, and Margaret.
Tob TAYLOR to Betsy BROWN - Feb 4, 1866. Children: Mary, Elisa, and Sarah.
Samuel MILLER to Elizabeth McLAIN - Feb 4, 1866. Children: Martha Ann, Alice, Casie, and Galveston.
Wesley GRAY to Lucretia HOBSON - Feb 11, 1866. Children: Artemesia, George, ___anbin, and John Presly.
Jeramiah MARMA to Sealy HILLY - Feb 11, 1866. Children: Ellen, Cordelia, James. Henry, and Violotta.

Gabriel KIZER to Nancy Jane BOWERS - Feb 11, 1866. Children: Nelson Smith and Lucy Jane Adison.
Jesse COWEN to Fanny JOHNSTON - Mar 24, 1866.
Wm. JOHNSON to Susan - Dec 28, 1865.
Lang JACKSON to Martha REDMAN - Jan 12, 1866.
John JACKSON to Mary REDMAN - Jan 12, 1866. Child: William.
Rial McFADEN to Phillis LACY - Jan 18, 1866.
Wilson HELMS to Missouri REDMAN - Jan 18, 1866. Children: Anna, Lang, and Emil.
Peter EMBERSON to Lucinda McFARLAND - Feb 25, 1866. Children: Aron, age 30; Thomas, age 25; Peter, age 23; Mary E., age 18; and Ella, age 16.
Aron EMBERSON to Amanda BAKER - Feb 12, 1866. Children: Robert, age 3, and Alexander, age 3 months.
George SIBLEY to Corinda BROWN - Feb 12, 1866. Children: Jacob A., age 9: George B., age 6; Rosanna, age 4; and John B., age 2.
Peter EMBERSON JONES to Mary A. GREY - Feb 25, 1866.
John EMBERSON to Martha HICKMAN - Feb 24, 1866. Children: Fanny, age 6; William, age 6; and Lousa, age 3.
Abram JOHNSTON to Cordelia JOHNSON - Apr 14, 1866.
Peter HUMBLE to Martha JACKSON - Jan 12, 1866.
Samuel REUBEN to Amanda THOMPSON - July 7, 1866. Children: Adam, John, and Lucy.
Richard WILLIAM to Hannah RAGLAND - Apr 29, 1866. Child: Mariah Ann, born Sep 29, 1861.
James LAWSON to Eliza ROBERTSON - Sep 8, 1866.
Daniel DANFORD to Jemima VANCROSE - Sep 30, 1866.
Robert EDWARDS to Melissa FIELDS - Nov 22, 1866.
Mortemer TAYLOR to Sarah J. MARSHALL - Nov 10, 1866.
George JILES to Amy JILES - Dec 4, 1866.

<u>Audrain County</u>, Book A.
Henry GOFFEN to Catherine FOWLER - Nov 27, 1865.
Elijah HARRISON to Sallie HARRISON - Dec 24, 1865.

John JAMISON to Susan BARCLY - Dec 28, 1865.
George MAULER to Ann MAULER - Jan 23, 1866.
Harry CARTER to Rosetta CARTER - Feb 16, 1866.
Robert LINSEY to Feba FRANKLIN - Feb 16, 1866.
Lewis RICE to Susanie RICE - Feb 14, 1866. Both were from Boone County. Child: Ann Elizabeth.
Harry BASKETT to Sallie BASKETT - Feb 18, 1866.
George CLARK to Catherin BROOKIN - Sep 24, 1866.
Matt BOYD to Winnie WADE - June 18, 1866.
Charles CUNNINGHAM to Carry WEST - Sep 30, 1866.
James HALL to Jane HALL - Dec 27, 1866.
Harrison REED to Eady DINGLE - Nov 19, 1866.
Alfred FLEMOUS to Nora McINTIRE - Sep 10, 1866.
John EUBANKS to Melinda BEATTY - Dec 20, 1866.
Jesse BRITT to Jane Cultey - Dec 20, 1866.
Randall WALKER to Sontee GORAM - Aug 25, 1866.
George GAMBLE to Perlinda MARTIN - Aug 24, 1866.
Samuel JACKSON to Manda GARRETT - Dec 20, 1866.
Rabert VASH to Catherine VASH - Feb 27, 1866. Children: Aaron, born in 1850; Sousie, born in 1853; Mary, born in 1859; and Sarah, born in 1860. This license also lists Robert's children by his first marriage to Rosetta: Henry, age 23; Charles, age 22; and Harriett, age 27.
Daniel F. LETCHER to Mary FALER - Feb 17, 1866. Children: Thomas, Mahala, Louisa, and Daniel.
Edward TOWNSEND to Martha FRENCH - June 9, 1867.
Jacob STURGEON to Rhoda NOBLE - June 16, 1866. The groom was formerly of St. Louis, and his age was given as 24, brides age was given as 20.
Ephraim PALMER to Annie WILLIAMS - May 10, 1866.
Squire BELL to Elvira BELL - Mar 30, 1866.
John MILLER to Mama MILLER - Mar 18, 1866.
Richard DULY to Martha DULY - Mar 26, 1866.
Gibson McDONALD to Hannah F. BELL - May 16, 1866.
John A. BRITT to Mary BRITT - Mar 26, 1866.
William Henry FASSETT to Frances ASHBERRY - May 21, 1866. Groom's age was give as 49, and the bride's age as 46. Children: Eliza, age 23; William Oliver, age 19; Charles Henry, age 17; John, age 10; Rachel, age 9; John

Willis, age 5, deceased; Robert Thomas, age 3.
Norris HUNTER to Lucinda CLARKE - Mar 25, 1866, Children: William, Eliza, Hiram, and Sarah A.
Thomas MITCHELL to Lucy J. BLUE - Apr 14, 1866. Children: Elizabeth and John C..
Levi RILEY to Catherine NICHOLAS - Apr. 14, 1866. Children: Benjamin, Mary E., and Henry.
____ BLUE to Elizabeth GALBRETH - Apr 14, 1866. Children: John W., Louisa, Hannah, Jane H., Thomas, Mary, and Mariah BLUE.
Henry MORRIS to Helen DARBY - Apr 14, 1866. Child: Eliza.
Henry DISHMAN to Mary HARRIS - May 19, 1867.
James PALMER to Maria WALKER - Sep 19, 1867.
John HENDERSON to Amanda PHILLIPS - Apr 12, 1868.
Norval BALL to Fanny HARDIN - Nov 24, 1867.
John MILLER to Judee TURLEY - Jan 8, 1868.
Elijah WRIM to Sarah JACKSON - Jan 30, 1868.
Nathan FAUCETT to Sarah BARNS - May 30, 1867.
Lewis JACKSON to Hannah MARTIN - July 29, 1868.
William JACKSON to Catherine HARRIS - Nov 29, 1867.
John CARRIER to Ann OLLISON - May 29, 1868.
Moses McMURPHY to Mary MATIN - Nov 18, 1868.
Henderson SMITH to Martha HADEN - Dec 3, 1868.
William DELONG to Mary BELL - May 17, 1869.
Daniel DORSOM to Lettie J. STELLE - Dec 24, 1869.
Henry DAVIS to Eliza CROCKETT - Nov 19, 1869.
Dennis GAY to Jane NICKENS - May 27, 1869.
John CUNNINGHAM to Lucy VAY - May 23, 1869.
James BOLEN to Jane McKINSEY - Mar 29, 1869.
Thomas FRUIT to Lucy PHILLIPS - Jan 15, 1869.
George THOMAS to Mary SKINNER - Dec 23, 1869.
Stephen JACKSON to Recy SPARKS - July 11, 1869. Groom of Callaway County.
Garrett WALKER to Malinda ROBINSON - July 11, 1869. Groom of Callaway County.
Oston PATE to Frances SOWSEN - May 19, 1870.
William BUNT to Laura CAMPBELL - Apr 11, 1870.
Alen Burgess WASHINGTON to Cassie TAYLOR - Oct 27, 1870.
John S. BASNZ (sic) to Harriet TURNER - Dec 1, 1870.
Hugh DILLARD to Caroline Cunningham - Mar 1,

Alexander HARRISON to Elizbeth DAVIS - Dec 25, 1870.
Solomon MILLER to Elizabeth VAN HORN - Apr 8, 1871.
Squire WILLIAMS to Netta JOHNSON - Dec 5, 1870.
Edward HOWARD to Eve SYACKET - Nov 23, 1871.
George Sterks to Cynthia STOKES - Oct 30, 1871.
Pleasant WEVER to Missouri HENDRICKS - Dec 25, 1871.
Henry TOWNLEY to Sara McDOWELL - Aug 2, 1871.
James BLUFORD to Sidney JONES - Oct 19, 1871.
George SELBY to Rebecca FORD - Mar 7, 1872.
Frank ARMSTEAD to Milly FORD - Mar 11, 1872.
Frank BASKET to Sally WILLIAM - Apr 7, 1872.
George GAMBEL to Eliza HENDERSON - Jan 14, 1872.
John F. HEAMS to Paulina MEADOWS - Apr 13, 1872.
Calvin CARTER to Magga THOMPSON - Apr 27, 1872.
John BALL to Nancy Jane RIVER - June 17, 1872.
John WHITE to Pink BUCKNER - June 19, 1872.
Henry CARTER to Henrietta PORTER - Dec 22, 1872.
Alexander GOODE to Maria PALMER - Sep 25, 1872.
Warren BROWN to Margaret OFFORD - Aug 14, 1872.
Meusses KNIGHT to Mary BRYANT - Nov 3, 1872.
Aaron WOOLDRIDGE to Mella POWELL - Oct 16, 1872.
Haralson FERGUSON to Alice CLARK - Feb 10, 1872.
Paton HARJUES (sic) to Mrs. Amanda BLEU - Apr 13, 1873.
Gilbert WOODWARD to Francis HARRISON - Aug 28, 1873.
George HENCH to Louisa ELLISEN - Aug 21, 1873.
Richard WEMS to Margaret CLEMENS - Oct 11, 1873.
Thomas TURNER to Julia D. THOMPSON - Aug 10, 1874.
Denis HALL to Rhoda THOMPSON - Dec 31, 1873.
George CUNNINGHAM to Miss Mattie - Jan 3, 1874.
Benjamin JOHNSON to Emmee HENDERSON - June 13, 1874.
Charles BROWN to Henrietta COOPER - June 20, 1874.
Jackson JAMESON to Lucy STULTZ - Nov 12, 1874.
James JAMESON to Cordie WALKER - Nov 5, 1874.

Benjamin WINN to Alice RITCHIE - Dec 29, 1874. Married at the residence of Joseph RITCHIE.
George JACKSON to Elizabeth JAMESON - Feb 28, 1875.
Alfred GRISWELL to Phillis JEWELL - June 6, 1875.
Silas MITCHELL to Bettie CARTER - Aug 6, 1875.
J. P. RIGHTSELL to Jane BASKETT - Dec 9, 1875.
Warren COOPER to Mariah CHURCHMAN - Feb 10, 1876.
John JOHNSON to Katy WASHINGTON - Jan 23, 1876.
James PRICE to Annie FRY - Feb 19, 1876.
William WRIGHT to Crecia OWENS - Feb 24, 1876.
Jerimah SIMS to Rose WILSON - Mar 11, 1876.
Turner THOMPSON to Martha MICKEE - May 18, 1876.
Oliver GASKINS to George Ann WILSON - Jan 20, 1876.
Cato SMITH to Margaret POWERS - June 7, 1876.
Richard PHILLIPS - Margaret JOHNSON - May 23, 1876.
Pleasant WEAVER to Amanda SORRELL - Aug 13, 1876.
Martin ROBINSON to Mary BUSH - Oct 17, 1876.
Warren BELL to Martha HARRIS - Mar 15, 1877.
Sarley BROWN to Mary ERVEN - Apr 5, 1877.
Isam SMALLY to Maria BANE - Apr 28, 1877.
Milton RICHARDSON to Annie WALKER - July 21, 1877.
Alfred B. DYNES to Rachael BATES - July 26, 1877.
Frank CHRISTIAN to Maggie GREENWAY - Aug 9, 1877.
Daniel LEROY to Ella BRIGHT - Aug 30, 1877.
William H. CARPENTER to Sallie PHILLIPS - July 5, 1877.
David CANADA to Maggie DUNLAP - Sep 9, 1877.
Scott BANE to Joanna BELL - Oct 14, 1877.
John JOHNSON to Lou Ann BENTON - Ovt 9, 1877.
Henry NIGHTINGALE to Lucy FRUIT - Oct 25, 1877.
Alonzo HAWKINS to Celia CANADA - Nov 29, 1877.
John EUBANKS to Caroline CUMMINGS - Jan 27, 1878.
L. F. SCOTT to Martha ADAMS - Feb 2, 1878.
Thomas McCLURE to Sophia DORSEY - Feb 22, 1878.
Demar WASHINGTON to Susan OTIE - Apr 23, 1878.

Martin BUCHUM to Melinda MEADOWS - Apr 11, 1878.
Warner GEORGE to Georgia Ann POWELL - Sep 11, 1874.
Francis NICKENS to Dica Isabel THOMPSON - Apr 20, 1878.
Charlie RITCHIE to Celia KERR - Mar 24, 1878.
Charles DAVIS to Maria LONG - July 18, 1878.
Thomas SMITH to Malinda EUBANKS - Sep 11, 1873.
George SCOTT to Sallie WATTS - Dec 21, 1875.
Swin (sic) DAVIS to Eunece COATS to Dec 18, 1874.
Silles HEULL - Susan CUNNINGHAM - May 23, 1873.
Thomas WHITE to Mary COOK - June 8, 1874.
Jesse BRITT to Minter COLLINS - Mar 2, 1878.
Benjamin CRIGLER to Jane SINCLAIR - Oct 19, 1878.
Simon BOOKER to Amanda JACKMAN - Nov 28, 1878.
Thos. WHITE to Martha ESAZLE - July 7, 1878.
Warren FISHER to Mariah BROWN - Sep 3, 1878.
John GATEWOOD to Melinda MICKEY - Jan 21, 1879.
Charles E. C. WALKER to Lou Elizabeth CARTER - Dec 26, 1878.
James BLUE to Nannie TAYLOR - Feb 7, 1879.
Robert BLUE to Susan Wells - Mar 9, 1879.
George HINCH to Fannie RICHARDSON - Mar 12, 1879.
Rolling MITCHELL to Elizabeth CARSON - May 18, 1879.
Daniel S. DUDLEY to Ellen ANDERSON - Sep 3, 1879.
Martin BEACHAM to Mildred ARNOLD - July 4, 1879.
Martin MITCHELL to Barbara HAINS - Jan 1, 1880.
Ruben JOHNSON to Lizzy JOHNSON - Dec 24, 1879.
Robert JOHNSON to Rebecca SMILE - Apr 10, 1878.
Wm. HOLT to Fannie LEFRIDGE - Dec 24, 1879.
E. W. WHAILY to Georga A. BROWN - June 18, 1877.
William CROWLEY to Harriett PREWITT - Mar 28, 1880.
Abram C. JOHNSON to Maggie REVIER - June 13, 1880.
Perry RED to Paulee ELLIS - Apr 25, 1880.
James DUDLEY to Ella HENDERSON - Apr 30, 1874.

Henry BUCKNER to Laura DAWSON - Oct Oct 11, 1880.
Robert TOMHIRSON (sic) to Fannie FAUCETT - Oct 21, 1880.
J. W. STEVENSON to Matilda HARRIS _ Nov 11, 1880.
David PUXTER to Caroline SHOCK - Nov 11, 1880.
George W. STEWARD to Endora BLUE - Aug 29, 1880.
Nelson BROOKINGS to Hennie DAVIS - June 1, 1880.
Henry LYNCH TO Lucy Jane COCKREL - Feb 23, 1881.
Solomon MARTIN to Fannie CASBY - May 13, 1881.
Alexander RIGHT to Mary MACK - June 13, 1881.
Mark LACY to Dicy HAMILTON - Mar 30, 1881.
Ford HOLODY to Martha MOORE - Aug, 1878.
P. P. G. PERRY to Elizabeth FISHER - Apr 28, 1881.
William ROLLIGS to Hattie WOLSY - Sep 25, 1878.
George YATES to Arena MARTIN - Nov 30, 1878.
Frank VINE to Emily FORRES - Dec 21, 1879.
James JOHNSON to Lizzie JONES - Mar 17, 1880.
George BIVIERS to Mary Susan Ellis - July 14, 1880.
Nathaniel BALL to Laurie CUNNINGHAM - Nov 10, 1880.
Jerry Mile ELLIS to Alsie BROWN - Mar 16, 1881.
Henry HANSADY to Louizy SAIL - May 25, 1881.
Turner JAMISON to Lida MARTIN - Apr 6, 1879.
Richard BALL to Jane DUNCAN - July 14, 1869.
  This marriage was not recorded until June 21, 1890.

CEMETERIES

<u>Mt. Olive</u>, Johnson County.   Located Sec 5, Twp 47, R 25, 2½ miles south of the county line.
BRADFORD, Porter H. - 1893 - 1940.
BRADFORD, Mrs. B. - 1876 - 1932.
COLLINS, ada - 1879 - 1947.
COLLINS, Amander - 1877 - 1945.
COLLINS, Mrs. Fannie - 1903 - 1945.
COLLINS, Fox - 1878 - 1940.
COLLINS, Jane - 1837 - 1910.
COLLINS, James - 1861 - 1914.
COLLINS, Robert - 1833 - 1918.
FORBUSH, Harriet - 1828 - 1938.
CROCKETT, William - 1845 - 1911.
FOY, Elmer - 1862 - 1917.
GRANT, Mary Elizabeth - d. 1948.
GOLES, Albert T. - 1861 - 1918.
GOLES, Bertha H. - 1870 - 1941.
GOLES, Grant W. - 1864 - 1927.
GOLES, R. H. Simpson - 1869 - no date.
GOLES, Ulysses - 1893 - 1948.
HARRISON, Matilda - 1908 - 1948.
JACKSON, Mattie BURTAN - d. 1941.
RALPH, Bessie - 1897 - 1946.
RALPH, Delia - 1873 - 1948.
RALPH, George - 1877 - 1926.
SANDFORD, Malinda - 1839 - 1908.
SANDFORD, William - 1838 - 1914.
SIMPSON, Alice - 1845 - 1912.
SIMPSON, Alice - 1868 - 1936.
STEVENS, Edward - 1877 - 1941.
WALKER, Bessie JoLee - 1911 - 1949.
WALKER, John - 1850 - 1932.
GOLES, Emmett "Toots", son of Hancel & Herthal B. - Dec 15, 1923 - Dec 14, 1976.
JOHNSON, George T. - Jan 1, 1869 - Mar 14, 1977.
JOHNSON, Lillie E., wife of George T., and a daughter of Harvey & Allie BROWN - Sep 29, 1904 - Nov 21, 1974.
BUSH, Phenix - Oct 23, 1895 - Nov 10, 1962.
COLLINS, Lula - d. Nov 20, 1957.
COLLINS, Zelota - d. Ovt 17, 1964.
DICKSON, Julia May - May 11, 1897 - May 16, 1968.

GOLES, Orcestes W. - Sep 21, 1891 - Dec 12, 1960.
HARRISON, Jacob E. - d. Sep 29, 1956.
JOHNSON, Robert Henry - d. Sep 29, 1956.
McKINLEY, Savannah COLLINS, wife of Bradford - Sep 28, 1900 - Sep 28, 1971.
RALPH, Monta - buried Aug 6, 1959.
GOLES, Hancel C. - Aug 15, 1895 - Aug 6, 1979.
GOLES, Herthel Bernice, wife of Hancel, daughter of Willfox & Lula (JOHNSON) COLLINS - Aug 12, 1904 - Nov 26, 1978.

Mt. Hope Church Cemetery, Boone County. Located on Mt. Hope Road. There is evidence of many unmarked graves.
DOXLEY, Charles Bell - 1885 - 1969.
JOHNSON, Everett - 1898 - 1981.
MATHEWS, Mintie - 1871 - 1964.
" William - 1882 - 1963.
BROWN, Matilda - 1912 - 1988.
" Gordon - 1906 - 1986.
BRANHAM, Joseph A. - 1916 - 1933.
JOHNSON, Lucinda - d. Oct 30, 1902, aged 70 yr.
DEVIER, Sallie - 1852 - Sep 17, 1905.
MITCHEL, Elvira - Oct 11, 1829 - July 21, 1934.
BROOKS, James E. - Aug 26, 1872 - Apr 27, 1920.
PERSINGER, Annie - Feb 7, 1855 - May 29, 1909.
PHELPS, Delilah Ann - May 18, 1835 - Feb 22, 1891.
JACKSON, Eliza, wife of A. - d. Dec 21, 1876, aged 42 yr., 11 mo., 10dy.
HUGHS, Eugene - June 20, 1874 - Aug 31, 1899.
BROWN, Lawrence A., son of Lillie - Nov 2, 1953 - Apr 3, 1977.
BROWN, Lillie M. - July 20, 1929 - Mar 30, 1988.
WILLIAMS, Dorsey C., US Army WWI - Sep 24, 1893 - Aug 20, 1980.
WILLIAMS, Rosa T. - Feb 18. 1891 - Aug 18, 1973.
WILLIAMS, Charles Russell - 1913 - 1975.
WILLIAMS, Bessie R. - 1903 - 1980.
WILLIAMS, Dora O. - Mar 2, 1874 - Dec 19, 1982.
BERRY, Amanda, wife of Octive BERRY - d. Nov 30, 1907, aged 50 yr.

BRANHAM, Mary O., daughter of G. B. & L. - d. Apr 20, 1876, aged 27 yr., 10 mo., 22 dy.
BOONE, Stadie - 1884 - 1953.
BOONE, James - d. Nov 25, 1943.
BAYNHAM, Medora - Feb 14, 1860 - Mar 10, 1903.
BURGETT, Annie M. - Nov 1861 - Nov 16, 1904.
BURGETT, Millie A., wife of G. M. - d. Jan 12, 1889, aged 50 yr., 5 mo., 12 dy.
BURGETT, Rev. Phillip A. J. - 1869 - 1950.
BURGETT, Jluia Ann, wife of Phillip - May 12, 1874 - Nov 12, 1912.
BURNHAM, ___?___ - Mar 19, 1882 - Apr 5, 1888.
CARTER, Harry - Feb 9, 1879 - Mar 14, 1962.
"   Melissa - Feb 1, 1877 - Nov 15, 1955.
CARTER, Leon A. - Dec 28, 1908 - Feb 9, 1930.
CARTER, Maude - July 23, 1911 - June 9, 1943.
CARTER, Raymond - 1903 - 1979.
CHAPPELL, Britton - 1821 - Mar 24, 1903.
CHILDS, Annie E., daughter of J. W. & Lizzie - Oct 21, 1903 - Mar 3, 1904.
CHILDS, Fannie - 1878 - 1924.
CHILDS, Earl T. - 1905 - 1907.
COLEMAN, Virgil K. - Apr 21, 1912 - Mar 24, 1965.
DAVIS, Albert - 1899 - 1964.
DAVIS, Maggie B. - 1878 - 1942.
DIXON, Noah - 1866 - 1912.
DIXON, Lina, wife of L. - no dates.
FARMER, Nell - June 9, 1900 - Jan 18, 1981.
FARMER, Ida M. - Aug 4, 1893 - Mar 22, 1970.
FERGUSON, Henry - 1918 - 1937.
FERGUSON, Lillian - 1893 - 1929.
FERGUSON, Mitchel - 1886 - 1972.
FERGUSON, Anna, wife of Mitchel - 1886 - 1972.
HART, Alexander - d. Aug 14, 1899, age 31 yr.
HAWKINS, Allen C. - 1895 - 1973.
HAWKINS, Myrtle, wife of Allen - 1899 - 1949.
HAWKINS, Lawrence B. - 1884 - 1969.
HAWKINS, Zelia, wife of Lawrence - 1888 - 1964.
JOHNSON, William - 1870 - 1948.
JOHNSON, Carey Mildred, wife of Wm. - 1870 - 1950.
KELLY, Lucinda - Dec 24, 1862 - Jan 12, 1916.
KELLY, H. T. - Oct 15, 1852 - Apr 10, 1907.
KOUNSE, George - d. Oct 22, 1889, aged 70 yr.
LOGAN, Ora B. - 1889 - 1958.

BRANDT, Flora, wife of Jno. - Aug 5, 1881 - Aug 18, 1888.
BRANDT, Shannon, son of Jno. & Flora - Aug 5, 1881 - May 27, 1903.
BRANDT, Eddie, son of Jno. & Flora - Nov 14, 1887 - July 16, 1905.
WILLIAMS, Emmet Florence - no dates.
ROGERS, Henry David - 1869 - 1951.
ROGERS, King David - no dates.
___?___, Mathew S. 18?3 - 1969.
ROGERS, Dorothy A. - Apr 1, 1879 - Jan 25, 1986.
ROGERS, Smith T. - July 13, 1887 - Nov 3, 1973.
ROGERS, Robert Roy, son of Smith & Dorothy - July 18, 1913 - July 11, 1991.
ROUTT, Alice Victoria ROGERS, daughter of Smith & Dorothy - Jan 26, 1922 - Apr 14, 1983.

Mt. Vernon Church Cemetery, Callaway County. Located Sec 28, Twp 45, R 11, southwest of Hots Summit, Missouri. This is the oldest black church, still in existence in Callaway County, the original members being slaves who met in a shed on the master's property.
ADAMS, Thomas - d. May 7, 1910, aged 52 yr.
RANEY, Sophia, wife of Lar - Aug 30, 1857 - Mar 31, 1909.
BASS, Isaac S. d. Dec 30, 1870. aged 22 yr. 1 mo., 10 dy.
BATES, Milan - 1841 - no date.
"   Martha - 1843 - 1919.
BAYNHAM, J. Winfre - 1886 - 1968.
BAYNHAM, Annie, wife of J. W. - 1886 - 1928.
BAYNHAM, Wilton F. - July 1, ? - Jan 11, 1977.
BENTLEY, Hattie - May 15, 1890 - Nov 25, 1950.
BRANHAM, Polly - 1831 - 1929.
BRANDON, Maude - Apr 10, 1889 - May 21, 1901.
BRANHAM, Charlie, son of G. B. & L. - d. Oct 11, 1889, aged 32 yr., 10 mo,. 27 dy.
BRANHAM, Manda A., daughter of G. B. & L. - d. May 20, 1876, aged 11 yr., 8 mo., 3 dy.
BRANHAM, Louisa, wife of G. B. - d. Jan 16, 1892. aged 65 yr.
BRANHAM, Price, son of G. B. & L. - d. Feb 2, 1876, aged 24 yr., 6 mo., 2 dy.

MILLS, Johanna - Sep 5, 1854 - May 17, 1923.
MURRAY, Adeline - d. Jan 28, 1914, aged 65 yr.
MURRAY, Annie - d. Jan   , 191 , aged 6 yr.
MURRAY, Ida - July 19, 1880 - Nov 22, 1932.
MURRAY, Leland - Dec 15, 1904 - June 21, 1960.
MURRAY, Lewie H. - 1900 - 1947.
"   Lillian M. - 1894 - 1939.
MURRAY, Nora - 1877 - 1969.
MURRAY, Robert E., son of Frank - May 2, 1902.
MURRAY, Martha - Dec 23, 1870 - June 29, 1940.
MURRAY, William O. - Jan 3, 1873 - Jan 17, 1947.
MURRAY, William O. - Jan 1, 1904 - July 29, 1972.
MURRY, Bettie - Nov 10, 1874 - Feb 1, 1900.
McKAMEY, Elizabeth MURRAY - June 3, 1872 - Sep 4, 1963.
MURRAY, James - d. Dec 7, 1912, aged 69 yr.
NARY, Sallie A. - Aug 16, 1836 - Aug 17, 1899.
NEAL, John H., son of Henry & Sallie - d. Apr 4, 1890, aged 19 yr., 11 mo., 27 dy.
OLIVER, Alice G. - Apr 12, 1864 - Spe 13, 1921.
OLIVER, De Andrew - d. Sep 28, 1911, aged 28 yr.
OLIVER, Edward, Co F 56th USC INF - no dates.
OLIVER, Edward Jr. - Feb 2, 1872 - Mar 16, 1976.
OLIVER, George - June 20, 1851 - Feb 26, 1917.
OLIVER, Phoebe - May 20, 1817 - Oct 15, 1900.
PATTERSON, Mattie BURGETT - Jan 29, 1896 - Sep 2, 1930.
RAMSEY, Nellie, wife of Arch - d. Apr 7, 1888, aged 74 yr.
REESE, Luella - 1895 - 1956.
REYNOLDS, Ann - d. June 14, 1876, aged 48 yr.
REYNOLDS, Clifford - 1934 - 1935.
REYNOLDS, Earl, Pvt 415 RES Labor BN QMC WWI - Aug 19, 1894 - Nov 15, 1962.
REYNOLDS, Florence - 1911 - 1936.
REYNOLDS, Hattie - July 4, 1864 - Mar 26, 1947.
REYNOLDS, Mary, wife of Hattie - May 2, 1865 - Dec 4, 1939.
REYNOLDS, Richard D. - Feb 1, 1871 - Feb 10, 1966.
REYNOLDS, Serepta J., wife of Richard - Aug 24, 1870 - Aug 8, 1945.

REYNOLDS, Wm. Otto - Jan 26, 1896 - no date.
REYNOLDS, Orva B., wife of Wm. - Mar 27, 1897 - Feb 15, 1971.
REYNOLDS, Scott - d. Mar 30, 1906, aged 84 yr.
REYNOLDS, James - d. May 1, 1879, aged 44 yr.
REYNOLDS, Viola - 1900 - 1936.
REED, James - 1888 - 1960.
SAMUELS, Olivia L. Apr 24, 1895 - Jan 17, 1971.
SIMMONS, Carl E.- Dec 20, 1948 - July 20, 1965.
SIMMONS, Joseph - 1901 - 1970.
SIMMONS, Martha - Feb 1, 1867 - May 14, 1921.
SIMMONS, Richard - Jan 8, 1860 - 1948.
SIMMONS, Amanda, wife of Richard - 1863 - 1936.
SIMMONS, Richard Jr. - Dec 1882 - Feb 8, 1897.
SIMMONS, William R., son of Joe & Iola - Aug 13, 1926 - Oct 9, 1939.
SIMMONS, George - 1855 - Jan 11, 1924.
SIMMONS, Hildle G. - Nov 2, 1919 - July 9, 1939.
SIMMONS, Richard, son of R. R. & M. S. - Dec 19, 1882 - Feb 16, 1897.
SIMMONS, Warner W. - 1891 - 1985.
"   Lucille - 1900 - 1965.
SMITH, Cyrus C. - Mar 24, 1850 - Apr 28, 1896.
SMITH, Joanna H., wife of Cyrus - Auly 28, 1907, aged 65 yr.
STANLEY, Benjamin - Dec 25, 1888 - Feb 21, 1919.
STANLEY, Marie - 1870 - 1942.
STOKE, George, son of S. H. & Elizabeth - Oct 15, 1873 - Aug 10, 1892.
TARLETON, Solomon, Co D 69th USCI - no dates.
TARLETON, Joseph H. - d. Dec 7, 1892, 50 yr., 8 mo., 12 dy.
WEBB, Effie - Mar 8, 1890 - Feb 15, 1916.
WHITE, Ruben - 1857 - 1924.
WHITE, Ellen, wife of Ruben - 1860 - 1908.
WILLIAMS, Fanny MURRAY FOLEY - d. Oct 19, 1896.
WILLIAMS, Charity - 1817 - June 27, 1911.
BRANHAM, Maud L. - Apr 10, 1889 - May 21, 1901.

<u>Pleasant Hill Cemetery</u>, Newton County. Located Sec 11, Twp 25, R 32.
BAKER, Coleman - Oct 21, 1837 - Feb 22, 1903.
BAKER, Oliver - d. Aug 25, 1966, aged 44 yr., 10 mo., 14 dy.

BAKER, Ophia - June 26, 1897 - Jan 8, 1969.
ALLEN, John - 1865 - 1922.
CARTER. Gertrude - no dates.
BARNETT, Luke - 1847 - Jan 1, 1909.
BRITT, Myrtle - 1883 - 1960.
BRITT, Wyatt - 1870 - 1910.
BROWN, Roy - Dec 5, 1906 - Nov 21, 1966.
BROWN, Juanita - Mar 4, 1904 - Dec 15, 1925.
McCLANAHAN, Orvil - no dates.
McCLANAHAN, Leo - no dates.
McCLANAHAN, J. W. - Sep 5, 1870 - Feb 7, 1918.
CALLAWAY, Edna - 1868 - 1963.
" Frank - no dates.
MARTIN, Billy Wayne - d. Mar 7, 1971, aged 38 yr., 2 mo., 11 dy.
MARTIN, Lottie - 1905 - 1970.
MARTIN, William A. - 1902 - no date.
COOPER, Eliza Dale - d. Oct 1, 1925, aged 75 yr.
COOPER, Ernest, 1879 - 1887.
COOPER, Fannie - 1882 - 1906.
COOPER, Matilda - May 8, 1868 - Sep 12, 1907.
COOPER, Ralph d. 1876 - 1908.
GARVIN, Biddie - 1888 - 1936.
GARVIN, David D. - 1872 - 1934.
GARVIN, Louvina G. - 1876 - 1942.
GILBERT, Charles P. - no dates.
CORK, Mary - no dates.
GIBSON, Francis - Feb 24, 1872 - Aug 8, 1914.
GIBSON, William - d. May 31, 1941.
EVANS, Naomi BRITT - 1906 - 1962.
GRANT, Amanda - d. 1937.
GRANT, Silas - d. 1912.
GROUCH, Anna - 1867 - 1911.
JACKSON, Emmes - no dates.
FROST, Fannie - no dates.
FROST, Gladys - d. July 3, 1931.
DENNIS, John - Sep 25, 1845 - July 12, 1914.
HOUSTON, Joanna - Feb 16, 1862 - Sep 19, 1902.
HOUSTON, S. H. - no dates.
GAGE, William - 1884 - 1911.
GAGE, Fred - d. July 7, 1947.
GAGE, Lewis - no dates.
GAGE, Mary - d. July 17, 1939, aged 89 yr.
GAGE, Neona - Feb 22, 1900 - Mar 13, 1901.
GAGE, Sterling - Apr 18, 1901 - May 31, 1972.

McPHERSON, A. - Aug 25, 1866 - Oct 6, 1906.
HOLMES, Guy - 1883 - Sep 22, 1918.
JONES, Commodore - Feb 17, 1900 - Feb 4, 1953.
OWENS, Savannah E. - 1884 - 1936.
MARSHALL, Will - 1866 - 1954.
MARSHALL, Erma - Jan 27, 1897 - Nov 8, 1920.
MARSHALL, William T. - 1906 - 1962.
HARRIS, Clifford - 1928 - 1947.
HARRIS, Malner J. - 1888 - Nov 18, 1966.
HARRIS, Mentie - 1892 - no date.
HARRIS, Wilburn - 1916 - 1967.
JEFFERSON, Alonzo - no dates.
JEFFERSON, Minnie - May 5, 1874 - Mar 22, 1913.
KIMBROUGH, John - no dates.
KIMBROUGH, Garland - no dates.
KIMBROUGH, Savannah H. - no dates.
JOHNSON, John H. - 1838 - 1900.
JOHNSON, Mollie - 1867 - 1920.
JOHNSON, William David - 1867 - 1942.
NORMAN, Carrie - 1890 - 1946.
POWELL, Charles O. - 1890 - 1950.
KINGCADE, H. M. - d. Sep 25, 1921.
KINGCADE, Marie - d. Jan 3, 1971, aged 70 yr., 9 mo., 11 dy.
KINGCADE, Orvial G. 1876 - 1950.
PHILLIPS, Jack - 1896 - 1912.
PHILLIPS, Maude - 1885 - 1917.
RANDOLPH, George Thomas - Apr 1, 1865 - May 4, 1904.
WOOLRIDGE, Floyd Allen - 1910 - 1916.
WOOLRIDGE, Harold Clay - 1908 - 1909.
SCOTT, Minor - d. June 26, 1955, aged 93 yr.
SCOTT, Rachel - d. July 15, 1908, aged 42 yr.
WHITE, Fred - May 8, 1900 - May 3, 1970.
STEWART, Grace - d. May 1, 1966, 66 yr., 3 mo.
RICH, Arthur - d. Sep 25, 1965, aged 69 yr, 11
WHITE, Thomas H., Cpl Kansas Inf Sp. Am. War - Nov 27, 1871 - Jan 14, 1952.
SMITH, Rev. George - no dates.
SMITH, Mandy - no dates.
SMITH, Mary - 1865 - Aug 7, 1901.
WILCOX, Henrietta - 1897 - 1959.
WILCOX, Cecil Burl - 1900 - 1962.
WILCOX, Dewey - no dates.
WILCOX, Roy - no dates.
WILCOX, Fred - 1891 - 1950.

SMITH, Houston - Pvt 805 Pioneer Inf. - no date.
TERRY, Arthur E. - 1907 - 1952.
TERRY, Edward - 1862 - 1916.
TERRY, Ella L. 1901 - 1968.
TERRY, Howard - 1904 - 1915.
TERRY, Mattie - 1869 - 1941.
TERRY, Ogretha - 1909 - 1943.
TERRY, Wilbur - 1900 - 1965.
WHEELER, Sam - Apr 25, 1815 - Apr 1, 1903.
WHEELER, Lewis - 1880 - 1961.

Berry Cemetery, Green County. Located Sec 20, Twp 30, R 24.
YOKUM, Lewis Frank - Mar 17, 1893 - May 31, 1914.
YOKUM, Effie - 1890 - 1967.
REAVES, Leo - 1911 - 1978.
JAMES, Charity - Mar 18, 1842 - May 31, 1914.
SIMMONS, Enoch - Aug 13, 1886 - Feb 1, 1900.
SIMMONS, Ralph - July 4, 1885 - May 16, 1904.
SIMMONS, Jasper - Nov 2, 1882 - Jan 11, 1908.
BERRY, Millard W. - Apr 16, 1920 - Nov 3, 1959.
BERRY, Della May, daughter of Wm. H. & Caroline - Feb 5, 1891 - June 15, 1917.
BERRY, Wm. H. - Aug 10, 1848 - Jan 31, 1917.
BERRY, Caroline M. - Aug 25, 1850 - Sep 8, 1914.
BERRY, Hubert W., son of Wm. H. & C. M. - Apr 26, 1879 - Mar 18, 1904.
BERRY, Birtie, son of Wm. H. & C. M. - May 2, 1882 - Jan 10, 1902.
BERRY, Sarah E., daughter of W. H. & C. M. - Sep 3, 1873 - Nov 24, 1894.
BOONE, Marie - Aug 5, 1819 - Dec 19, 1893.
BERRY, Drucella - no dates.
BOYD, A. - no dates.
HERRON, Susan V., wife of Aaron - Dec 25, 1860 - Apr 11, 1912.
WALLS, J. A. & Vine - no dates.
WALLS, Chas. - no dates.
WALLS, Press - no dates.
WALLS, Joe - no dates.
WALLS, Bob - no dates.
WALLS, Baby - no dates.
HARVEY, Maud Lee - 1881 - 1924.

HARVEY, Rev. H. - 1851 - 1918.
HARVEY, Sarah A., wife of H. - July 10, 1857 - Nov 25, 1906.
HARVEY, Lulie E., daughter of H. & S. E. - July 8, 1876 - Mar 4, 1889.
HARVEY, William E., son of H. & S. E. - Mar 11, 1883 - Feb 16, 1889.
HUDDLESTON, Rachel A. - Feb 9, 1821 - Jan 3, 1902.
MASON, John - d. Sep 24, 1888, aged 51 yr.
JONES, R. S. - Nov 28, 1854 - Dec 20, 1892.
DECKS, Elizabeth - d. Jan 14, 1905, aged 71 yr.
PERYMAN, Jocy Bell, daughter of B. & M. A. - Aug 28, 1881 - June 19, 1882.
OLIVER, Alma L., daughter of D. W. & N. - d. Mar 27, 1884, 7 mo.

The following names and dates were compiled from other sources:

BERRY, Luther - Apr 27, 1893 - Oct 21, 1951.
BERRY, Mammie Tressie - July 13, 1889 - Feb 5, 1967.
BERRY, Frank - no dates.
BERRY, Helen Drucella, daughter of L. & M. T. - Jan 26, 1918 - July 26, 1947.
BERRY, infant of Mr. & Mrs. Charles BERRY.
ALLEN, George - no dates.
BRAY, John - Feb 20, 1880 - Apr 25, 1958.
CARLOCK, Babbie Darnell, son of Dalmus - d. 12 hours.
DANFORTH, Nelson - 1851 - no date.
ELLISON, Mollie - 1865 - no date.
REAVES, Leo - Apr 23, 1911 - Aug 6, 1978.
MURRAY, Fannie - no dates.
REAVES, Cassie - no dates.

<u>Anderson Cemetery</u>, Harrison County. Located Sec 7, Colfax Twp..
Two slaves were brought to Missouri by their owner, William ANDERSON.
"Aunt Cynthia" - born Hart County, KY., d. about 1858.
ANDERSON, Henry Clay - June 29, 1850, Hart County, Ky. - death date unknown.

Colored Cemetery, Louisville, Lincoln County.
BELL, Ross N. - 1925 - 1957.
BELL, Albert - 1890 - 1970.
"   Nora - 1890 - 1974.
COPENHAVER, Charity Ann, wife of Robert, married Jan 8, 1891; 1848 - May 1915.
BARBER, Homer, MO Pvt 342 Serv BN - June 10, 1932.
BARBER, Rufus - 1887 - 1957.
KERR, Edward L. - May 24, 1919 - Mar 4, 1963.
KERR, Donald - 1947 - 1947.
PALMER, Cordelia - Aug 10, 1884 - Dec 6, 1945.
PALMER, James - Apr 20, 1883 - Feb 7, 1968.
PALMER, America - Sep 4, 1904 - July 11, 1932.
CHAPMAN, Rhoda - Mar 1894 - May 1941.
CHAPMAN, Cora - Apr 14, 1878 - Sep 16, 1932.
CHATMAN, John - Apr 7, 1904 - Feb 8, 1981.
PARSONS, Charley - 1874 - 1949.
ELDER, Maggie F. - Mar 6, 1885 - Dec 19, 1940.
"   George I. "Nish" - May 11, 1876 - Nov 30, 1967.
ELDER, Perry - 1897 - 1960.
MOORE, Lewis - 1859 - July 1942.
STEEL, Tori Summer - b. & d. 1977.
CROCKET, John - Mar 1, 1863 - Dec 13, 1934.
Overton, Ada - Feb 27, 1904 - Aug 10, 1941.
OVERTON, Robert - Oct 10, 1851 - Aug 13, 1933.
OVERTON, Sherman Sr. - July 22, 1894 - Aug 10, 1978.
OVERTON, Isaac Willie, MO Pvt 547th ENGR Const. BN WWI - Oct 18, 1927 - Jan 13, 1963.
OVERTON, Burton Allan - 1892 - 1949.
OVERTON, Albert T. - b. & d. 1947.
SALMON, Gertrude - 1892 - 1937.
SALMON, Clemon - 1912 - 1925.
SALMON, Mayme - 1928 - 1931.
WILLIS, Helen Mae - 1929 - 1930.
WILLIS, Martha - 1897 - 1940.
REYNOLDS, Lucy, wife of R. L. - Feb 22, 1854 - Sep 19, 1919.
DIXON, ___ia - June 1850 - Sep 1940.
McGINNUS, William - Jan 15, 1854 - Sep 10, 1921.
McGINNUS, Mary, wife of Wm. - Nov 12, 1862 - Apr 17, 1929.
McGINNUS, Ruby Inez, daughter of Wm. & Mary -

Dec 24, 1898 - Feb 5, 1915.
McGINNUS, Children of Wm. & Mary - 1898 - 1915:
Viola, O'Della, Pauline, Ruby. Marvin Claud
- 1886 - 1964.
DRYDEN, Lorence - 1900 - 1967.
DRYDEN, William H., Pvt 28th Co 7 BN 163 Depot
Brig. WWI - Jan 29, 1890 - Oct 10, 1918.
FISHER, James - Oct 11, 1955, aged 70 yr., 2 mo., 4 dy.
WATTS, Daniel - 1895 - 1918.
ROBINSON, Sue L. - 1901 - 1978.
WEBB, Mother Mag. - d. July 2, 1911, age 60 yr.
WEBB, L. O., Cpl Co O 62nd USCT - Sep 30, 1840 - July 6, 1910.
McGINNIS, In memory of John and Mary - no dates.
McGINNIS, Katie, wife of Isaac - Mar 20, 1860 - Dec 24, 1905.
McGINNIS, D. C. - Mar 1862 - Jan 1936.
McGINNIS, Rhodie - May 1860 - Mar 1936.
McGINNIS, Charles - Aug 1866 - July 1948.
McGINNIS, Claude - 1886 - 1964.
McGINNIS, Waler - Jan 15, 1897 - Apr 21, 1919.
HAYGOOD, Fred - Mar 20, 1835 - Sep 10, 1913.
UPTEGROVE, Carrie B. - Sep 6, 1907 - Nov 6, 1925.
McGINNUS, Arthur - Feb 28, 1889 - Nov 4, 1919.
WILLIAMS, C. Coffman, son of Sarah - May 20, 1891 - July 6, 1910.
TURLEY, Cornelia - d. Apr 15, 1938, aged 70 yr.
TURLEY, Iona - June 8, 1903 - Apr 27, 1930.
TURLEY, John W. - 1869 - 1962.
TURLEY, Lizzie - 1876 - 1966.
TURLEY, Robert, Mo Pvt 163 Depot Brig. WWI - Feb 25, 1902 - Feb 25, 1942.
ROLLINS, Mary E. - Nov 1861 - May 21, 1930.
ROLLINS, Edward - no dates.
ROLLINS, Rufus - 1885 - 1959.
SCOTT, Larry Ell. - 1907 - 1973.
SCOTT, Arthur Davis, MO Pvt US Army WWI - Nov 5, 1890 - Dec 26, 1973.
SCOTT, Harry - Mar 1888 - June 1972.
THOMPSON, Arthur - Aug 1901 - Sep 1941.

<u>Negro Cemetery</u>, Monroe County. Located Sec 28,

Twp 53, R 8.
HUTCHEN, Scott, MO Pvt 5 Co 164 Dep. Brig. WWI - Jan 2, 1897 - Oct 19, 1957.
HUTCHEN, Lark - 1880 - 1961.
HUTCHEN, Nellie - no dates.
ANDERSON, Alex - b. Augusta County, Va., 1842 - May 13, 1893.
LUE, Lizie, wife of J. W. LUE - d. Aug 6, 1888, aged 23 yr., 6 mo.
MITCHELL, Edward Jr. - d. Aug 15, 1925, aged 35 yr., 8 mo.

Bethel Cemetery, Howard County. Located west of Franklin, Missouri.
HENRY, Lloyd L. J. - Mar 5, 1987 - Mar 29, 1989.
GREEN, George L. Sr. - Mar 11, 1872 - July 15, 1937.
GREEN, Minnie L. - 1874 - 1955.
WRIGHT, Nannie GREEN - Apr 10, 1896 - Oct 18, 1958.
GREENE, Rosa B. - Apr 29, 1897 - June 23, 1983.
GREENE, Arthur A. - 1913 - 1940.
GREEN, A. H. Sr. - 1889 - 1937.
GREENE, Carol S. - Sep 12, 1932 - Jan 9, 1951.
BURRIS, Alice - May 1867 - May 1926.
BROWN, Thomas A. - Apr 20, 1884 - Apr 5, 1945.
" Edna - Dec 14, 1890 - Aug 17, 1965.
BROWN, Nelson, husband of Nanie - 1893 - 1952.
SPENCE, George, MO Pvt 806 Pioneer Inf. WWI - d. Feb 10, 1934.
JONES, Charles, US Army WWII - Mar 14, 1922 - Aug 31, 1978.
ESTILL, Susan, wife of Strother - d. Nov 20, 1908, aged 52 yr., 2 mo., 20 dy.
ESTIL, Kit - 1874 - 1967.
RAY, Cliff - Sep 3, 1882 - Aug 7, 1980.
WHEELER, Ora Bell - June 5, 1894 - Dec 18, 1918.
GIBSON, Anna C. - 1895 - 1974.
ESTILL, Wallace - d. Aug 26, 1917, age 42 yr.
ESTILL, Charles - d. Dec 25, 1908, 19 yr.
REED, Monroe - 1884 - 1965.
GERRARDT, Eldridge, MO Sgt Co D 350 Machine Gun Batt. WWI - May 5, 1891 - Dec 22, 1953.
JOHNSON, Don, Co D 62nd US Col Inf - no dates.

WILLIAMS, Helen P. - 1911 - 1971.
MEYERS, James, son of F. B. - Aug 4, 1889 - Mar 5, 1919.
MEYERS, Frank Burnett, MO Supply Sgt 65th Pioneer Inf - d. Mar 21, 1928.
KINGSTON, Loyd - Aug 10, 1926 - rest of stone destroyed.
ARNOLD, Coy - d. July 5, 1907, aged 83 yr.
JORDON, Roberta - Aug 27, 1932, aged 33 yr.
GIBSON, John - 1899 - 1947.
TALBOT, Minnie - Apr 30, 1880 - Feb 15, 1929.
JACKSON, S. M. T. Lillian, wife of Willard - Mar 22, 1895 - illegible.
BROWN, Mary E. Mar 5, 1859 - Jan 12, 1916.
BROWN, James G. - Nov 5, 1849 - July 18, 1908.
BROWN, James W. - Jan 9, 1879 - May 9, 1901.
BROWN, John B. - 1884 - 1952.
REARSON, Billie - Aug 13, 1890 - Oct 8, 1951.
FLETCHER, Florence - d. Oct 16, 1930, aged 36 yr.
PEARSON, Richard - dates illegible.
CHIPLEY - only base of the stone is here.
TAYLOR, Herbert - 1886 - Dec 24, 1910.
CASEN, Charlie - May 22, 1888 - Jan 8, 1911.
CASON, Clarence - no dates.
BIBB, Chrissie R., son of A. BIBB - Feb 28, 1903 - Feb 25, 1904.
BIBB, J. - d. Dec 25, 1904, aged 51 yr.
" Lucy - d. June 29, 1903.
STAPLETON, John - 1850 - 1938.
JOHNSON, Robert - Dec 23, 1856 - Aug 15, 1885.
" Livie - Jan 15, 1853 - Aug 1880.
LANDRUM, Martha - d. Feb 8, 1890, aged 57 yr.
BOOTHAN, Thomas - May 10, 1860 - Oct 18, 1891.
JACKSON, Howard - Apr 13, ? - Mar 12, ?.
CREAM, Cooper - May 15, 1888 - Aug 15, 1909.
CHIPLY, Marcie - Feb 8, 1838 - Oct 11, 1890.
CHIPLY, Marion, mother - no dates.
CHIPLY, __?__, father - no dates.
CHIPLY, Thomas - Sep 16, 1889 - Sep 2, 1890.
CHIPLY, Oscar - Jan 3, 1886 - Oct 8, 1890.
BLANKENBAKER, Jay - d. Nov 10, 1922, aged 75 yr.
HAWLINS, Dennis - d. Mar 4, 1916, aged 55 yr.
CHIPLY, __?__, daughter of A. L. & L. - d. Oct 7, 1881, aged 6 mo., 12 dy.

Hill - Beatty Colored Cemetery, Moniteau County.
Located Sec 7, Twp, 47, R 14.
HILL, Cora Bell, wife of Noah - July 18, 1887 - Nov 6, 1900.
HILL, Noah - July 24, 1889 - Jan 4, 1905.
BEATTY, George W. - Sep 15, 1817 - Sep 22, 1877.
BEATTY, Harriet, daughter of G. W. & A. BEATTY - Mar 4, 1863 - Apr 20, 1874.

Finnis Creek Cemetery, Saline County. Located one mile west of highway 65, about five miles south of Marshall.
ADAMS, Green Jr.   ADAMS, Isaac
ADAMS, Mary Ann   ADAMS, Green Sr.
ADAMS, Gracie
ADAMS, Sarah - 1880 - 1959.
LEWIS, Rev. W. E. - Nov 1, 1862 - 1928.
LEWIS, Penelope - Apr 22, 1863 - Dec 8, 1958.
LEWIS, Percy - 1891 - 1940.
LEWIS, Rev. Richard A. - 1888 - no date.
LEWIS, Julia - 1887 - 1952.
COLLINS, Betty - 1866 - 1934.
COLLINS, Joseph - 1849 - 1934.
WILLIAMS, Vivian - Nov 2, 1913 - Jan 5, 1952.
MOFFIT, Mary - Feb 22, 1886 - Jan 20, 1960.
LAWRENCE, Lester Fox - Oct 15, 1889 - July 6, 1947.
LAWRENCE, Lucy - Jan 15, 1889 - 1965.
NANCE, Kathryn - d. 1857.
FRANKLIN, Edward - Sep 2, 1907 - July 30, 1971.
LAWRENCE, Stanley Thomas - Dec 9, 1897 - Nov 3, 1957.
LAWRENCE, Annie - 1872 - 1964.
LAWRENCE, Richard Sr. - Apr 4, 1870 - Nov 7, 1942.
LAWRENCE, Clarence - Dec 29, 1893 - Dec 17, 1958.
LAWRENCE, Leonard A. - 1909 - 1961.
LAWRENCE, Lester - June 28, 1903 - Feb 16, 1920.
LAWRENCE, Booker - Nov 9, 1909 - Nov 25. 1972.
MOLDEN, Michael - July 26, 1926 - Jan 13, 1976.
DANIELS, Lizzie - 1897 - 1936.
LAWRENCE, Ella   LAWRENCE, Sam
LAWRENCE, Samuel - 18?? - 1913.

CROBARKER, Arthur - 1873 - July, 1944.
CROBARKER, Martha - 1875 - 1932.
RICH, Julia   CHISM, Nettie
BROWN, Henderson   CHISM, James
BROWN, Edward   JACKSON, Jim "Pap"
BROWN, George   MALONE, Bessie
ALEXANDER, Leonard - Apr 4, 1888 - Feb 14, 1967.
ALEXANDER, Buford - July 25, 1910 - Apr 24, 1975.
ALEXANDER, Eliza   LEWIS, Charley
ALEXANDER, Richard   LEWIS, Mary
GREEN, Tony Jr.   ALEXANDER, John - d.
GREEN, Tony M. Sr.   1941.
GREEN, Annie - d. Nov 12, 1936.
GREEN, Richard - 1840 - 1928.
GREEN, Lizzie - 1854 - 1922.
JACKSON, Lucy - Mar 22, 1883 - Mar 10, 1951.
SMITH, Georgia A. - 1880 - 1971.
SMITH, James A. - Jan 13, 1871 - 1947.
MOLDEN, Georgia - Aug 24, 1906 - Jan 13, 1955.
GARRETT, Jack - 1870 - no date.
BROWN, Tom   SNOODY, Alfred
BROWN, Eva   MOLDEN, Michael
JACKSON, Bertha - Mar 9, 1904 - Sep 3, 1974.
SPEARS, Magaline   MOLDEN, Katherine
SPEARS, Rev. Wellington
SPEARS, Emma   SPEARS, Julia
SPEARS, Garfield - Feb 15, 1907 - Aug 16, 1961.
MATHEW, Isabel - d. June 3, 1890, aged about 35 yr.
MATHEW, Charley   BROWN, William
CHISM, Dan   BROWN, Fannie
LAWRENCE, Nellie BROWN JACKSON - Mar 1, 1891 - Dec 6, 1961.
JACKSON, Aaron - June 1, 1888 - Oct 5, 1925.
JACKSON, Juanita - Aug 26, 1923 - Nov 1, 1925.
LAWRENCE, Anthony   LAWRENCE, Charles
LAWRENCE, Robert Anthony - Oct 29, 1948 - July 14, 1950.
BARNES, Sam - July 15, 1879 - July 17, 1948.
SMITH, James R. Jr. - Apr 9, 1939 - July 16, 1940.
SMITH, Isreal   SMITH, Mildred
STEWART, Mary   STEWART, Benton
STEWART, Willie   SMITH, Johnie

MOLDEN, Susan
PAYNE, Julia
PAYNE, Malinda
LAWRENCE, Jennie
LAWRENCE, Bettie
HOLMES, Lavenia
SMITH, Waite

MOLDEN, Fanny
MOLDEN, Robert
PAYNE, Julia
LAWRENCE, Johnie
HOLMES, Shed
HOLMES, Susie

CROBARKER, William Lester - Oct 7, 1873 - Oct 12, 1964.
CROBARKER, Emma Jane - Apr 6, 1877 - Feb 27, 1955.
WILLIAMS, Ada CROBARKER - May 30, 1891 - Feb 10, 1984.
LEWIS, Canary C. - Aug 4, 1902 - Dec 6, 1971.
SMITH, Ella Mae - d. May 22, 1974.
SPEARS, Willia Mae BROWN _ Apr 14, 1909 - Aug 15, 1977.
SPEARS, Francis Edmond - Mar 18, 1905 - Nov 28, 1979.

South Cemetery, Livingston County. Located one mile east of the intersection of Highways 36 and 65.
BROWDER, William - Sep 8, 1856 - date illegible.
WHITE, Ellen - Apr 14, 1864 - Nov 2, 1886.
JONES, Edward C. - Mar 25, 1873 - Sep 17, 1936.
SHIELDS, Alexander - d. Jan 6, 1912, aged 62 yr.
MONTGOMERY, Elizabeth - May 19, 1896 - Aug 7, 1970.
CLINKSCALES, family marker.
ELLIS, Charles Franklin - d. Mar 17, 1972, aged 102 yr., 4 mo., 27 dy.
ELLIS, Carrie Mae - 1887 - 1956.
STEWART, Deward W., MO Tec. 4 182 Port. Co. T. C. WWII - Mar 22, 1912 - June 20, 1961.
BRADFORD, Francis M., son of H. & R. - d. Mar 8, 1882, Aged 19 yr., 5 mo., 5 dy.
BALLEW, Arthur - d. Dec 5, 1878, aged 66 yr.
BALLEW, Harriet, wife of Arthur - no dates.
ANDERSON, Robert - Aug 5, 1928.
"   Luella - Oct 2, 1923.
ANDERSON, Ralph, Cook in US Army - Nov 24, 1890 - Nov 18, 1874.
JOHNSON, Caesar - d. May 29, 1882, aged 82 yr., 2 mo.

ROZELLE, Lloyd - 1900 - 1944.
BROWDER, William - d. Nov 29, 1924, aged 52 yr.
ROZELLE, Frances - 1912 - 1944.
GREEN, Monie BURNETT, Mo Pvt Engineers WWI - Jan 29, 1894 - Feb 4, 1948.
GREEN, Pearl - May 29, 1887 - Dec 6, 1968.
GREEN, Lucky - Sep 18, 1887 - Dec 27, 1967.
GREEN, Francis M., Mo Sgt Co M 65 Pioneer Inf. WWI - Nov 24, 1884 - Jan 20, 1959.
BERRY, Patrick - d. 1908.
BERRY, Katie - d. 1908.
McDONALD, Hannah - d. 1913.
BERRY, Harvey - 1895 - 1954.
PAYNE, Eva CREWS - 1878 - 1950.
PRICE, James H. - 1898 - 1953.
SCHOLLS, Eileen W. PRICE - 1901 - no date.
ANDERSON, Alonzo John - 1894 - 1966.
ANDERSON, Beatrice H. - 1900 - no date.
MIDGYETT, Charlotte J. - 1921 - 1953.
BANKS, Hawley, son - 1899 - 1948.
BANKS, Lois L. - 1901 - 1929.
BANKS, Ruth, mother - 1872 - 1955.
BANKS, James, father - 1867 - 1952.
COVELL, Gussie - 1872 - 1921.
WILLIAMS, Gay Bell - Mar 28, 1867 - Mar, 1923.
SNEED, Maniza - Mar, 1866 - Dec 9, 1940.
ALEX, Elmer - 1877 - 1950.
ALEX, Jesse - Jan 25, 1883 - Mar 16, 1918.
ALES, Henry - d. May 4, 1915, 70 yr.
ALEX, Mother Victoria - July 31, 1853 - May 7, 1948.
JOHNSON, Lottie - Oct 15, 1875 - Mar 1, 1877.
WOLFSKILL, Rachel - Aug 15, 1837 - Mar 13, 1915.
WOLFSKILL, Clarence Arthur - May 3, 1885 - June 6, 1899.
GILBERT, Edward - 1873 - 1959.
"   Eliza GILBERT - 1885 - 1941.
PARKER, George, Mo Pvt Stu Army Trng Co WWI - Mar 14, 1898 - Oct 5, 1967.
PARKER, Sophia - Feb 13, 1855 - June 10, 1928.
TROSPER, Kathryn - 1907 - no date.
TROSPER, Roy B. - 1904 - Sep 1976.
JONES, William - 1874 - 1953.
ESTES, Harold T., Mo Pfc 804 Pioneer Inf WWI - June 17, 1892 - Mar 24, 1949.

ESTES, Charles - Dec 11, 1884 - Dec 27, 1947.
ESTES, Edward - Apr 26, 1881 - Apr 29, 1935.
LEWIS, Malinda - no dates.
HARRIS, Rev. John W. - Aug 15, 1876 - Jan 17, 1948.
HOLMES, William, Mo Cpl. 3 Depot SVC Co ASC WWI - Mar 17, 1892 - Aug 15, 1968.
SAWYER, Myrtle N. - Mar 16, 1880 - Nov 24, 1969.
SAWYER, Lucillius A. - Sep 14, 1878 - May 21, 1967.
HILLMAN, Virgil - Jan 7, 1873 - Oct 28, 1853.
HARDIN, Thomas, Co 11 67th, Co C 65th USC - d. July 5, 1913.
HARDIN, Melisa - Dec 17, 1853 - July 3, 1935.
BROWN, Ethel Lee, mother - Jan 1, 1876 - June 22, 1929.
COWHORN, Alfred - d. May 1892, aged 75 yr.
LEWIS, Lawrence S. - Mo Pfc Co D 14 Inf Regt. Korea - Dec 11, 1928 - Aug 14, 1953.
BANKS, Thomas H., father - 1869 - 1958.
BANKS, Lula E., mother - 1868 - 1910.
BANKS, Bessie L., nurse, 1897 - 1948.
SAWYERS, Rev. Daniel - Jan 8, 1937 - May 17, 1921.
SAWYERS, Anna Eliza, wife of Rev. D. S. SAWYERS - Sep 20, 1839 - Jan 13, 1922.
SAWYERS, Mary Anna, daughter of D. S. & A. E. - Dec 1, 1875 - May 7, 1896.
KILES, Carolyn Lee - 1940 - 1943.
JOHNSON, Gertrude E. - 1862 - 1917.
WINFREY, Caddie Carrer, daughter of Alex & Rachel - Mar 30, 1887 - Jan 18, 1910.
PATRICK, Nancy - d. Aug 14, 1885, aged 60 yr.
KILES, Mathew - Mo Pvt S. A. T. C. Western University - Aug 17, 1929.
KILES, Mary F., daughter of M. & N. KILES - Mar 7, 1867, aged 10 mo., 7 dy.
KILES, Ann Eliza, daughter of J. M. & N. A. - d. Jan 16, 1882.
KILES, Jas. M. - 1871 - 1936.
ANDERSON, Fred E. - Dec 20, 1924 - May 26, 1967.
ANDERSON, Bert L., father - Aug 2, 1890 - Jan 24. 1962.
MONTGOMERY, Lottie L., mother - 1878 - 1935.

DIXON, C. H. - Aug 2, 1862 - Nov 2, 1918.
BURTON, Mary A. - d. Feb 23, 1893, aged 84 yr.
BURTON, James - 1855 - no dates.
" Julia - d. Oct 19, 1926, age 68.
GILLIAM, Jane - Oct 29, 1854 - Feb 11, 1923.
CASWELL, Charlotte - June 1, 1836 - Feb 11, 1923.
WITCHER, Sandy V., Mo St Mi U. S. N. R. WWII - July 7, 1905 - Nov 25, 1955.
WARE, Orville W. Mo Tec 4733 Engineers WWII - Jan 4, 1918 - Nov 25, 1955.
TOLSON, Ada Mae, daughter - 1909 - 1963.
" Millie Ann, mother - 1882 - 1954.
JACKSON, William - 1859 - 1946.
PAGE, Cora J. - Apr, 1875 - Mar, 1941.
JOHNSON, Mary I., wife of J. W. - Oct 14, 1865 - Sep 11, 1886.
HUDSON, Eliza - Dec 24, 1823 - Jan 23, 1905.
CLAYTON, Albert, Co C 52nd U S C T -no dates.
BELL, Pleasant - d. 1894, aged 66 yr.
" Phoebe - d. 1906, aged 71 yr.
BELL, Jesse, - d. 1893, aged 33 yr.
BELL, Sylvester - d. 1904, aged 15 yr.
BELL, James - d. Jan 11, 1899, aged 16 yr.
BELL, Minnie - d. Dec 5, 1899, aged 8 yr.
HICKS, Jones - Co M 83rd U S C - no dates.

<u>Oak Chapel Cemetery</u>, Callaway County. Sec 15, Twp 46, R 11.
CAVE, Elwood - Sep 1, 1881 - Sep 30, 1967.
SCOTT, Clayton, son of Sam - d. Aug 20, 1966, aged 50 yr.
SCOTT, Sam - no dates.
SCOTT, Anna Lucille - 1901 - 1971.
LEWIS, Manuel T. - Jan 19, 1944 - May 15, 1957.
CAVE, James Frederick - b. & d. 1973.
DULLE, John - 1926 - 1981.
NEVINS, Mabel - May 17, 1925 - Feb 1, 1962.
NEVINS, Burton O. - 1888 - 1960.
" Bessie - 1891 - 1966.
NEVINS, Georgia, wife of Monroe - June 2, 1877 - Aug 3, 1953.
NEVINS, Monroe - 1867 - 1939.
NEVINS, Thomas - 1842 - 1930.
" Julia - 1845 - 1930.
NEVINS, Baxter SR. - 1880 - 1925.

NEVINS, Baxter Jr. - 1908 - 1920.
NEVINS, Robert, son of Thos. & Julia - d. Oct 31, 1888, aged 14 yr., 3 mo., 27 dy.
WILKERSON, Leslie, son of Francis & Susan - May 20, 1883 - Nov 6, 1904.
BERRY, Earl - 1912 - 1983.
BERRY, Della V. - 1895 - 1956.
DAVIS, John W., Mo Pvt 1 CL 317 AMM Train 92 div - d. 1930.
DAVIS, Will - 1873 - 1972.
" Emma - no dates.
GRUBB, William - d. Apr 11, 1873, aged 70 yr.
GRUBB, Lucinda - d. Sep 29, 1872, aged 16 yr., 1 mo., 12 dy.
KEMP, Noah R. - 2 Jan 1872 - June 8, 1872.
KING, Ovie, Mo Pvt Co D 805 Pioneer Inf WWI - Jan 9, 1897 - Mar 14, 1953.
LOGAN, Mary A. - Sep 3, 1955 - Feb 16, 1963.
" Thelma - July 7, 1954 - Feb 16, 1963.
" Carrie M. - July 28, 1953 - Feb 16, 1963.
McBRIDE, Arnold Ray, Pfc US Army Korea - Jan 9, 1929 - Oct 4, 1964.
McBRIDE, John Henry Leroy - d. Mar 30, 1957, aged 37 yr., 3 mo.
McBRIDE, Rev. Albert - Feb 14, 1896 - Apr 23, 1975, married Dec 13, 1915.
McBRIDE, Leola, wife of Albert - d. Nov 25, 1895.
NEVINS, Parker - 1905 - 1930.
SCOTT, Orice - no dates.
SCOTT, Shela Mae - 1883 - 1960.
SCOTT, Milton L. - 1875 - 1964.
SCOTT, Pauline - 1912 - 1969.
SCOTT, Margie Emma - 1904 - 1974.
VAUGHAN, Alsey, faithful friend and servant of the Robert A. HUDSON family - 1844 - 1930.
WHITTLER, Betty Lou - 1932 - 1974.
WHITTLER, John M. - 1888 - 1984.
" Mattie - 1903 - 1982.
GUTHRIE, Jos. B. - d. Jan 15, 1883, aged 3 yr.
LEE, Nacorey D. - b. & d. 1979.

Namraseh Cemetery, Chariton County. Located Sec 17, Twp 52, R 18.
LOCKE, Zeland - d. Jan 31, 1882, aged 70 yr.

BANKS, Worley, Mo Pvt 805 Pioneer Inf - d. Oct 18, 1918, aged 21 yr.
LOCKE, Martha, wife of John - d. May 10, 1877, aged 20 yr., 10 mo., 18 dy.
___?___ - Nov 29, 1919 - Sep 22, 1924.
HOMAN, John - d. June 30, 1881, aged 62 yr.
STEWARD, Lewis - d. Apr 3, 1896, aged 35 yr.
JACKSON, Easter J., wife of Ambrous - d. Sep 9, 1899, aged 70 yr.
JACKSON, Robert - d. Oct ?.
FINNELL, Harriet, wife of Richard - d. Oct 4, 1897.
FINNELL, Susie B., daughter of Richard and Harriet - d. July 3, 1903, aged 23 yr., 4 mo., 13 dy.
FINNELL, Burvell, son of John & Leona - d. Apr 17, 1903 - May 7, 1913.
PETTIGREW, John Henry, son of Wash & Birdie - d. June 9, 1903, aged 7 yr.
WILSON, James, Mo Pvt 805 Pioneer Inf - d. June 9, 1920.

Colored Cemetery, Pike County. Located in Sec 31, Twp 51, R 4.
CARTER, Phoebe Ann, wife of Edmond - Feb 10, 1841 - Feb 15, 1885.
CARTER, Edmond - June 1, 1838 - Feb 2, 1920.
PEARL, Thomas - May 15, 1844 - Apr 11, 1904.
PEARL, M. C. - Aug 18, 1880 - July 9, 1898.
PEARL, Lottie Lee M., daughter of Thomas & Elizabeth - d. Mar 3, 1893, aged 14 yr., 9 mo., 13 dy.
BELL, Mildred N. - Feb 18, 1920 - Oct 29, 1920.
SHEPHERD, Ada - 1879 - 1930.
FRAZER, Elizabeth, wife of William - Oct 15, 1818 - Mar 18, 1881.
PEARL, Mrs. Amie E. - d. 1918.

Crow's Fork, Callaway County. Located Sec 5, Twp 47, R 8.
GRAVES, William H. - d. May 21, 196?, aged 44 yr., 1 mo., 6 dy.
GRAVES, Virginia - d. Apr 17, 1969, aged 47 yr.
ALLEN, John Robert - d. Dec 20, 1965, aged 20 yr.
WOOLERY, Martha - d. Feb 19, 1966, age 43 yr.

GALBREATH, Louise G. - d. Nov 3, 1962, age 48 yr.
NICHOLS, Fred, Pvt US Army WWI - d. May 4, 1891 - Aug 19, 1963.
PAYNE, Emmitt, Mo Mech AM BN 92 Div - d. Apr 23, 1938.
McGUIRE, Jack - 1892 - 1990.
PAYNE, James M. Jr., US Air Force Korea - Oct 28, 1931 - June 15, 1988.
PAYNE, James "Bud" - 1915 - 1970.
PAYNE, Sadie V. - May 11, 1915 - July 24, 1981.
GALBREATH, Bessie - 1887 - 1973.
GALBREATH, Vincent C. - 1958 - 1959.
GALBREATH, Lavoris - Nov 3, 1934 - 1982.
GALBREATH, Clifford - 1916 - 1979.
BELL, Willie - 1900 - 1978.
McGUIRE, Eddie - 1919 - 1989.
PATTERSON, Gertrude - 1902 - 1980.
COOK, James - d. Oct ?.
WILLIAMS, Nenny - d. Sep 20, 1932.
WILLIAMS, Robert - d. Oct 14, 1962, age 65.
BELL, Jack - d. Aug 13, 1903, aged 75 yr.
BELL, Emmealine, wife of Jack - d. Feb 15, 1906, aged 60 yr.
BELL, Sindie A., daughter of J. & E. - d. Apr 7, 1882, aged 17 yr., 1 mo., 19 dy.
McGUIRE, William, Pvt Co D 415 Eng Det WWII - Aug 29, 1919 - Aug 30, 1954.
DUDLEY, George - d. Nov 24, 1968.
BUCKNER, Willis - 1914 - 1974.
JOHNSON, Frank Edward, Mo Pfc HHC 20 Inf American Dev, Vietnam - July 5, 1948 - May 12, 1969.
GALBREATH, Frank - 1894 - 1977.
SCOTT, Belle - d. 14 June ? , aged 27 yr., 3 mo., 2 dy.
BELL, Arch - 1867 - 1940.
" Susie - 1873 - 1940.
BELL, Elmer, WWII - 1904 - May 23, 1970.
A survey taken in 1982 included other grave markers not found in 1993. They are:
GALWITH, John - d. Nov 13, 1946, aged 75 yr.
GRAVES, Hallie - d. May 26, 1972, aged 34 yr., 18 dy.
McGUIRE, William - 1900 - 1965.
MITCHEL, Richard - d. Apr 12, 1967, aged 94

yr., 1 mo., 23 dy.
PATTERSON, Clarence - d. Jan 4, 1975, aged 57 yr., 8 mo., 3 dy.
SMITH, Howard - 1862 - 1957.
SMITH, Emma, wife of Howard - Sep 19, 1856 - 1958, aged 102 yr.
WILLIAMS, Albert - d. Aug 31, 196?, aged 65 yr.

Loutre Island Negro Cemetery, also known as the George Washington Cemetery, Montgomery County. Located Sec 15, Twp 45, R 5, on the west side of Highway 19.
CLABORN, Marlow, Pvt US Army WWI - July 25, 1896 - Mar 16, 1976.
CLABORN, Kitty - Dec 25, 1857 - Mar 12, 1945.
CLAYBORN, Ledy - Aug 4, 1891 - May 20, 1896.
PROCTOR, August - d. Aug 9, 1936.
" Maggie - d. Feb 25, 1938.
PITMAN, Julius - d. Dec 13, 1918.
" Cordelia - no dates.
PRICE, Anderson - d. June 13, 1902.
PRICE, "Aunt Sarah" - "Born a slave in 1855, died in 1947, she set a good example for members of her race".
LONG, Katherine Corine - May 21, 1908 - Dec 5, 1951.
Mitchel, Maggie, daughter of H. & P. - Feb 18, 1869 - Apr 25, 1901.
ROSE, Albert - July 4, 1841 - Nov 12, 1919.
JEFFERSON, Hester M. - 1890 - 1959.
MURE, Charlie - 1910 - 1931.
MURE, Walter - 1914 - 1926.
SHARP, Margarett TREVINO - Jan 6, 1927 - Apr 13, 1974.
RITTER, Herman S., Sgt US Army WWII - Mar 10, 1907 - June 25, 1985.
RODGERS, James C. - 1907 - 1987.
JENKINS, Irene - d. 1935.
DAWSON, Don, Mo Pvt Co F 7 US Vol Inf Spanish American War - Oct 27, 1874 - Feb 22, 1969.
HOLLAND, Wheeler - 1883 - 1958.
" Callie - 1889 - 1956.
" Willie - 1927 - 1941.
GILLETTE, Darlene J. - Aug 29, 1920 - Dec 27, 1963.
KEMP, Bob - 1886 - no date.

KEMP, C. R. - 1933 - 1965.
KEMP, B. G. - 1937 - 1970.
KEMP, Sylvin A. - d. Nov 20, 1973, aged 27 yr. 5 dy.
KEMP, A. E. - 1936 - 1970.
KEMP, Leon - 1911 - 1973.
" Cora A. 1914 - 1966.
KEMP, Monique - 1928 - 1980.
KEMP, Theodore R., US Army WWII - July 22, 1909 - May 1, 1988.
KEMP, Juanita - no dates.
KEMP, Pearl - no dates.
KEMP, Roy - no dates.
KEMP, Viola - no dates.
KEMP, Warner - Apr 2, 1870 - July 28, 1913.
LAWRENCE, Carter - no dates.
RITTER, Delbert - Oct 10, 1908 - Aug 17, 1982.
RITTER, Jimmy & Lula - no dates.
McCOY, Lula V. - Mar 13, 1891 - Apr 9, 1964.
McCOY, Howard - 1896 - 1972.
MITCHELL, Arvel - no dates.
MITCHELL, Harvey - no dates.
MITCHELL, Hershell - no dates.
MURE, Earthly - Apr 11, 1880 - no date.
" Jack - Oct 15, 1878 - Aug 9, 1970.
MURE, Walter - 1914 - 1926.
PANEL, Bill - no dates.
PANEL, Esther - no dates.
PAYNE, Ben - no dates.
PITMAN, Lewis - no dates.
CONNER, Mattie - June 25, 1890 - Oct 5, 1968.
CONNER, Edward R. Mo Cox USNR WWII - Feb 26, 1924 - Apr 25, 1973.
CONNER, Arthur, Mo Pvt US Army WWI - Oct 22, 1895 - Mar 2, 1974.
COLE, Annie, wife of Harvey - Nov 1, 1876 - Jan 29, 1898.
GLOVER, George - no dates.
GLOVER, Louis - no dates.
ALLEN, Esther - 1903 - 1963.
CARTER, Ellar GANOR, wife of Harrison - 1857 - Jan 20, 1894.
CLABORN, Carrie - no dates.
CLABORN, Charlie - no dates.
CLABORN, Elizabeth - d. Feb 14, 1955, aged 83

yr., 4 mo.
CLABORN, York - no dates.
CLAYBORN, Zylphia - no dates.
CONNOR, Gussie - 1926 - 1973.
ROBINSON, John & Myrtle - no dates.
TREVINO, Arthur - no dates.
WARNER, Charles - no dates.
WARNER, David L. - 1900 - 1975.
" Mrs. David - 1904 - 1967.
WARNER, John - no dates.
WARNER, Katie - no dates.
WARNER, Rhuie - no dates.
YANCY, Fannie - no dates.
WARNER, Odie Mae - d. 1926.

<u>Salt Creek Cemetery</u>, Howard County. Located past the Sulpher Springs Church which is off Highway 240.
JENNING, Stella Mae, wife of Howard - May 18, 1894 - Feb 20, 1984.
JENNING, Howard - Aug 20, 1894 - Feb 20, 1983.
RAY, Ernest - 1888 - 1982.
HITT, Margaret BELL - 1924 - 1966.
BENTLEY, Alfred - 1911 - 1990.
TOLSON, Kizzie - d. Aug 1, 1921, age 80 yr.
ROBINSON, Minnie - 1874 - 1912.
JENNINGS, Jane - d. Nov 20, 1920, aged 65 yr.
JENNINGS, Andy - 1846 - 1927.
JENNINGS, Charles Edward, son of Howard & Stella - Aug 18, 1921 - June 26, 1938.
THORNTON, Ada - 1884 - no date.
THORNTON, Edgar - 1876 - 1942.
FERGUSON, Blanche - 1893 - 1966.
STAPLETON, George W., Mo Pvt 357 MG BN 92 Div WWI - Apr 8, 1896 - Dec 22, 1941.
STAPLETON, Maggie - 1931 - 1934.
PAYNE, Ernest O. - 1893 - 1919, d. US Gen. Hospital, Denver, Colorado.
PAYNE, Nina B. - 1867 - 1947.
" Jesse - 1874 - 1955.
PAYNED, B. E. - 1894 - June 25, 1911.
" George - no dates.
RAY, Herman - 1880 - 1954.
RAY, Enmom - 190? - 1987.
JENNINGS, Edmond - d. Mar 10, 1901.
" Fannie - d. Feb 3, 1899.

Colored Cemetery, Lincoln County. Located off Highway JJ, southwest of Elsberry, Missouri.
BEALMEAR, Edward G., Indian Corp. 2nd Inf. - d. July 26, 1939.
CHRISTIAN, D. L. - May 3, 1859 - Aug 23, 1913.
DAVIS, Willie - 1894 - 1956.
MOLLER, Henry, Co I 18th USCI - no dates.
MOLLER, Eugene - 1911 - 1954.
EDW____, Sandy - d. Apr, ?, aged 71 yr.

Wright Family Cemetery, Cooper County. Located outside of Speed, Missouri.
WRIGHT, Charlie - d. 1931.
WRIGHT, Sallie, his wife - no dates.
WRIGHT, "Sank" - no dates.
WRIGHT, Will   WRIGHT, Annie
WRIGHT, Thomas   WRIGHT, Lucy
WRIGHT, Ida, wife of "Sank".
WRIGHT, Nora   WRIGHT, Floyd
BANTY, Will   BANTY, Ella
SHIELDS, Julius   SHIELDS, Anna
SHIELDS, Robert, son of Julius & Anna.
HALE, William   HALE, Robert
CRUMP, Steve   SMITH, Jim
CRUMP, Katherine, wife of Steve.
SMITH, Ada, wife of Jim SMITH.
CRUMP, Leslie & Nelson - sons of Steve & Katherine CRUMP.
SMITH, Sadie, daughter of Jim & Ada.
SMITH, Garfield, son of Jim & Ada Smith.
BANTY, Zella   WILLIAMS, Bob
WILLIAMS, Ida, wife of Bob.
WILLIAMS, William & Martha, children of Bob & Ida.
WILLIAMS, Carl Eugene, infant son of Carl & Ida.
CLAY, Essie, daughter of Tom & Lucy.
JACKSON, Catherine, daughter of Sadie SMITH JACKSON.
JACKSON, Harry, son of Catherine JACKSON.
WRIGHT, Calab   WRIGHT, Jim
WRIGHT, Alpha, wife of Jim.
BANTY, Clarence   WRIGHT, Laura
WRIGHT, Sylvester, son of Jim.
WILLIAMS, Infant of Earl & Juanita.

WRIGHT, Quincy, son of Jim & Alpha.

<u>Church of God Colored Cemetery</u>, Pike County.
Located Sec 35, Twp 51, R 3.
CLARE, H. C. - 1872 - 1927.
CLARE, Mary E. - 1886 - no date.
WELLS, Milton - Oct, 1855 - June 1943.
WELLS, Peachy, wife of Milton - Sep 15, 1864 - Sep 12, 1933.
McGINNIS, James H. - 1881 - 1952.
McGINNIS, Nettie - 1879 - no date.
HARRISON, Alvin - 1874 - 1944.
" Celia - 1858 - 1933.
" Simon - 1855 - 1930.
WILLIS, Ida - no dates.
WILLIS, House - no dates.
GRIMMETT, Alverina - Apr 15, 1892 - May 18, 1983.
GRIMMETT, James - Mar 12, 1886 - Sep 28, 1964.
PARSONS, Lorn M.- Nov 6, 1865 - Feb 7, 1927.
PARSONS, Minnie - Feb 10, 1874 - July 13, 1954.
PARSONS, Eddie M. - 1890 - 1969.
PARSONS, Frances M., father - July 8, 1860 - 1939.
PARSONS, Emeline, mother - Mar 10, 1863 - Oct 13, 1922.
McGINNIS, John F. - 1858 - 1935.
McGINNIS, Jane, wife of John - 1865 - (after 1945).
PARSONS, Noah   DRYDEN, Olli
PARSONS, Ella   CLARE, Frank
PARSONS, Marlin   DORSEY, an infant
McGINNIS, Arbie   DORSEY, Bob
WELLS, two infant children of Ralph WELLS.
McGINNIS, Katherine "Kitty".

<u>Keytesville City Cemetery</u>, Black Section, Chariton County.
LEWIS, Helen - 1914 - 1917.
LEWIS, Evelt - 1904 - 1923.
WILLIAMS, Ceola - 1895 - 1924.
" William - 1892 - 1938.
BISH, Isabel S. - May 1, 1894 - Jan 2, 1922.
ALLEN, Dennis - 1890 - 1969.

POTTS, Dora - 1902 - 1982.
HAYES, Nancy - June 1, 1849 - Feb 14, 1921.
ELLIOTT, Benjamin - d. Feb 14, 1894, aged 76 yr., 11 mo., 21 dy.
EWING, Francis, daughter of Thomas & Elizabeth - d. Aug 17, 1899, aged 21 yr., 7 mo., 1 dy.
WOODS, James, Mo Pvt 349 MG BN 92 Div WWI - June 15, 1887 - June 21, 1951.
POTTS, Marvin A. - 1921 - 1942.
POTTS, Lucy - 1863 - 1926.
BUTLER, Nathaniel, Mo Mech 804 Pioneer Inf - d. Aug 7, 1937.
HUGHES, Allen, Pvt 1 Cl 530 Sev BN Engr. Corps - May 27, 1928.
PARRISH, Edward M., Mo Sgt 317 AM TN 92 Div 92 WWI - Nov 20, 1888 - Mar 25, 1947.
DUNCAN, Carrie - 1872 - 1952.
ALLEN, Glenn - 1859 - 1936.
" Maria L. 1863 - 1921.
COWDEN, Christina - Oct 9, 1903 - Mar 9, 1918.
CHRISTOPHER, Willis - d. Oct 27, 1895, age 56.
CHRISTOPHER, Linnie, daughter of W. & M. A. - d. July 29, 1897, aged 14 yr., 6 mo., 27 dy.
TURNER, Ernest, son of W. & E. - d. July 22, 1888, aged 11 yr., 4 mo., 11 dy.
GUTHERIDGE, Selector - 1904 - 1972.
" Arleta - 1903 - 1972.
PAGE, Mary W. - no dates.
TOLSON, Steve, Mo Pvt 415 Res. Labor BN QMC WWI - Dec 13, 1890 - June 24, 1966.
WOODS, Lue, Mo Pvt US Army WWII - Mar 7, 1898 - Feb 23, 1960.
WHEELER, Oswald, Sgt US Army - WWII - 1910 - 1980.
WHEELER, Rebecca - 1892 - 1974.
" Bush - 1890 - 1961.
WHEELER, Jesse Warner, Mo Tec 4 170 Port BN TC WWII - Mar 13, 1921 - Mar 14, 1966.
DAVIS, Frances R., wife of Isaac - d. Apr 18, 1893, age 48 yr., 9 mo., 15 dy.
EWING, Nancy - d. May 30, 1889, aged 60 yr., 3 mo., 3 dy.
CROCKETT, Mary Jane - no dates.
WHEELER, Nan - 1854 - 1932.
WILLIAMS, Nadine - Mar 26, 1891 - Dec 16, 1945.
" Samuel - Aug 15, 1887 - Mar 17, 1938.

WILLIAMS, Lawrence, Mo SK3 USNR WWII - Dec 13, 1925 - Sep 29, 1948.
MONROE, Oscar P. - June 3, 1887 - Apr 24, 1937.
MONROE, Ben - 1858 - 1915.
MONROE, George E., Mo Bglr Co. D 351 Mach. Gun BN WWI - May 7, 1888 - Jan 9, 1958.
HERNDON, Eliza, wife of Samuel - d. Sep 28, 1898, age 73 yr.
MARMADUKE, Richard - d. Mar 14, 1884, aged 1 yr., 2 mo.
SWEATMAN, Edna R. - 1918 - 1965.
AKERS, Charles - Apr 25, 1865 - Oct 9, 1918.
WHEELER, Peyton, father - 1859 - 1936.
" Cora, mother - 1875 - 1943.
" Ogdalena - Feb 27, 1900 - Dec 21, 1911.
" Martha - 1904 - 1950.
" Margin - 1898 - 1971.
" Carrie - 1908 - no date.
THIRKELS, Richard Henry Jr., US Navy WWII - 1923 - 1980.
LEWIS, A. M. Rev. - d. Mar 11, 1904, age 55 yr., 7 dy.
EWING, Jessie W. - d. Oct 4, 1882, age 12 yr., 5 mo.
EWING, three infant sons of T. H. & E. - d. Apr 8, 1882.
EWING, Thomas - d. Oct 31, 1887, aged 48 yr.
DAMERON, Charley - Dep 24, 1874 - Feb 21, 1888.
JENKINS, Carrie - 1877 - 1941.
JENKINS, Dora - no dates.
WHEELER, Jeanetta B. - Apr 14, 1899 - Nov 6, 1972.
DUNCAN, Walter B. - Jan 6, 1920 - June 28, 1972.
MORRIS, Dimple Page - 1897 - May 26, 1922.
PATTON, Ernest - 1907 - 1975.
MILLER, Earl Lee - Mar 17, 1905 - Sep 30, 1966.
AKERS, Virginia MILLER - July 23, 1911 - Feb 13, 1973.
PATTON, Jack Thomas - 1903 - 1976.
PATTON, Margaret M. - 1913 - 1975.
BASE - rest of stone in gone.
MILLER, Diana, wife of Urin - d. July 28, 1901, aged 83 yr., 4 mo.
WASHINGTON, Thomas - 1911 - 1975.
WASHINGTON, Thomas E. - 1941 - 1963.

JOHNSON, Charles V. - 1932 - 1963.
JOHNSON, Mac Lee - 1913 - 1969.
ALLEN, Charlotte E., wife of James K. P. - 1858 - 1918.
BROWN, Georgia A. - 1876 - 1946.
" George W. - 1875 - 1948.
SMITH, Vaughn L. Nov 8, 1908 - no date.
SMITH, Howard - 1928 - 1981.
SMITH, H. Rosetta - 1911 - 1968.
BENTLEY, Ella F. - June 12, 1892 - Jan 11, 1981.
JOHNSON, James M. - Aug 14, 1909 - Nov 2, 1961.
HEARIOLD, M. Feddie - Jan 1, 1865 - Nov 4, 1919.
HEARIOLD, Taylor - Nov 2, 1861 - July 18, 1941.
HEAROLD, Krumb T. - Aug 4, 1887 - Aug 10, 1911.
CARTER, Ann G. - 1869 - 1939.
" William - 1870 - 1937.
SCROGGINS, Nancy A., wife of Lafayette - d. Jan 4, 1899, aged 62 yr., 8 dy.
CHRISTOPHER, Anna - Jan 4, 1880 - no date.
" Ernest - Oct 10, 1879 - Sep 5, 1942.
CHRISTOPHER, Robert P. - 1899 - 1978.
CHRISTOPHER, Victoria H. - 1911 - 1981.
CHRISTOPHER, Evans - 1885 - 1950.
CHRISTOPHER, Oletha - 1890 - 1957.
" Robert - 1878 - no date.
BROWN, Gladys C. - 1910 - 1963.
BUTLER, Lillian C. - Feb 27, 1903 - July 2, 1971.
FRAZIER, Joe - may 5, 1900 - Nov 16, 1950.
MARTIN, Laura - 1895 - 1951.
MARTIN, Aron, Mo Pfc 83 C Co T C WWI - Oct 7, 1887 - July 8, 1947.
PRATHER, Kittie - 1853 - 1929.
BOONE, Emma, wife of G. - d. June 14, 1890, aged 42 yr. 5 mo., 16 dy.
STARKS, Samuel - 1874 - 1917.
FRISTO, Wm. - no dates.
REDDING, Tonia Michele - Nov 8, 1963 - Sep 25, 1964.
GLASGOW, Bertha A. - 1909 - 1961.
GLASGOW, Nathaniel - Feb 20, 1878 - Apr 26, 1952.
GLASGOW, Ardella, wife of N. - Oct 11, 1886 -

Sep 14, 1950.
GLASGOW, Gussie H., Mo Pfc Co C 318 Med BN WWII - Nov 29, 1908 - July 2, 1958.
GLASGOW, Gean, Mo Pvt US Army WWII - Sep 11, 1914 - May 7, 1961.
GLASGOW, Orville C., Mo Pfc 3395 QM Truck Co WWII - Nov 3, 1924 - Mar 7, 1967.
CHILDS, Susie - Mar 28, 1911 - Aug 9, 1969.
GLASGOW, Ida Helen - 1919 - 1981.
CHRISTOPHER, Archie Sr. - Feb 14, 1872 - Feb 17, 1952.
CHRISTOPHER, Archie Jr. - Mar 19, 1913 - Oct 1, 1950.
CHRISTOPHER, Rebecca S. - Feb 10, 1871 - Jan 8, 1944.
GLASGOW, Berge N., Mo Pfc US Army WWII - Jan 27, 1921 - Feb 23, 1974.
PAGE, wm. McKinley - 1900 - 1976.
HUGHES, Lilly - Feb 19, 1888 - Jan 21, 1972.
WHITE, James - 1891 - 1969.

<u>Pleasant Hill Cemetery</u>, Lincoln County. Located in Hurricane Twp.
COFFER, Samuel - 1841 - 1922.
DAVIS, Ellis - d. May 7, 1947, aged 45 yr.
DAVIS, Treie B. - Mar 15, 1891 - Jan 18, 1914.
DAVIS, Quintis B. - Jan 10, 1846 - no date.
DAVIS, Jane - 1850 - Jan 15, 1907, married Dec 27, 1866.
DEMPLES, Hazel - Mar 4, 1892 - Sep 24, 1914.
JOHNSON, Lee - June 5, 1886 - Jan 6, 1908.
MARSH, Amanda - d. Dec 2, 1914, aged 53 yr.
MARSH, Fred - dates illegible.
MORRIS, Shed - d. Feb 8, 1917, aged 77 yr., 1 mo., 24 dy.
MORRIS, Reavilnew - d. Nov 9, 1916, aged 18 yr., 3 mo., 3 dy.
SMITH, Dave - 1881 - 1936.
STEELE, William, Mo Pvt I Cl 517 AMM Train 93 Div - d. Nov 16, 1929.
WILLIAMS, George - d. Oct 27, 1902, aged 75 yr.
WILLIAMS, Charlotte - dates illegible.
WASHINGTON, Emily, wife of Edward - d. Spe 4, 1898, aged 63 yr.

WASHINGTON, India - Sep 15, 1860 - no date.
WASHINGTON, John H. - Aug, 1803 - Feb 29, 1913.

Hillsdale Community Cemetery, Howard County. Located on county road #429.
JACKMAN, Laura - 1905 - 1906.
JACKMAN, Haller - 1911 - 1912.
DAVID, Charlie - 1906 - 1919.
ARNOLD, Mima - May 23, 1868 - Aug 28, 1908.
SHIPES. Lizzie L. - d. Dec 24, 1905, aged 4 yr., 7 mo., 24 dy.
ARNOLD, Finis - Aug 1, 1865 - Oct 24, 1916.
ARNOLD, Charley D. - Aug 16, 1894 - Jan 30, 1917.
ARNOLD, Robert C., Mo Pvt Co C 164 Depot Brig WWI - Feb 20, 1892 - Aug 9, 1970.
WILLIAMS, William - 1929 - 1990.
WILLIAMS, Herman - 1894 - 1969.
WILLIAMS, Frankie - 1898 - 1941.
LEE, Romie - d. 1934.
STEMMONS, Ethel L. - Apr 29, 1900 - May 27, 19??.
GATEWOOD, John - d. Apr 23, 1915, aged 76 yr.
STEMMONS, Josephine - Oct 28, 1900 - Dec 23, 1932.
STEMMONS, Herman A. - Aug 17, 1897 - Oct 24, 1969.
BROWN, Barbara jo - 1946 - 1992.
ARNOLD, Eugene - d. May 1914.
ARNOLD, Lucy - d. Aug 15, 1912, aged 62 yr.
HILL, Annie - 1919 - 1969.
PETTY, Allen - 1944 - 1991.
JONES, Carol Carlotta - Nov 26, 1968 - Mar 11, 1987.
YARD, __?__, d. 1964.
PETTY, Roger, US Army WWII - Mar 18, 1923 - Sep 14, 1980.
PETTY, Everett, Pvt US Army WWII - Nov 16, 1919 - Nov 27, 1976.
PETTY, Stacy R. - 1969 - 1976.
PETTY, Corine - 1927 - 1976.
TURNER, Floyd E. - 1909 - 1977.
STEMMONS, Maydene - 1895 - 1989.
BARNETT, Roberta - 1878 - 1967.
HILL, __?__ - 1878 - 1955.

HILL, Rosa - 1889 - 196?.
RICKETTS, Lilbert, Mo QM Corp WWII - June 25, 1918 - Mar 11, 1966.
JACKMON, Fletcher - 1883 - 1965.
JACKMAN, John Pat - 1886 - 1958.
RICKETT, Mattie - Jan 7, 1961, aged 82 yr.
McQUITTY, Ellery - 1903 - 1957.
JACKMAN, Billie L. - 1952 - 1952.
JACKMAN, Robert H. - 1927 - 1980.
BURRIS, Alfred - 1906 - 1966.
BURRIS, Vernon A. Jr. - 1928 - 1986.
BURRIS, Roscoe, Pvt US Army WWI - 1898 - 1985.
BURRIS, Gilbert Lee - Feb 12, 1932 - apr 15, 1956.
BURRIS, Luella - Feb 2, 1905 - Nov 27, 1975.
" Vernon - Jan 25, 1909 - no date.
JACKMAN, Shirley - b. & d. 1948.
JACKMAN, Donald Dean - b. & d. 1948.
JACKMAN, Christine - 1953 - 1958.
JACKMAN, Lenze L., Tec 5 WWII - June 30, 1920 - July 26, 1991.
STEMMONS, Wm. L. - 1890 - 1949.
STEMMONS, Thomas - 1868 - 1951.
ROBINSON, Betsy, wife of J. - 1871 - 1918.
STEMMONS, Ellery Sr. - Dec 15, 1900 - Nov 12, 1989.
MARSHALL, Frank - 1879 - 1921.
" Roxie Sep 17, 1882 - June 12, 1950.
STEMMONS, Frank - July 15, 1892 - Nov 17, 1964.
" Eva - Aug 17, 1894 - Oct 16, 1975.
STEMMONS, James R. - 1926 - 1958.
CLASBY, Jesse C. - d. Apr 19, 1947.
JACKMAN, Elijah - 1878 - 1945.
JACKMAN, Nina B. - 1895 - 1963.
EUBANKS, Wm. E. - Apr 12, 1928 - July 25, 1974.
BOOTH, David Leonard, Mo Pvt 805 Pioneer - no dates.
EUBANKS, J. H. - 1864 - 1942.
" Sallie - 1869 - 1959.
" Elizabeth - 1910 - 1925.
McKEE, Adison - Aug 17, 1866 - Feb 21, 1934.
WILLIAMS, John L., Pvt Col 2 Mo Inf Spanish American War - Oct 3, 1880 - Jan 6, 1969.
McKEE, Terry - Oct 24, 1874 - Apr 4, 1981.
McKEE, Paul R. - June 15, 1907 - July 15, 1981.
McKEE, David Leonard - Oct 27, 1918 - no date.

BOOTH, Joseph - 1892 - 1973.
BARNETT, William H. - 1899 - 1970.
BURRIS, John H. - May 6, 1924 - Sep 18, 1971.
McKEE, Ora L. - 1909 - 1984.
"   Jim - 1900 - 1975.
RAY, Willa - 1909 - 1966.
EUBANKS, Janet L. - d. 1963.
BURRIS, Corenne - 1893 - 1964.
STAPLETON, Lelia - 1897 - 1971.
STAPLETON, Virgil, Mo Pvt US Army WWI - Dec 20, 1889 - May 12, 1955.
RAMOS, Geraldine - 1924 - 196?.
McKEE, Sylvester - 1941 - 1942.
JACKMAN, Lillie - no dates.
EUBANKS, Devolia - d. June 23, 1943.
O'DON, Allien - Sep 11, 1939 - Jan 4, 1970.
ROBINSON, Rosevelt - 1925 - 1972.
STEMMONS, Lou Ada - Sep 17, 1879 - May 1, 1966.
McKEE, Elzia W., Pvt US Army WWI - Feb 15, 1894 - Jan 13, 1992.
ENGLISH, Doris EUBANKS - Feb 28, 1930 - Jan 18, 1984.
HUBBARD, Albert G., III - Nov 9, 1952.
HUBBARD, Alvin M., son - 1854 - 1973.
EUBANKS, Joe E. - 1936 - 1953.
EUBANKS, Willis S. - June 24, 1941 - Feb 15, 1968.
McKEE, Linda Joyce - Apr 27, 1953 - Jan 26, 1959.
McKEE, Clara Odell - July 27, 1896 - Apr 3, 1970.
McKEE, Elzia - no dates.
ROBINSON, Wilma - 1931 - 1939.
ROBINSON, Noble L. C. - 1900 - 1959.
ROBINSON, Jesse Mae - 1900 - 1971.
RAY, Alfred - 1904 - no date.
"   Margaret - 1895 - 1950.
BURRIS, Ada - Oct 31, 1892 - July 24, 1979.
"   Homer - Dec 17, 1895 - May 23, 1973.
McQUITTY, Bessie M. - May 25, 1893 - Oct 31, 1961.
McQUITTY, Forrest L. - May 22, 1896 - no date.
EUBANKS, Recolia - May 14, 1902 - Feb 10, 1989.
EUBANKS, Robert B., Sr. - Sep 26, 1898 - Mar 12, 1985.
MILLER, Jonell Adonis - Jan 29, 1988 - Apr 27,

1988.
BENSON, Opal M. - June 21, 1911 - no date.
" Estill - Mar 25, 1913 - no date.
EUBANKS, Odessa HILL - 1915 - no date.
EUBANKS, Millicent - 1913 - no date.
EUBANKS, Eursel - Mar 31, 1903 - Apr 13, 1988.
" Mary Magglen - Nov 17, 1907 - no date.
JACKMAN, Brooksie - 1899 - 1956.
JACKMAN, Blenda Joyce - b. & d. 1953.
HILL, Ann HOWARD - Aug, 1889 - Dec 18, 1895.
HILL, Joseph P., son of H. & C. - d. Oct 26, 1884, aged 14 yr., 3 mo., 11 dy.
JACKSON, Allice, daughter of A. & N. - d. Jan 19, 1883, aged 25 yr., 3 mo., 22 dy.
JACKSON, Elizabeth, daughter of A. & N. - Aug 17, 1878, aged 17 yr., 11 mo., 3 dy.
JACKSON, Nancy, wife of A. - rest of stone is buried.
JACKSON, Ellis, daughter of H. & M. - d. Aug 18, 1883, aged 19 yr., 6 mo., 17 dy.
HILL, Amy JACKMAN, wife of Prior HILL- d.July 19, 1883, aged 71 yr.
BORNETT, Charlie - d. Feb 22, 1889, aged 20 yr., 2 mo.

Mt. HEBRON Cemetery, Lafayette County. Located north of Odessa, Missouri.
BELLES, Gill Eve - July 14, 1829 - Mar 4, 1902.
" Marinda A. - Apr 3, 1841 - Jan 22, 1908.
BUTT, Thomas, d, Aug 4, 1882, age 63 yr., 3 mo., 11 dys.
BUTT, Martha, daughter of Thomas & Margaret - Sep 9, 1852 - Apr 25, 1870.
WHITSETT, Wm. A. - 1874 - 1930.
WILMOT, Fannie L. BELLES, wife of R. A. - d. Dec 20, 1891, aged 26 yr., 2 mo., 1 dy.
WATERHOUSE, Hezekiah - Sep 4, 1823 - Oct 17, 1894.
WATERHOUSE, Lucinda - Sep 16, 1829 - May 26, 1903.
WHITSETT, J. Oliver - Aug 31, 1840 - Mar 22, 1913.
WHITSETT, Kirby S. - Sep 11, 1874 - Sep 14, 1896.

WHITSETT, Samuel T. - Dec 17, 1809 - May 7, 1864.
WHITSETT, Martha A., wife of S. T. - Nov 27, 1812 - Mar 31, 1895.
WHITSETT, Elizabeth - Apr 3, 1809 - Nov 20, 1895.
WHITSETT, Uncle Billy (Wm. M.) - d. Jan 18, 1883, aged 77 yr., 4 mo., 2 dy..
SLOSS, Sarah Jane - Feb 13, 1828 - Sep 1, 1840.
STOCKTON, F. W. - Aug 16, 1838 - May 27, 1893.
STOCKTON, Elizabeth, wife of F. W. - d. Feb 10, 1878, aged 36 yr., 6 mo., 14 dy..
STOCKTON, Sallie S., wife of F. W. - d. July 20, 1883, aged 42 yr., 3 mo., 3 dy..
SMITH, Albert D., son of S. & M. N. - Feb 28, 1867 - Jan 31, 1871.
REYNOLDS, J. W. - Oct 24, 1824 - Oct 5, 1904.
TUCKER, James F. - Aug 17, 1835 - May 10, 1871.
TUCKER, Robert M., son of J. F. & R. W. - Aug 23, 1870 - Mar 17, 1881.
SMITH, Martha, wife of Samuel - d. Oct 1, 1875, aged 41 yr., 10 mo., 11 dy..
SMITH, Samuel - Apr 6, 1834 - Mar 27, 1895.
MARSHALL, Mathew A. - Dec 16, 1885 - Apr 30, 1912.
MARSHALL, R. P. - Jan 9, 1839 - Apr 16, 1918.
" Jane F. S. - Apr 6, 1844 - Dec 6, 1920.
MOORE, Cordelia, wife of J. C. - 1836 - 1924.
MOORE, J. C. - d. July 30, 1905, aged 66 yr..
MOORE, Wm., son of J. C. - 1860 - 1923.
PRICE, Edward - Nov 12, 1801 - Apr 1, 1873.
MEGLASSON, Mary A., wife of W. T. - Apr 5, 1839 - Feb 4, 1882.
MARSHALL, Absalom - 1807 - 1872.
" Dolly - 1803 - 1897.
MARSHALL, Wm. Beatty - June 23, 1871 - Dec 30, 1902.
MARSHALL, Chas. S., son of R. P & J. F. - Apr 17, 1877 - Sep 19, 1902.
PRATHER, Mary S. July 18, 1860 - Dec 23, 1909.
" Chatham E. - May 29, 1860 - Apr 27, 1931.
DAWSON, John W. - Mar 9, 1880, aged 31 yr., 9 Mo., 22 dy..
DAWSON, Mary - May 31, 1879, aged 29 yr., 10

mo., 16 dy..
HOUX, George - Mar 8, 1797 - July 9, 1881.
"   Eliza A. Apr 7, 1808 - Nov 6, 1883.
HOUX, Charlotte - d. Aug 7, 1863, aged 69 yr., 10 mo., 5 dy.
HOUX. William - d. Dec 1, 1887, aged 88 yr., 9 mo., 9 dy.
GRAHAM, J. W. - Dec 23, 1833 - Jan 17, 1904.
"   Athelia - Apr 16, 1844 - Apr 27, 1914.
GREEN, John S. - Aug 19, 1849 - Oct 24, 1889.

SLAVE SCHEDULES

These schedules list only the slave owner and any slave over the age of 99 by name. For other slaves, their age, sex, and color were listed.

Cole County, 1850.
William C. YOUNG - 50 - m - B; 20 - f - B; 15 - m - M; 10 - f - M; 4 - m - M.
Thomas MILLER - 62 - f - B; 37 - f - B; 25 - f - M; 15 - f - M; 10 - f - B; 10 - f - B; 6 - m - B; 42 - m - B; 4 - f - M; 2 - m - M; 2/12 - m - B; 2/24 - f - B.
Charles MERIDITH - 55 - f - B.
Thomas L. BOLTON - 20 - f - B; 17 - m - B; 16 - f- B; 10 - f - B.
Whitley F. FOWLER - 30 - m - B; 17 - f - B; 17 - f - B; 1 - m - B; 2/12 - m - B.
Gustavus A. PARSONS - 20 - f - B; 15 - f - B.
James W. MAY - 26 - f - B; 12 - m - B.
Alfred BAYSE - 53 - f - B.
Levi GUNSAULUS - 13 - f - B.
William H. FURGERSON - 15 - f - B; 12 - f - B; 50 - m - B.
Jefferson L. ROGERS - 45 - m - B; 30 - m - B; 25 - f - B; 12 - m - B; 21 - m - B.
Benjamin PACE - 14 - m - B; 12 - m - B.
Enos B. CORDELL - 50 - m - B; 45 - m - B; 19 - m - B; 14 - m - B; 22 - m - B; 25 - m - B; 45 - f - B; 26 - f - B; 6 - m - B; 4 - f - B; 1 - f - B.
Henry CORDELL - 35 - f - B; 14 - f - B.
James LUSK - 31 - f - B; 16 - m - B.
David S. GREEN - 25 - m - B; 23 - m - B; 19 - m - B; 45 - f - B; 8 - m - B; 7/12 - m - B.
A. M. DAVISON - 23 - f - B; 21 - m - M; 20 - m - B; 10 - f - B; 7 - f - M; 5 - m - M.
B. H. McCARTY - 25 - f - M; 21 - f - B; 4 - f - B; 1 - f - M; 12 - m - B.
W. B. READ - 15 - m - M.
G. W. HOUGH - 44 - f - M; 25 - f - B; 2 - m - B; 8/12 - f - M.
John H. EDWARD - 35 - f - B; 16 - f - B; 27 - f - B; 28 - m - M; 15 - m - B.
William WELDEN - 35 - f - B.

C. F. EDWARD - 32 - m - B; 24 - m - B; 10 - m - B; 10 - m - B; 9 - m - B; 4 - m - B; 4 - m - B; 26 - f - B; 22 - f - B; 12 - f - B.
John S. McCRACKEN - 45 - m - B; 45 - f - B; 25 - f - B; 7 - f - B.
C. M. BOLTON - 21 - f - M; 14 - f - B; 21 - f - B.
Joseph BOGGS - 50 - f - B; 29 - f - B; 10 - f - M; 29 - m - B; 8 - m - B; 6 - m - B; 3/12 - m - M.
Wm. BRADBERRY - 14 - f - B.
Jacob P. MAUS - 40 - m - B.
Alex GORDEN - 34 - m - B; 31 - f - B; 29 - f - M; 24 - m - B; 19 - m - B; 12 - m - B; 9 - m - B; 9 - f - B; 7 - f - B; 4 - m - B; 3 - m - B.
William M. KERR - 40 - m - B; 40 - m - M; 40 - f - B; 30 - f - B; 25 - m - B; 20 - f - B; 16 - m - B; 10 - m - M; 9 - m - B; 4 - m - M.
Isaac PALMER - 58 - m - B; 52 - m - B; 50 - f - B; 35 - f - B; 34 - m - B; 34 - m - B; 30 - f - B; 30 - f - B; 28 - f - B; 22 - m - B; 20 - m - B; 18 - f - B; 17 - f - B; 16 - f - B; 16 - f - B; 14 - f - B; 14 - f - B; 12 - f - B; 12 - m - M; 10 - f - B; 7 - m - B; 5 - m - B; 2 - f - B.
George W. WADE - 24 - f - B; 22 - f - B; 18 - m - B; 18 - f - B; 10 - f - B.
Wm. B. STARK - 55 - m - B; 48 - f - B; 32 - f - B; 23 - f - B; 13 - f - B; 9 - f - B; 11 - f - B; 8/12 - f - B.
Wm. N. RICE - 42 - m - B.
Tennessee MATHEWS - 39 - m - B; 9 - m - B; 9 - m - B; 15 - f - B.
John D. CURRY - 60 - m - B; 60 - f - B; 25 - f - B; 18 - f - B; 12 - f - B; 5 - f - M; 1 - f - M.
Abraham FULKERSON - 34 - f - B; 4 - m - B.
Job GOODALL - 32 - m - B; 32 - f - B; 7 - m - B; 5 - m - B; 4 - m - B; 1 - m - B.
John PARE - 30 - f - B; 5 - m - M; 3 - m - B.
Calvin GUNN - 55 - m - B; 55 - f - B; 25 - f - B.
Milton J. MAHAN - 12 - f - B.
Philip T. MILLER - 33 - f - B; 21 - m - B; 23 - f - B; 9 - f - B; 3 - m - B.

Austin A. KING - 22 - m - B; 21 - f - B; 5 - m - B; 3 - m - B; 1 - f - B; 17 - f - B; 12 - f - B.
Wm. E. DUNSCUMB - 45 - f - B; 18 - f - M; 16 - f - M; 38 - m - B.
Wm. A. ROBARDS - 38 - m - B; 35 - f - B; 13 - f - B; 11 - m - B; 9 - m - B; 7 - f - B; 5 - m - B; 3 - m - B; 3 - m - B; 6/12 - f - B.
Hiram H. BABER - 12 - m - B.
Ephraim B. EWING - 20 - m - B; 22 - f - B; 1 - f - B.
Robert GALE - 23 - m - B.
James GLENN - 30 - f - B; 55 - m - B; 25 - m - M.
Daniel DUNCAN - 25 - f - B.
Henry DUNCAN - 30 - f - B; 10 - f - B; 10 - m - B.
Samuel CLAY - 60 - m - B.
B. A. RAMSEY - 24 - m - B; 22 - m - B; 20 - f - B; 16 - f - B; 13 - f - B; 8 - m - M; 1/12 - m - M.
John GORDEN - 15 - f - B; 5/12 - f - B.
Wm. GORDEN - 36 - m - B.
John OWENS - 24 - f - B; 17 - f - B; 17 - m - B.
Robert GALE - 45 - f - B.
Henry BUCKNER - 28 - m - B.
Lafayette SONE - 18 - m - B; 18 - f - M; 2 - m - M; 4/12 - f - M.
James C. SHORT - 11 - f - M.
J. H. PLUMMER - 35 - m - B; 12 - m - B; 8 - m - B.
Jeremiah MADDEN - 75 - f - B.
James CAMPBELL - 30 - f - B.
John CLIBOUN - 60 - f - B; 32 - f - M; 30 - m - M; 28 - f - M; 26 - m - M; 24 - f - B; 20 - f - M; 15 - m - M.
John BERRY - 25 - m - M; 21 - f - M; 18 - m - B; 13 - m - M; 10 - f - B; 6 - f - M; 5 - f - M.
James TOMLINSON - 23 - f - B; 3/12 - f - M.
Nathan PROCTER - 19 - f - B; 17 - m - B; 15 - f - B.
James CAMPBELL - 45 - f - B; 18 - m - B; 19 - f - B; 15 - f - B; 14 - f - B; 13 - f - B.
Wm. W. RALSTON - 29 - m - B; 17 - f - B.

Lucinda BARBER - 23 - f - B; 5 - m - B; 19 - m - B.
Lanman SHORT - 40 - f - B; 8 - m - B; 6 - f - B.
William H. SHORT - 7 - f - B.
Thomas J. WILBOURN - 20 - f - M; 8 - f - B; 1 - m - M.
Jason HARRISON - 25 - f - M; 8 - m - B; 6 - m - M; 3 - m - M; 1 - f - B.
Mary A. COLGAN - 18 - f - B.
A. W. AMOS - 1 - f - B; 1 - m - B.
Joseph RUSSELL - 14 - f - B; 13 - m - B; 5 - m - B.
Robert A. SHORT - 15 - f - M.
Mary TOMLINSON - 35 - m - B.
James MORROW - 23 - m - B.
Samuel E. SHORT - 13 - m - M.
Joseph SHORT - 16 - m - M; 8 - f - B.
Jeremiah DIXON - 72 - f - B; 32 - f - B; 15 - f - B; 24 - m - M; 17 - m - M; 21 - m - B.
Samuel MAHAN - 37 - f - B.
Martha BOLTON - 54 - m - B; 65 - f - B; 45 - f - B; 40 - f - B; 35 - f - B; 21 - f - B.
Henry DIXON - 7 - f - B; 6 - f - B; 4 - f - B.
Martha BOLTON - 14 - m - B; 7 - f - B; 10 - f - B; 9 - m - B; 7 - m - B; 8 - m - B; 7 - f - B; 2 - m - B; 1 - m - B; 4/12 - f - B; 6 - f - B; 5 - m - B; 4 - m - B; 2 - f - B; 5 - m - B.
Edward W. WARD - 45 - f - B; 15 - f - B; 12 - f - B; 10 - m - B.
Nicholas J. WINSTON - 50 - m - B; 45 - f - B; 40 - f - B; 17 - m - B; 19 - m - B; 10 - f - B; 9 - m - B; 6 - f - B; 2 - f - B; 26 - f - B; 3 - m - B.
Lanson ROBISON - 19 - f - B; 9 - m - B.
A. W. CEAMAL - 60 - f - B; 40 - f - B; 18 - m - B; 18 - m - M; 16 - f - B; 8 - m - B; 10 - f - B.
Warren DIXON - 55 - f - B; 40 - f - B; 35 - m - B; 32 - f - B; 17 - m - M; 15 - m - B; 7 - f - B; 5 - f - B; 1 - f - M; 1 - m - B.
Samuel L. SMITH - 48 - m - B; 35 - m - B; 25 - f - B; 12 - f - M; 3 - f - B.
John W. BOLTON - 42 - f - B; 40 - f - B; 22 - m - B; 16 - f - B; 13 - f - B; 6 - m - B.
Emely HEUIT - 16 - f - B.

James WILLIAMS - 45 - m - B; 35 - m - M; 38 - f
- B; 30 - m - B; 18 - m - M; 16 - m - B; 14 -
m - B; 14 - f - B; 10 - m - B; 9 - f - B; 7 -
f - B; 5 - m - B; 1 - f - B; 2/12 - f - B.
Thomas BOLTON - 50 - m - B; 44 - f - B; 30 - f
- B; 30 - f - B; 30 - m - B; 21 - m - B; 16 -
f - B; 14 - f - B; 11 - f - B; 13 - m - B; 12
- m - B; 11 - f - B; 10 - m - B; 8 - m - B; 6
- f - B; 4 - f - B; 2 - m - B.
Lawrence SHUBERT - 10 - f - M.
James BARBERRY - 48 - m - B; 45 - f - B; 20 - m
- B; 12 - m - B; 8 - f - B; 6 - m - B; 4 - m
- B; 2/12 - f - B.
William BOLTON - 52 - m - B; 30 - f - B; 27 - m
- B; 25 - m - B; 27 - f - B; 25 - f - B; 22 -
f - B; 15 - f - M; 14 - f - M; 10 - f - B; 5
- f - M; 2/12 - f - M; 13 - m - B; 9 - m - B;
9 - m - B; 5 - m - B; 4 - m - B; 1 - m - B.
James W. MORROW - 10 - f - B; 24 - f - B; 8 - f
- M; 6 - f - M; 3 - f - B; 1 - f - B
John C. GORDEN - 28 - f - B; 13 - f - M; 5 - m
- B; 5 - m - B; 1 - f - B.
Wm. A. DAVISON - 30 - m - B; 30 - m - B; 27 - f
- M; 5 - f - B; 28 - m - B; 29 - m - B; 25 -
m - B; 20 - m - B; 25 - m - B; 3 - m - B;
6/12 - m - B; 10 - f - M; 8 - m - B.
Thomas M. WINSTON - 40 - f - B; 16 - m - M.
G. B. WINSTON - 15 - m - B; 11 - f - B.
James V. SONE - 22 - m - B; 22 - f - B; 3 - m -
M; 6/12 - m - B.
John MOORE - 35 - f - B; 28 - f - B; 29 - f -
B; 18 - m - B; 20 - f - B; 15 - m - B; 14 - m
- B; 8 - m - B; 7 - f - B; 2 - m - B; 2 - m -
B; 3 - m - B; 2 - m - B; 2 - m - B; 1 - m -
B; 2/12 - m - B.
Robert EWING - 60 - m - B; 40 - f - B; 25 - m -
M; 22 - f - B; 23 - f - b; 21 - m - B; 20 - m
- M; 18 - m - B; 16 - m - B; 13 - m - B; 13 -
m - B; 10 - f - B; 8 - m - B; 6 - f - B; 5 -
m - M; 5 - f - M; 5 - m - B; 3 - f - B; 2 - f
- B; 6/12 - m - M; 2 - m - B; 1/12 - m - B;
11/12 - m - M.
Elizabeth KENNON - 16 - f - M; 7 - f - M.
June CORMETT - 23 - f - B; ? - f - B.
John ISHAM - 26 - m - M.
Peter E. DAVIS - 3 - f - B.

Daniel DUNCAN - 30 - m - B; 21 - m - B.
Wm. DUNCAN - 48 - f - B.
Ava NORFLEET - 48 - f - B; 36 - f - B; 28 - m - B; 22 - m - B; 10 - f - M; 12 - m - B.
Sira DUNCAN - 68 - m - B; 53 - f - B; 27 - m - B; 9 - f - B.
Abram NORFLEET - 24 - f - B; 2 - m - B; 9/12 - f - B.
Isaac BOND - 30 - m - B; 13 - m - B; 3 - f - B.
John McKENZIE - 29 - m - B; 26 - m - B; 50 - f - B; 23 - m - B; 18 - m - B; 12 - m - B; 7 - m - B; 4 - f - B; 2 - m - B; 26 - f - B; 26 - f - B; 16 - f - B; 1 - m - B; 1/12 - m - B; 2 - f - B.
Thomas T. ASHBY - 16 - f - M.
Wm. CRAIG - 36 - f - B.
Wm. K. WINSTON - 55 - f - M; 15 - f - b; 51 - m - B.
Wm. B. RAGSDALE - 50 - m - B.
Ephraim CLARK - 16 - f - B.
John HANLEY - 8 - f - B.
Shelby MARTIN - 40 - f - B; 5 - m - B; 2 - m - B.
Wm. B. WALTHALL - 60 - f - M; 26 - m - B; 17 - f - M; 13 - m - B; 10/12 - m - M.
PRICE, McKEE & Co. - 38 - m - B; 38 - m - B; 36 - m - B; 23 - m - B; 25 - m - B; 18 - m - B; 90 - m - B; 90 - m - B; 75 - f - B; 60 - m - B; 50 - m - B; 50 - m - B; 50 - m - B; 50 - m - B; 45 - m - B; 45 - m - B; 50 - m - B; 40 - m - B; 28 - m - B; 22 - m - B; 22 - m - B; 14 - m - B; 50 - m - B; 50 - f - B; 50 - f - B; 45 - f - B; 30 - f - B; 30 - f - B; 30 - f - M; 35 - f - M; 35 - f - B; 18 - f - B; 35 - f - B; 22 - f - M; 16 - f - B; 16 - f - M; 12 - f - B; 8 - f - B; 8 - f - B; 8 - f - B; 6 - f - B; 4 - f - M; 4 - f - B; 2 - f - B; 8 - m - B; 7 - m - B; 6 - m - B; 5 - m - B; 5 - m - B; 4 - m - B; 5 - m - B; 5 - m - B; 4 - m - B; 3 - m - B; 1 - m - B.
Fanny CASEY - 18 - f - B.
Wm. DURHAM - 18 - m - B; 12 - m - B; 14 - f - B.
Sally F. HOWARD - 26 - f - B.
John W. WELLS - 55 - f - B; 20 - m - B; 14 - f - M.

Thomas GREGORY - 35 - f - B; 5 - f - M; 3 - m - B.
William HICKAM - 50 - f - B; 33 - f - B; 22 - f - B; 11 - m - M; 10 - m - M; 6 - f - B; 3 - f - B; 4/12 - m - B.
Reuben GARNETT - 70 - f - B; 50 - m - B; 38 - m - B; 29 - f - B; 17 - f - B; 10 - f - B; 9 - f- B; 9 - f - B.
James McKEE - 16 - m - B; 15 - f - B; 10/12 - f - B.
Mary MASON - 7 - m - B.
John USHER - 41 - f - b.
Isham DURHAM - 9 - m - B; 12 - f - B.
William G. MINOR - 30 - f - B; 17 - f - B; 6 - f - M; 4 - m - M; 6/12 - m - M.
Joseph HIGGINS - 30 - f - M; 17 - m - M; 35 - m - M; 17 - m - B; 10 - m - M; 11 - m - B; 1 - m - M; 8 - m - M.
James HIGGINS - 22 - f - B; 7 - m - M; 1 - f - M.
Elizabeth WALSER - 28 - f - B; 16 - m - B; 7 - f - M.
Samuel LEGG - 24 - f - b; 21 - m - B.
Sarah LANE - 50 - f - B; 46 - f - M.
John KENNEY - 50 - m - M; 46 - f - M; 4 - m - B.
James MOAD - 12 - f - B.
John JOHNSON - 46 - m - B.
Hiram HASKINS - 43 - f - B; 13 - m - B; 12 - m - B; 9 - m - B; 6 - m - B; 2 - f - B.
Robert BASNETT - 35 - m - B.
Thomas TERRY - 14 - f - B.
Joel C. MELTON - 44 - m - B; 42 - m - B; 30 - f - M; 16 - f - M; 14 - m - B; 10 - m - B; 8 - m - M; 2 - m - M; 2 - m - M.
Josiah LAMPKIN - 24 - f - M; 4 - m - M.
Thomas L. PRICE - 42 - f - B; 41 - m - B; 14 - m - B; 29 - m - B.
Avey PRICE - 36 - m - B.
Robert GLOVER - 50 - m - B; 50 - f - B; 14 - m - B; 29 - m - B.
John JOHNSON - 60 - m - B.
Henry E. DIXON - 50 - m - B; 38 - m - B; 23 - m - B; 19 - f - B; 12 - m - M; 11 - f - B.
Michael D. CLARK - 40 - f - B.
John HANLEY - 25 - f - B; 15 - m - B; 10 - f -

B; 8 - f - B; 8 - f - B; 5 - m - B; 1 - f - B.
Waller BOLTON - 58 - m - B; 52 - m - B; 47 - f - B; 46 - m - B; 35 - m - B; 34 - m - B; 28 - m - B; 31 - f - B; 30 - f - B; 29 - f - B; 24 - f - B; 24 - f - B; 20 - f - B; 17 - f - B; 15 - f - B; 14 - f - B; 13 - m - B; 11 - m - B; 11 - f - B; 9 - m - B; 7 - f - B; 5 - f - B; 5 - m - B; 5 - m - B; 2 - f - B; 1 - f - B; 2 - m - B.
Merriweather BOLTON - 100 - f - B; 45 - f - B; 45 - m - B; 40 - m - B; 20 - m - B; 18 - f - B; 15 - m - B; 12 - f - B; 10 - m - B; 8 - f - B.
Elizabeth ROPER - 52 - f - B; 40 - m - B; 26 - f - M; 18 - m - B; 30 - f - B; 28 - f - B; 14 - f - B; 13 - f - B; 11 - f - B; 10 - f - B; 8 - m - B; 7 - f - B; 5 - f - B; 3 - f - B; 3 - f - B; 1 - f - B; 25 - f - B; 15 - f - B.
George W. LOCKET - 54 - f - B; 32 - f - B; 25 - m - B; 25 - m - B; 18 - m - B; 18 - f - B; 8 - f - B; 5 - f - B; 4 - f - B; 3 - m - B; 1 - f - M.
Theodore STANLEY - 40 - m - B; 38 - f - M; 38 - f - B; 28 - m - B; 26 - m - B; 24 - f - B; 24 - m - B; 23 - f - B; 21 - f - M; 15 - m - B; 14 - f - B; 11 - m - B; 9 - f - B; 6 - m - B; 3 - f - B; 3 - f - B; 2 - m - B; 2 - m - B; 1 - m - B; 1 - m - B; 60 - f - B; 60 - f - M; 60 - m - B; 60 - f - B; 1 - m - B; 45 - f - B; 45 - m - B; 45 - m - B; 32 - m - M; 30 - m - B; 25 - f - M; 24 - f - B; 6 - f - M; 16 - f - B; 9 - m - B; 9 - f - B; 7 - m - M; 5 - f - B; 4 - m - B; 2 - f - B; 2 - m - B.
Mary S. TOMPKINS - 60 - f - B; 30 - f - B; 25 - m - B; 24 - m - B; 15 - f - B.
John ANDERSON - 12 - f - B.
Wm. H. EANS - 55 - f - B; 48 - f - B; 20 - f - B; 18 - m - B; 8 - f - B; 5 - f - B; 2 - m - B; 1 - m - B.
James A. MAHAN - 30 - f - B; 9 - m - B; 7 - m - M; 7 - f - B.
Levi DIXON - 57 - m - B; 28 - m - B; 20 - m - B; 20 - m - B; 17 - m - B; 16 - m - B; 25 - f - B; 10 - f - B; 5 - f - M; 5 - m - B; 3 - m - B.

D. H. LINN - 10 - m - B.
William SCOTT - 55 - m - B; 26 - m - B; 22 - m - B; 29 - f - B; 25 - f - B; 14 - m - B; 6 - f - B; 4 - f - B; 2 - m - B.
Robert W. WELLS - 40 - m - B; 30 - m - B; 30 - f - B; 25 - m - M; 24 - f - M; 22 - m - M; 18 - f - M; 16 - m - B; 9 - f - B; 8 - m - B; 7 - f - B; 5 - m - B; 3 - f - B; 1 - f - B.
Margaret LISLE - 18 - f - B.
Ann WALKER - 18 - f - B.
Julia C. PLUMP - 26 - f - B; 3/12 - m - B.
Sally COFFELT - 35 - m - B; 26 - f - B; 6 - f - B; 4 - m - B; 1 - f - B.
Rob't G. SIMINGTON - 25 - f - B; 6 - m - B; 6/12 - m - B.
Catherine ROBERSON - 25 - f - B; 16 - m - B; 13 - m - B.
Mary JAMES - 14 - f - M; 12 - f - B.
Catherine KELLY - 10 - f - B.
H. H. NEUMAN - 34 - f - B; 25 - f - M; 9 - f - M; 3 - f - B.
Wm. D, KERR - 35 - f - B; 13 - f - M.
Lewis BOLTON - 51 - m - B; 44 - f - B; 55 - m - B; 30 - m - B; 28 - m - B; 26 - f - M; 24 - f - M; 21 - m - B; 18 - m - B; 17 - m - B; 16 - m - B; 14 - m - B; 13 - f - B; 12 - m - M; 35 - f - M; 8 - m - B; 8 - m - B; 8 - f - B; 5 - m - B; 4 - m - B; 4 - f - B; 2 - m - B.
Peter G. GLOVER - 42 - m - B; 30 - f - B; 25 - f - B; 13 - f - B; 10 - m - B; 9 - f - B; 7 - m - B; 7 - f - B; 6 - m - B; 5 - f - B; 3 - m - B; 2 - f - B.
G. C. MEDLEY - 17 - m - M.
Maria SHARP - 17 - f - B.
Henry DIXON - 30 - m - B; 25 - m - B; 13 - m - B; 12 - m - B; 1 - m - B; 35 - f - B; 34 - f - B; 14 - f - B.
Wilson BROWN - 35 - f - B; 14 - m - B; 11 - f - B; 8 - f - M; 5 - f - B.

Osage County, 1850.
George HOOPS - 21 - m - B.
David HOOPS - 40 - f - B; 30 - m - B; 23 - m - B; 18 - m - B.
Reuben TERRELL - 52 - m - B; 50 - f - B.
Elijah JONES - 20 - f - B; 2 - m - B; 1 - m - B.

Thomas DAVIS - 15 - m - B.
C. W. HOLTONKNIDER - 25 - m - B; 20 - f - B.
Thomas ANDERSON - 30 - m - B; 21 - f - B; 12 - m - M; 9 - f - B; 5 - f - B; 2 - m - B; 5/12 - m - B.
Gilbert CRISMAN - 52 - f - B; 32 - m - B; 26 - f - B.
Lucy DAVIS - 43 - f - B; 18 - f - B; 3 - m - M.
Thomas BACCUS - 10 - m - B.
James THORNTON - 39 - f - B; 25 - f - B; 12 - f - B; 7 - m - M; 5 - m - M; 5 - m - M; 4 - f - M; 3 - f - M.
Andrew BRANSON - 47 - f - B.
Robert P. HOWERTON - 65 - f - B; 55 - f - B; 22 - f - B.
Thomas MILLER - 26 - f - B; 27 - f - B; 8 - m - B; 4 - m - B.
David BRANSON - 24 - f - B.
Eli McJALTON - 28 - f - M; 27 - m - B; 20 - m - B.
Hercules W. NEILL - 10 - f - M.
Henry WOODY - 25 - m - B; 25 - f - B; 25 - f - B; 13 - f - M; 6 - f - B; 4 - f - M; 3/12 - f - B.
Leander RAINEY - 23 - f - M; 4/12 - m - M.
William T. BIRCH - 17 - m - B; 13 - f - B.
Newton CASEY - 52 - m - B; 12 - f - M.
Hugh WILSON - 45 - m - B.
William LAMKIN - 45 - f - B; 20 - f - B; 13 - m - B; 6 - f - M; 1 - f - B.
Nathan ORME - 36 - f - B; 16 - m - M; 14 - f - M; 3 - f - M.
Harrison HOLLOWAY - 14 - f - B.
Samuel LAMBETH - 26 - f - B; 24 - m - B; 21 - m - B; 10 - f - M; 6 - f - M; 4 - f - B; 1 - f B; 1 - m - M.
Mathew AGEE - 17 - f - M.
David WILLSON - 50 - m - B; 18 - m - B; 14 - f - B; 12 - m - B.
John GILES - 50 - f - M.
Ryland GILES - 11 - f - B.
John WILLSON - 33 - f - B; 20 - m - M; 7 - f - B; 5 - m - B.
Ellen WILLE - 85 - f - B.
Thomas F. BAKER - 16 - f - M.
John McLAUGHLIN - 37 - f - B, 23 - m - B; 7 - f

- B; 5 - m - B.
William LAUGHLIN - 24 - f - M.
William C. RENNOLDS - 39 - f - B.
Edward LEWIS - 14 - m - B.
Tia TATUM - 12 - m - M.
John DODDS - 18 - f - B.
Washington ROSSEN - 19 - m - B; 19 - f - B; 6 - f - B.
Samuel ROVER - 45 - m - B; 38 - f - B; 15 - m - B; 13 - f - B; 7 - f - B; 4 - m - B; 7/12 - m - B.
John BERRY - 56 - f - B; 17 - m - B; 14 - f - M.
Frederick DAVIS - 25 - f - B; 21 - f - B; 21 - m - B; 20 - f - B; 6 - f - B; 4 - m - B; 2 - m - B; 6/12 - f - B; 7/12 - f - B.
Williamson MOSEBY - 51 - f - B; 18 - m - B; 12 - f - B; 7 - m - B.
Joseph AUD - 15 - f - B; 12 - m - B.
Brawley A. HANCOCK - 30 - m - B, 30 - f - B; 25 - m - B; 21 - m - M; 16 - f - B; 14 - f - B; 12 - m - B; 8 - m - B; 6 - m - B; 6 - f - B; 4 - m - B; 3/12 - f - B.
Charles PHELPS - 40 - f - B; 11 - f - B.
Jesse WETON - 80 - f - B; 65 - f - B; 38 - m - M; 30 - m - B; 30 - f - B; 29 - f - B; 17 - m - B; 10 - m - B; 8 - m - M; 7 - f - B; 5 - m - B; 3 - f - B; 2 - f - M; 4/12 - f - B.
Martha Hull - 35 - m - B; 40 - f - B; 36 - m - B; 36 - f - B.
Rachel SHOBE - 36 - m - B; 36 - f - B.
John M. DOWNLEY - 28 - m - B; 20 - m - M; 15 - f - M; 25 - f - B; 4 - f - B.
Armstrong DUDGEON - 32 - f - M; 20 - m - B; 12 - f - B; 7 - f - B; 3 - f - B; 2 - f - B.
Benjamin LAUGHLIN - 45 - f - B; 45 - f - M; 26 - m - B; 22 - m - M; 18 - m - B; 16 - m - B; 14 - m - B; 2 - m - B; 15 - f - M; 12 - f - B; 8 - f - B; 4 - f - B.
Jacob FISHER - 26 - m - M; 21 - m - B; 13 - m - B; 25 - f - B; 15 - f - B; 5 - f - B; 3 - f - B; 2 - f - B; 6 - f - B.
William CLARK - 26 - m - M.
Lewis WELTON - 42 - f - B; 30 - f - B; 21 - m - B; 20 - f - B; 10 - f - B; 9 - f - B; 5 - f - B; 1 - m - B;

Mary Ann HULL - 35 - m - B; 25 - f - M; 6 - m - B.
John SHIPLEY - 23 - f - B; 2 - f - B.
Nancy WALLACE - 40 - f - B; 12 - f - M.
Bernhard BRUNS - 38 - m - B; 35 - f - M; 3 - f - B.
Coleman LEAL - 24 - f - B; 18 - m - B.
Edward GILLION - 46 - m - B; 45 - f - B; 20 - f - B.
Joseph WILLIAMS - 32 - f - B; 14 - f - B; 10 - f - B; 5 - f - B.
Deborah NEAL - 8 - f - B; 6 - f - B; 60 - f - B.
James S. DODDS - 13 - f - B.
Elisha RADIKEN - 24 - f - B; 6 - m - M; 3 - f - M.
Elizabeth HOOVER - 18 - f - B.
Rosanna M. SMITH - 30 - m - B; 21 - m - B; 17 - f - B.
Giles LEE - 17 - f - B.
George D. SMITH - 10 - m - B; 6 - m - B.
Wm. P. MABIN - 30 - m - B; 30 - m - B; 30 - m - B; 30 - m - B; 86 - m - B; 50 - m - B; 50 - m - B; 18 - m - B; 14 - m - B; 5 - m - B; 25 - f - B; 3 - f - B; 18 mo., - f - M; 24 - f - B; 42 - f - B; 25 - f - M; 25 - f - M; 27 - f - M; 30 - f - M; 60 - f - B; 62 - f - B; 47 - f - B; 45 - m - B; 27 - f - B; 8 - f - B; 6 - f - B; 4 - f - B; 2 - f - B.
William BOLTON - 30 - m - M; 18 - m - B.

BURIAL RECORDS

Danforth Cemetery, Greene County. Located Sec 7, Twp 29, R 20.
GLOVER, William Irvine, son of W. A. - Oct 23, 1902 - Jan 3, 1903.
ZIEGLER, Infant of D. P. - d. Mar 11, 1903, age 1 wk.
CHAUDLEY, Paul, infant son of S. C. - d. May 6, 1903.
FITCH, Infant - d. Aug 17, 1903.
FRENCH, Nannie - d. May 16, 1904, aged 59.
RITCHEY, Child of John - d. Sep 5, 1905, age 6 mo.
CRESON, George - Mar 5, 1818 - Jan 22, 1906.
McQUIRE, William - d. Apr 1, 1906, aged 24 yr.
SIMMONS, Marie, infant of Charles - d. Apr 6, 1906.
COATS, Mrs. Albert - d. June 21, 1907, aged 24 yr.
BALL, Mrs. Jim - buried June 22, 1907.
CROWDUS, Catherine - d. Jan 4, 1909, at the home of her grandson, John TILLMAN.
O'LAUGHLIN, Ellen - buried Feb 16, 1909.
EDDINGS, Mary - d. age 20, buried Feb 16, 1909.
CRENSON, Sarah, d. Feb 15, 1909, age 76.
WEAVER, Mrs. Osa - d. Mar 19, 1909, age 43.
PRICE, Nannie, wife of J. T. - d. Apr 26, 1909, age 23, at the home of her father, Winfield DILLARD.
RINGEBURG, Carl Leroy - d. Sep 8, 1909, age 9 mo.
GLEN, Infant daughter of J. E. - d. Sep 24, 1909.
CORNELISON, Rena - d. Oct 7, 1909, age 3.
BRISTOW, Mrs. - d. Nov 17, 1904.
GORNELL, Mrs. R. - d. Mar 11, 1909, age 75.
RANDLES, Laura M. - 1912 - 1960.
ROOLER, Lucy - no dates.
SADDLER, Lon - no dates.
TUSSEY, John - 1883 - 1930.
McALILEY, Mary E. - Nov 27, 1899 - July 7, 1902.
WARD, Linny - Oct 2, 1866 - Feb 20, 1933.
WICKS, Barbara - d. July 18, 1942.
PRICE, Tom - d. June 15, 1964.
PHILLIPS, Vera "Estelle" - d. Dec 5, 1964.

SMITH, Reggie - d. Mar 11, 1957.
SMITH, Claud - d. Oct 16, 1955.
TEED, Bertha Lee GREEN, daughter of Frank & Hattie Caroline GREEN - no dates.
HAYDEN, Lily - Sep 28, 1902 - Sep 24, 1905.
COMSTOCK, Nancy - Oct, 30, 1885 - May 1, 1918.
SAVILLE, Dr. Frank - d. Dec 1937, age 62.
WEAVER, Oscar - d. Dec 14, 1946, age 106.
OWENS, Laura Edith - Jan 30, 1899 - June 30, 1983.
ROGERS, Elmer d. Oct 4, 1981, age 84.
JOHNSON, Mrs. H. F. - d. July 14, 1891.
CROUSE, Mrs. Peace - buried Oct 14, 1900.
DEEDS, George - d. Aug 18, 1901.
FITCH, Lizzie, daughter of William - d. Mar 6, 1902, age 1.
BRIDGEMAN, Katherine PRICE - Sep 27, 1924 - Oct 31, 1983.
WALLS, Regina Capucine, Mom - Aug 22, 1965 - Nov 17, 1987.
WALLS, Gayla Patrice - Feb 28, 1970 - Feb 17, 1987.
JEFFERIE, Mary E. - d. Dec 28, 1950.
JOHNSON, Er_dous - no dates.
JEFFRIES, Harvey - 1895 - 1928.
" Jennie - 1900 - 1985.
AYERS, Rev. Wm. GREEN - June 15, 1852 - Dec 8, 1920.
HORN, Robbie Lucille, daughter of G. S. - Oct 25, 1909 - Feb 13, 1963.
PRICE, Joe Lloyd - Sep 28, 1930 - Oct 27, 1972.
PRICE, Leon S. - July 13, 1929 - July 2, 1966.
PRICE, Ethel P., Mother - 1900 - 1986.
PRICE, Oscar, Father - 1892 - 1954.
HENDERSON, Lula LOVE - 1906 - 1945.
PRICE, Mathew Grant - 1947 - 1975.
PRICE, Mary - no dates.
JEFFERS, Clarrisa - d. Apr 3, 1912, age 26.
REID, Mary H. - no dates.
CRESON, Albert, son of John & Susan - Aug 15, 1877 - Aug 15, 1898.
GAULT, Harvey W. - Jan 23, 1817 - Dec 8, 1879.
JEFFRIES, John W. - d. Nov 14, 1870, aged 2 yr., 10 mo., 10 dy.
KING, Dennis Roy - d. Oct 19, 1941, age 1 mo., 18 dy.

McMILLIN, Eason - no dates.
McMILLIN, Roy - no dates.
PRICE, Infant daughter of S. J. & Elizabeth - Mar 14, 1906 - Mar 17, 1906.
RANDLES, Clarence E. - 1910 - no date.

<u>Oregon County Black Burials</u>. The only known grave sites are in white cemeteries. Bailey Cemetery, located in Sec 13, Twp 24, R 4, contains two such graves:
SIMPSON, Susan - no dates.
SIMPSON, Infant - no dates.
The other, unnamed cemetery is located about ½ mile from Thayer, Missouri, and contains one grave:
RAGAN, Lou - d. Feb 5, 1875, aged 53 yr.

<u>North Cemetery</u>, Chillicothe, Livingston County.
ANDERSON, Jennie - d. Aug, 1935.
ANDERSON, Roscoe - d. 1901.
ANDERSON, Ruth M. - 1876 - 1965.
ANDERSON, William H. - 1877 - 1935.
BALLEW, Charles - 1836 - no date.
BALLEW, Caroline - 1841 - 1919.
BALLEW, Hal J. - d. June 15, 1928.
BANKS, Mary - 1887 - no date.
BANKS, Mary Via - 1872 - 1938.
BANKS, V. Walter - 1888 - 1938.
BEACH, Herbert - Oct 1, 1875 - Mar 19, 1918.
BERRY, Zenobin - 1887 - no date.
BLACK, Oscar - 1880 - 1953.
BLACK, Beronice - 1879 - 1950.
BLAND, Benjamin F. - Sep 6, 1895 - Mar 19, 1960.
BOTTS, Edward J. - d. Dec 6, 1892.
BOYLE, Olivia LEEPER - 1892 - 1951.
BROWN, Edward Clem - 1892 - 1955.
BROWN, Edna V. - 1889 - 1978.
BROWN, William Edward - 1858 - 1942.
BROWN, Elgin J. - 1867 - 1946.
BROWN, G. W. - Feb 6, 1860 - Aug 28, 1946.
BROWNIE, ? - Feb 25, 1851 - 1899.
BURRELL, Monroe - no dates.
CABBEL, Hattie - d. 1933.
CRAIN, William - 1879 - 1966.
CRAIN, Albert C. - 1884 - 1919.

CRAIN, Irene B. - 1886 - 1959.
CREWS, Joanna - d. Nov 23, 1902.
CREWS, Wilson - 1861 - 1878.
CURRY, Thornton - 1851 - 1929.
DOXEY, Neoma - Oct 4, 1922 - Nov 11, 1936.
ELLIS, Anna - 1872 - 1922.
GRAHAM, Henry - no dates.
GRAHAM, Emil - 1830 - 1895.
GRAHAM, Lucy - 1849 - 1910.
GRAHAM, Charley - 1869 - 1885.
GRAHAM, Henry - 1839 -1888.
GROSS, Jane - 1826 - 1903.
GROSS, Charles - 1829 - 1907.
HERRIFORD, Karl Kennett - Nov 17, 1906 - Nov 26, 1906.
HICKS, John - no dates.
JOHNSON, Sadie M. - 1883 - 1948.
JOHNSON, Charles H. - Jan 9, 1857 - Oct 15, 1953.
LITTRELL, James - no dates.
LITTRELL, Hannah - Mar 15, 1845 - Nov 3, 1858.
LITTRELL, Jordan - 1822 - Nov 11, 1878.
LITTRELL, George B. - Apr 12, 1845 - Sep 4, 1861.
LITTRELL, Main L. - Apr 11, 1843 - June 6, 1863.
LONGDON, Emma G. - Nov 12, 1855 - 1937.
LOHGDON, R. H. - 1851 - 1930.
LONGDON, Ben - no dates.
LONGDON, Bertha - no dates.
MILLER, Rhoda - d. June 13, 1903.
MONROE, Harriet - 1836 - 1901.
MUNROE, Anne - Feb 8, 1822 - no date.
PATTERSON, Ann - d. 1919.
PATTERSON, Hattie - 1882 - 1932.
ROUNDTREE, Davy - d. Jan 21, 1914.
ROUNDTREE, Mary A. - d. Oct 28, 1927.
ROWLAND, Wallace W. Jr. - 1870 - 1931.
SCOTT, Thomas - 1847 - 1933.
SCOTT, Mary E. - 1850 - 1939.
SHIRLEY, Mary - d. Aug 3, 1878.
SMITH, Rosa - d. 1931.
SPEARS, James Mathew - Feb, 1828 - Sep 13, 1894.
STEWARD, Leon - 1907 - 1968.
STEWART, Alberta Irene - 1913 - 1938.

Unknown, Jane - d. 1887.
WALLER, Sarah M. - June 18, 1861 - May 1, 1892.
WALLER, Lewis G. - 1847 - 1928.
WALLER, Henry Oliver - Sep 5, 1880 - Sep 30, 1926.
WILLIAM, Virgil E. June 15, 1877 - Feb 19, 1941.
WILLIAM, Thos. B. - 1874 - 1930.
WILLIAMS, Henry - 1845 - 1927.
WILLIAMS, Fannie B. - 1857 - 1939.

<u>Yale Cemetery</u>, Barton County. Located near Mindenmines, east of the Missouri-Kansas boarder.
ADAMS, George - no dates.
ADAMS, Robert, son of George - d. Jan 26, 1904, aged 1 yr., 26 dy.
ANDERSON, Malinda - d. Sep 10, 1900, age 54.
BAKER, George - Feb 11, 1856 - no date.
BARLEY, Mary Rosa - Oct 8, 1910, age 7.
BEATON, Gus - no dates.
BROWN, Lula - d. May 9, 1903, age 26.
BUCKNER, Wm. - 1873 - 1915.
CADELL, Annie - d. Feb 27, 1907, 53.
CALLAWAY, Henry Z., son of George - 1893 - Mar 28, 1904.
COBB, Laura - 1864 - 1917.
COBB, W. M. - no dates.
DORSEY, Richard & Jo Anna - no dates.
DORSEY, Tenezebe - no dates.
DORSEY, Willie - d. May 27, 1909, age 11.
DRAKE, Paul - d. July 28, 1910, age 1 yr., 6 mo.
FITZGERALD, Gilbert - d. Jan 26, 1903.
GAMBLE, Sam - July 30, 1903 - Feb 16, 1904.
GAMBLES, Samuel - no dates.
GILMORE, Sidney - 1883 - 1923.
GOLSTON, Henry - 1861 - 1914.
HAMILTON, Cloyd - 1881 - 1915.
HAFTON, Dolly, daughter of J. W. - d. Apr 28, 1906, age 5 mo..
HAMILTON, Ioma, daughter of James - d. Mar 13, 1907, age 2 yr..
HARRIS, Harlo - d. Dec 24, 1926, aged about 20 yr.
HARRIS, Mary - d. 1922.

HARRIS, Hattie - Aug 17, 1864 - Dec 17, 1913.
HARVEY, Frank - killed - buried Nov 14, 1905.
HOWARD, Agatha - d. Mar 10, 1903, age 1.
HOWARD, Cornelius - 1882 - 1915.
HOWARD, Oliver - 1889 - 1915.
HUDSON, Dennis - no dates.
JACKSON, Mary - d. Sep 14, 1906, age 34.
JACKSON, Bailey - no dates.
JACKSON, Pollie, wife of A. L. - 1861 - 1913.
JACKSON, Mollie - no dates.
JACKSON, Timothy - d. Mar 24, 1911, age 42.
JARRETT, Amy - d. Feb 5, 1906, age 45.
JOHNSON, Benjamin - no dates.
JOHNSON, Willie - Jan 30, 1903 - Mar 20, 1909.
JONES, Henry - stillborn on Dec 22, 1928.
KENNEDY, Genola - d. 1945, age 2.
KENNEDY, Isaac - no dates.
KENNEDY, Rosie - no dates.
KNIGHT, Sam - Jan 28, 1902, age 22.
LEWIS, Callie - no dates.
LEWIS, Ella May - d. Aug, 1915.
MAPLES, Ella - no dates.
MAPLES, Spencer - no dates.
McGEE, Infant - d. May 15, 1905.
McINTIRE, Mary - 18?2 - 1921.
MILLER, Judd O. - no dates.
MILLER, Lott LITTLETON - Jan 12, 1868 - Sep, 1921.
MILLER, Margaret SHAW - 1874 - Mar 3, 1911.
MILLER, Mary Letha - d. Jan 5, 1903, age 11.
MILLER, Ruth - d. Sep 19, 1910, age 1.
MUNDY, Sadia - d. Jan 12, 1906, age 29.
MURDOCK, Lucy - no dates.
MURDOCK, Thomas - no dates.
MONTGOMERY, John - d. Aug 28, 1910, age 54.
MONTGOMERY, Walter - d. Feb 26, 1907, age 22.
MOORE, Bettie - d. July 17, 1902, age 39.
PALMER, Donnie - no dates.
PALMER, Frank - no dates.
PARKER, George - d. Mar 21, 1903, age 33.
SANDERS, Fannie - d. Mar 25, 1904.
SANDERS, Jessie A. - 1894 - 1913.
SIMMONS, Willie - 1901 - 1921.
SIMS, Jeffery - no dates.
SMITH, Viola - no dates.
SLAUGHTER, Ollie - 1887 - 1925.

STEPHENS, Beatrice HARRIS - Oct 22, 1901 - Oct 6, 1937.
STERNES, Sam - d. Mar 16, 1906, age 27.
TINDRELL, Launa - 1891 - 1920.
TONEY, Bessie WHITE - no dates.
TONEY, Lee - d. Oct 1, 1906, age 34.
TOWNSELL, Willam - d. Oct 23, 1904, age 21.
VAUGHN, June - d. Dec 19, 1904, age 35.
WARDEN, Infant - d. Jan 21, 1904.
WEAVER, Charles - d. July 31, 1905, age 60.
WHEATON, George - no dates.
WHEATON, Laura - d. May 20, 1911, age 30.
WHITE, George - 1872 - 1915.
WHITE, Jeff L. - Apr 4, 185? - Oct 5, 1914.
WHITE, March, a resident of Kansas - d. Nov 26, 1904.
WHITE, Sarah - no dates.
WHITEHEAD, L. W. - 1865 - 1920.
WILLIAMS, Terry - d. Jan 5, 1907, age 57.
YARBROUGH, John - no dates.
YARBROUGH, Mannie - no dates.
YOUNG, Allen - 1891 - 1918.
PARMELT, Kenneth d. July 3, 1910, age 7 mo..
This is the only white person buried in this cemetery.

<u>Southside Cemetery</u>, Fulton, Callaway County. There are no records for this cemetery prior to 1917, when the city took over management, even though there are much older graves. Only those burials which took place before 1933 were extracted from the records.
TAYLOR, Ernest - d. June 16, 1917.
CATO, Infant of Mary Cato - d. June 24, 1917.
CURTIS, Bertha - d. Aug 28, 1917.
BROWN, Mrs. Oscar - d. Sep 9, 1917.
RENFRE, Mary - d. Sep 17, 1917.
HOLT, Ike - d. Dec 21, 1917.
JOHNSON, Fannie - d. Jan 5, 1918.
BUFORD, Susan - d. Jan 5, 1918.
STEWART, Winnie - d. Jan 1, 1918.
JORDAN, Clifford - d. Feb 22, 1918.
STARKS, Mrs. John - Mar 18, 1918.
WIGGENS, Rev. - Apr 16, 1918.
CARTER, Ennis - May 7, 1918.
RAMSEY, Amie - d. July 17, 1918.

WALKER, Prince - d. July 19, 1918.
BROOKS, Henry - d. Aug 21, 1918.
BUSH, Mattie - Sep 21, 1918.
GIVENS, Abe - d. Oct 11, 1918.
YOUNG, Jack - d. Nov 11, 1918.
SWAN, Effie - d. Nov 11, 1918.
CURTIS, Noland - d. Jan 1, 1919.
WADE, J. C. - Apr 1, 1919.
THOMAS, Genevieve - d. Apr 6, 1919.
HUNTER, Samuel - d. Apr 7, 1919.
CRAGHEAD, James - d. May 31, 1919.
JOHNSON, Flora - d. June 21, 1919.
COOPER, Clotile - d. Aug 12, 1919.
McDONALD, Alfred Lee - d. Aug 15, 1919.
SCROGGINS, Henry - d. Aug 30, 1919.
SCOTT, Rose - d. Sep 1, 1919.
TAYLOR, Pearl - d. Jan 3, 1920.
NICHOLS, Charles - d. Jan 7, 1920.
GIVENS, Simon - d. Feb 6, 1920.
FISHER, Curtis - d. Feb 15, 1920.
KING, Lucile - d. Feb 17, 1920.
JEFFERSON, Anne - d. Mar 9, 1920.
JEFFERSON, May Gladys - d. Apr 13, 1920.
JEFFERSON, Willie May - d. May 10, 1920.
WALKER, Kirkley - d. June 4, 1920.
MITCHELL, Frank - d. June 10, 1920.
HUBBARD, Mattie Pearl - d. June 24, 1920.
WILHITE, Victoria - d. July 5, 1920.
BURTON, Fannie - d. Aug 27, 1920.
CLANTON, Emma - d. Oct 29, 1920.
SMITH, Mrs. Arneda - d. Nov 16, 1920.
STARKS, Leroy - d. Dec 31, 1920.
HENDERSON, America - d. Jan 14, 1921.
WILSON, Mary A. - d. Jan 28, 1921.
CASON, Julia - d. Jan 31, 1921.
MONROE, Lizzie - d. Feb 8, 1921.
McKAMEY, John - d. Feb 19, 1921.
BLACK, Infant of James BLACK - d. Feb 23, 1921.
HAYES, Bettie - d. Mar 23, 1921.
HENDERSON, Grace - d. June 6, 1921.
BROWN, Martha - d. June 21, 1921.
NEILL, Harry - d. Oct 4, 1921.
HUDSON, Arlee - d. Nov 5, 1921.
ROSS, George - d. Nov 10, 1921.
KING, Mima - d. Jan 6, 1922.
GIBBS, Emmett - d. Mar 9, 1922.

CAMPBELL, Andrew William - d. Mar 11, 1922.
BROWN, Calvin - d. Mar 11, 1922.
LYNES, Frances - d. Apr 1, 1922.
FARRIS, Charles - d. Aug 9, 1922.
ELLINGTON, Ruth - Sep 16, 1922.
CASON, Susan - d. Sep 24, 1922.
WALKER, Mitchell - d. Nov 5, 1922.
BOWEN, Infant of W. H. - Nov 14, 1922.
BENNETT, Emma Jane - d. Nov 15, 1922.
WHITE, Chasie - d. Feb 1, 1923.
CUNNINGHAM, Della - d. Feb 9, 1923.
JEFFERS, A. J. - Mar 12, 1923.
RANDALL, William - d. Mar 23, 1923.
WHITE, John - d. Apr 7, 1923.
COOPER, Estrell - d. May 3, 1923.
SCOTT, Hattie May - d. May 29, 1923.
HOLT, Infant of Wm. C. - d. June 15, 1923.
REYNOLDS, Alonzo - d. June 22, 1923.
TAYLOR, Infant of Hattie May - d. July 24, 1923.
KING, Walter - d. Aug 8, 1923.
BOYD, Henry - d. Aug 15, 1923.
WILHIITE, Luvich - d. Sep 17, 1923.
EMERSON, Lucile - d. Oct 10, 1913.
FERRELL, James Howard - d. Oct 13, 1923.
JACKSON, Lou - d. Oct 24, 1923.
FISHER, Frances - d. Jan 3, 1924.
WILSON, William - d. Mar 25, 1924.
HENDERSON, Ina - d. May 5, 1924.
WALKER, Prince - d. May 7, 1924.
LOGAN, Hannah - d. May 26, 1924.
BROWN, Ernest - d. June 30, 1924.
NICHOLS, Awood (sic) - d. July 2, 1924.
JEFFERSON, Frank - d. Aug 8, 1924.
BAILEY, John - d. Aug 11, 1924.
LAWSON, Infant of Zenie - d. Aug 21, 1924.
STARKS, Louise - d. Sep 12, 1924.
BROWN, James - d. Oct 27, 1924.
THRELKELD, Cecil - d. Oct 27, 1924.
CASON, Mary Eliza - Dec 13, 1924.
PAYNE, Ray Milton - d. Jan 20, 1925.
KIBBY, Ella - d. Jan 20, 1925.
KING, Robert - d. Jan 31, 1925.
BROWN, Linzie - d. Jan 31, 1925.
BENNETT, Silas - d. Mar 2, 1925.
JEFFREY, Roy - d. Mar 3, 1925.

THOMAS, Ernest - d. Mar 4, 1925.
NICOLSON, Sadie - d. Mar 11, 1925.
THOMAS, Ella - d. Apr 6, 1925.
JEFFERSON, Annie - d. Apr 11, 1925.
FISHER, George Washington - May 5, 1925.
BROWN, Wm. Oscar - d. May 11, 1925.
SCROGGINS, Martha - d. May 23, 1925.
FOSTER, Clifford - d. May 29, 1925.
BROWN, Alice - d. June 9, 1925.
FISHER, Mary - d. June 15, 1925.
CURTIS, Frankie - d. July 11, 1925.
PATTERSON, Melcena - d. July 31, 1925.
JOHNSON, Martha - d. July 31, 1925.
LYNES, Caroline - d. Oct 3, 1925.
BAKER, Susan - d. Nov 24, 1925.
CHAMBERS, Nellie - d. Jan 11, 1926.
CURTIS, Goldie - d. Feb 15, 1926.
NEVINS, Mrs, Maria - d. Feb 27, 1926.
SCOTT, Julia - d. Mar 3, 1910.
DICKERSON, Cora - d. Apr 1, 1926.
COOK, Samuel - d. Apr 1, 1926.
COOPER, Ike - d. Apr 3, 1926.
TURNER, Hester Roxine - d. Apr 9, 1926.
TURNER, Massen - d. Apr 12, 1926.
NICHOLS, Harriet - d. Apr 24, 1926.
WADE, Susie - d. May 26, 1926.
HALMAN, Charles - d. May 29, 1926.
COOK, Frank - d. June 8, 1926.
JACKSON, Julia - d. June 23, 1926.
RAMSEY, Henry - d. Aug 19, 1926.
HAWKINS, John - d. Oct 26, 1926.
WILSON, Willie - d. Nov 6, 1926.
WILKERSON, Lewis John - d. Nov 20, 1926.
LAMBERT, Joseph - d. Nov 23, 1926.
DAVIS, Nannie BROWN - d. Jan 18, 1927.
LAWSON, Andrew - d. Mar 1, 1927.
JORDAN, Edna Gertrude - Mar 17, 1927.
WHITE, Charles - d. Mar 24, 1927.
KIBBY, Mrs. Kitty - d. Apr 15, 1927.
FLOOD, Mary Susan - d. July 31, 1927.
JOHNSON, Alfred - d. Mar 2, 1927.
KING, Roy - d. Aug 18, 1927.
BUSH, Henry - d. Sep 29, 1927.
COOPER, Opal - d. Nov 3, 1927.
KING, Anna May - d. Dec 6, 1927.
PERKINS, Leon - d. Jan 10, 1928.

CHANEY, Clen - d. Jan 30, 1928.
COOPER, Ellen - d. May 4, 1928.
PARKER, George W. - d. June 2, 1928.
ROSS, Clarens G. - d. June 30, 1928.
SCOTT, Mary E. - d. July 2, 1928.
KING, Renie - d. July 9, 1928.
GALBREATH, Mollie - d. Aug 30, 1928.
GALBREATH, Clarence - d. Oct, 12, 1928.
NICHOLS, George - d. Oct 20, 1928.
McNIGHTER, Ida May - d. Nov 2, 1928.
LYNES, Emma - d. Nov 13, 1928.
SMITH, Willie - d. Nov 23, 1928.
JACKSON, Perry - d. Nov 27, 1928.
BUSH, Martha Lizzie - d. Dec 1, 1928.
STARKS, Helen B. - d. Jan 6, 1929.
WHITE, Charles B. - d. Jan 19, 1929.
THOMPSON, Tanty - d. Feb 4, 1929.
MILLER, Betty - d. Feb 13, 1929.
CURTIS, Charles - d. Mar 29, 1929.
NICKENS, Solomon - d. Apr 27, 1929.
KING, Minnie Pearl - d. Apr 30, 1929.
TURNER, Eunice - d. Apr 30, 1929.
HEADSTETH, Bertha May - d. May 5, 1925.
VALENTINE, John - d. July 18, 1929.
YOUNG, Vianne - d. Aug 16, 1929.
CASON, Lucy - d. Aug 21, 1929.
WILKERSON, Mary - d. Oct 19, 1929
SHY, Emily - d. Oct 21, 1929.
CRAIGHEAD, Elmer - d. Oct 21, 1929.
DUDLEY, Milton Lawrence - d. Nov 11, 1918.
McNIGHTER, Armstead - d. Nov 18, 1929.
GRAY, Joseph - d. Dec 28, 1929.
CAVE, Alex - d. Jan 11, 1930.
SMITH, Douglas - d. Feb 18, 1930.
PAYNE, Sarah Francis - d. Feb 22, 1930.
HART, Johnny - d. Mar 3, 1930.
BLYTHE, Nellie May - d. Mar 11, 1930.
BELL, Henry - d. Mar 19, 1930.
BROWN, Alma - d. Mar 31, 1930.
KING, Francis - d. Apr 15, 1930.
BROWN, Everett - d. Apr 15, 1930.
ELLINGTON, Marvin, infant - d. May 26, 1930.
COOPER, Daniel - d. May 31, 1930.
RAMSEY, Martha - d. June 14, 1930.
SMITH, Susie - d. July 12, 1930.
WHITE, John - d. July 25, 1930.

WILKINS, Stephen - d. Aug 28, 1930.
BRANHAM, Lewis - d. Aug 3, 1930.
SCOTT, Arthur, age 44 - d. Sep 9, 1930.
STARKS, John, age 68 - d. Oct 7, 1930.
HOLLAND, Edward, age 30 - d. Sep 20, 1930.
THOMAS, Martin M., age 21 - d. Oct 14, 1930.
BRITT, Rachel, age 20 - d. Oct 25, 1930.
HARRIS, Martha, age 33 - d. Nov 2, 1930.
KING, Law, age 47 - d. Feb 21, 1931.
WOODS, Louise, age 74 - d. Mar 4, 1931.
BELL, Arminte, age 79 - d. May 9, 1931.
PRICE, Mima, of Holts Summit, Mo., age 72 - d. Aug 3, 1931.
STARKS, Safronia, age 56 - d. Dec 8, 1931.
PAYNE, Trot Earl, of Glasgow, Mo., age 39 - d. Dec 28, 1931.
BRADFORD, Vadney, age 29 - d. May 14, 1932.
MORTON, Anderson, age 42 - d. July 17, 1932.
WILKINS, Enos, age 64 - d. July 18, 1932.
SIMPSON, Amanda, age 59 - d. Aug 22, 1932.
LYNES, Arthur, age 44 - d. Oct 11, 1932.
LEWIS, Alma Louise, stillborn - d. Nov 8, 1932.
KIBBY, Albert, age 34 - d. Dec 17, 1932.

FREE BLACKS

Extracted from the 1840 Census.

Barry County:
Randolph CARTER - 1-2-0-0-1; 0-1-0-0-1.

Boone County:
John, a free colored - 0-0-0-0-1; 0-0-0-0-1.
Moses DUNCAN - 0-0-0-1.
Peter PARKER - 0-0-0-0-1; 0-0-0-1.
Richard WALKUP - 0-0-0-1.
Malinda, a free woman - 1; 1-0-1.

Chariton County:
Eli, a free man of color - 1-0-0-2; 1-1.
David JOHN - 1-0-0-1; 0-1-0-0-2.

Clay County:
Nancy HUTCHEN - 0-1-1; 1-1-0-1.
Joshua HUTCHEN - 1-1; 1-0-1.
Joseph COLLETT - 4-0-0-1; 0-3-0-1.
Cato BIRNHAM - 0-0-0-0-1.
David MORTON - 0-0-0-1.
Peter GARDNER - 0-0-0-0-1.
Agnes AGA - 0; 0-0-0-0-1.
Spencer SEALS - 0-0-1.
Ambrose SCOTT - 0-0-0-0-1; 0-0-1.
Thomas ESTES - 0-20-1-1; 1-1-0-1.

Cole County:
Luke FERGUSON - 1-0-1-1; 0-0-1.
Siraws FULKERSON - 0-0-0-1; 0-0-1.

Cooper County:
Charles RUTHERFORD - 0-0-0-1.

Franklin County:
Sally, a colored woman - 0-2; 0-0-0-1.
Moses STAUNTON - 0-0-0-0-1.
Anderson - 0-0-0-1.
Benjamin BANNISTER - 0-0-1; 0-0-0-0-1.

Howard County:
Phillis DAVIS - 1-0-0-1; 2-2.
Cason ARNOLD - 0-3-0-0-1; 0-1-0-1.
L. JERRY - 0-0-0-1; 0-1-0-1.

Lafayette County:
Fanny, a free woman - 2; 1-0-0-1.
George, a free man - 1-0-1; 5-0-0-1.

Lewis County:
Eden SINCLAIR - 0-0-0-1.
Jack MYERS - 0-0-0-1; 0-0-0-1.

Lincoln County:
William GREEN - 0-0-0-0-1; 0-0-0-0-1.

Madison County:
Robert ISOM - 1-3-0-1; 2-1.
Cornelius CAMPBELL - 2-0-0-0-1; 0-0-0-1.
William NISWONGER - 0-1-0-0-1; 2-0-1-0-1.

Marion County:
Joshua DUNLAP - 0-1-0-1-1; 1-0-1.

Newton County:
Nelson KINGKADE - 0-1-0-1; 0-0-1.

Perry County:
Joseph DIXON - 0-0-0-1; 2-1-1-0-1.
Joseph COLE - 0-0-0-1.

Pike County:
Lucy MACKEY - 0; 0-0-0-1.
Jino TAYLOR - 1; 1-0-0-1.

Polk County:
Daniel STROTHER - 0-0-1-0-1; 0-1-0-0-1.

Ralls County:
Leonard POTTER - 0-0-0-1.

Randolph County:
Eliza MONT - 2-1; 2-0-1.
Edward WILDON - 0-0-0-1; 1-0-1.

St. Charles County:
Serra, a free woman - 0-0-1-1; 0-2-1-0-1.
Melville, free colored - 0-2-1; 1-1-1.
Dick OWENS - 0-0-0-1.
Mary MOMBRA - 0-1-1; 1-0-1-1.
Perry CORK - 0-0-0-0-1.

Ste. Genevieve County:
Lewis MOLLEY - 2-0-0-1; 1-2-0-1.
Yaco OBERCHON - 0-0-0-0-1.
Joseph BEQUET - 1-0-0-0-1; 0-0-0-0-1.
Antoine RECALY (sic) - 1-0-0-0-1; 0-0-0-1-2.
Michael BADO - 0-0-1; 0-0-0-1.
Clarece, free colored - 0-1; 0-0-1.
Ned LOGAN - 0-0-0-0-1; 0-0-0-0-1.
Calagie, free colored - 2-2; 1-0-0-1-1.
Peter MORESE - 1-0-0-0-1; 0-0-0-0-1.
Molley WINCENT - 0-1; 0-0-0-0-1.

St. Louis:
J. D____ - 0; 0-0-1.
Matilda ANDERSON - 2-0-1; 0-0-1-1-1.
George W. STOCKTON - 0-0-4-1; 2-0-0-1.
Fanny GLASCOW - 0; 0-0-0-1.
Mary HOURE - 0-0-0-0-1; 0-1-0-1.
Milla CONN - 0; 2-1-1.
Robert SMITH - 0-1; 0-0-1.
Francis La BUSHE - 0-0-1-1; 2-2-2-1.
Gillind JEFFERSON - 0-0-0-1; 0-0-0-1.
Lance AMOS - 2-0-0-1; 0-0-1-1.
Peter MAXWELL - 0-1-0-0-1; 2-0-2-0-1.
Lewis CARSON - 0-0-1; 1-0-1.
Peter WEIR - 3-0-1; 1-1-1.
Marian GUITAR - 0; 0-0-1.
Jacob BUTLER - 0-0-1.
Felisete CROCKET - 1-0-1.
Alexander BALLISIEN - 0-0-2; 2-1-1-0-1.
Julia LEVEAN - 0; 0-1-0-0-2.
Ellen BEMARE - 0; 0-0-0-1.
Winnette DIXON - 1; 0-2.
Angimine GOBEL - 0; 0-1-1.
Shadrock DUNCAN - 2-0-0-1; 2-0-0-1.
Antoine MORINE - 1-0-1; 0-0-1-0-1.
Matilda CLARK - 1-1-4-1; 0-0-2.
Jane RUSSEL - 0-2; 4-1-1-0-1.
Montreve HOWSELEY - 0-1; 0-1.
William MOSES - 0-1; 0-1.
Lewis NASHE - 1-0-1; 1-1.
Robert CASTLE - 0-0-0-1; 0-0-0-1.
George JOHNSON - 0-0-1; 0-0-1.
Nelson CARR - 0-0-1; 0-0-1.
Washington KENNEDY - 1-0-1; 0-1-1-1.
Cave PETERS - 1-0-1; 0-2.

109

Philip GNIYAR - 0-0-0-1; 1-2-1-0-1.
Jeffrey G. ISLE - 0-0-1; 1-2.
William DOUGHLAS - 0-1-1-1; 3-1-0-1-1.
Frederick GROTEGUTH - 0-0-0-1; 0-0-0-1.
Clara BALDWIN - 0; 0-0-1.
Dolly WILLIAMS - 1; 0-0-2-0-1.
Daniel BANKS - 0-0-0-1; 0-0-0-1.
Margaret MARAT - 0; 0-0-1.
Norval BUCKNER - 0-0-1; 0-0-1.
Henry MORINE - 0-2-1; 1-2-2;
Charles ANDERSON - 3-1-1; 2-0-2.
Elizabeth SMITH - 0; 0-0-0-0-2.
Lucinda JONES - 0; 0-1.
Parker RANN - 1-0-0-1; 0-0-1.
Illegible (pg. 109) - 2-0-0-1; 1-0-1-1-1.
Illegible (pg. 109) - 0-0-0-1; 2-2.
Illegible (pg. 109) - 1-2-1-1; 2-1-1-0-1.
Edwin LABLEDIE - 2-0-1; 0-1-0-0-1.
Joseph GWAGEL (sic) - 2-2-0-1; 1-2-0-1.
Gabriel VITAL - 2-0-1-1; 0-1-1.
Isaac GARRISON - 0-0-0-1.
John HILL - 0-0-1; 0-0-1.
Elizabeth KENECT - 1-3-0-1; ?.
Easter BEBEE - 0-0-0-1.
Delphi_ RAMSEY - 0; 0-0-0-1.
John LEWIS - 3-0-0-1; 1-2-1.
Lewis PRICE - 1-0-1-1; 0-0-1-1-1.
Jerry DUNCAN - 1-0-0-1; 2-1-0-2.
Reuben HOLMES - 0-0-1; 0-0-1.
Sarah STEWART - 0-0-0-1; 0-1-1.
Thomas BUTCHER 0-0-1; 0-0-1.
Henry JOHNSON - 0-1; 0-0-1.
James D. BONHER - 0-2-1; 2-1.
Nathan RIEDE - 0-0-1; 0-0-0-1.
Lavina BANISTER - 2-2; 0-0-1.
James WILLIAMS - 1-0-0-1; 0-0-0-1.
Jane JACKSON - 1; 1-0-0-1.
William DAY - 0-0-1; 0-0-1.
William STONEHAND - 0-1.
Mary POTTER - 3-1. 0-0-0-1.
Francis BRADWATER - 0-0-1-1; 0-0-1.
Catherine VION - 0-1; 0-1.
Jane HEDGES - 0; 0-0-1.
Francis ROUBEDEAN - 0-0-1; 0-0-1.
Matilda BERTRANDE - 1; 0-1-0-1.
Philip CHENIE - 1-1-1; 0-0-1-0-1.

Margaret J. LEWIS - 0; 1-1-0-1.
Franklin LEE - 0-0-1; 0-0-0-0-1.
Pleasant JACKSON - 0-0-0-0-1.
Elizabeth DICKENSON - 0; 0-0-1.
John BRANHAM - 0-0-0-2; 0-1-0-1.
John B. MEACHUM - 1-4-1-1; 1-1-0-1.
Mary WASH - 0; 0-0-0-1.
Julia WEIR - 0; 0-1-1.
Henry COTTON - 0-1-1-1; 1-0-0-0-1.
Thomas, free colored - 0-0-0-0-1; 0-0-0-0-1.
James E. ROBINSON - 0-1; 1-1.
Matilda CHAUTEAU - 2; 0-0-1-0-1.
Maria SEXTON - 0-0-1; 1-0-0-1.
Hannah DEARIN - 0-1-1; 0-0-0-1.
Lilly LAW - 0-0-0-1; 0-0-0-1.
Moses ISAACS - 1-1; 0-0-1.
Jane CARTER - 0-1; 0-0-1.
Lavina BANISTER - 2-2; 0-0-1.
Susan MARSHALL - 1; 1-0-1.
Bob MUSICK - 0-1-0-1; 1-0-1.
David BUTLER - 0-0-0-1; 1-1-0-1.
Antoine CRAVIER - 0-0-1; 0-1.
John TAYLOR - 1-0-0-1; 1-0-1.
Milly BLUE - 0; 0-1-0-1.
Isabella WRIGHT - 0; 1-1-1.
Harriet HENRY - 0-0-1; 1-0-2.
John WINSTON - 1-0-0-1; 0-1-0-1.
Matilda DUBUEY - 0; 3-0-2.
W. LISNEY - 1-1-1; 0-1-1-1.
Felix FRANKLIN - 2-1; 0-1-1.
Benj. HART - 1-0-0-0-1.
D. MARTIN - 0-0-0-0-1; 0-0-0-1.
Easter ALEXANDER - 2; 0-1-2-1.
J. WHITE - 0-0-3; 0-0-1.
Fannie LEWIS - 0; 0-0-1.
W. HAMILTON - 0-2; 0-0-1.
H. TAYLOR - 0-0-3-2-1; 0-0-0-2.
Shepherd SMITH - 0-0-1; 0-0-0-1.
A. PUTFIELD - 0-0-0-1; 0-0-1-1.
Jacob PUTFIELD - 0-2-2.
Sophea HOYLE - 0-2-2; 0-1.
John MURRAY - 0-3; 1-1.
Lity PARKER - 1-0-1.
Caroline JOHNSON - 0; 0-1-1.
Pheobe STUBBS - 0-1-1; 1-1-0-0-1.
Ceasar JOHNSON - 0-1-0-0-1; 0-0-0-0-1.

Edward DIXON - 0-0-1; 0-1.
Chas. JACKSON - 0-0-1; 2-1.
Jonathan DUNCAN - 0-0-1-0-1; 0-1-0-0-1.
I. YOUNG - 2-0-0-1; 0-0-1.
Stephen ANDERSON - 0-0-0-0-1; 0-1-0-0-1.
Eliza JOHNSON - 0-1; 0-1-1.
Maria SOWERS - 1-1; 0-1-1.
Jinny CABLANNCE - 0; 0-0-2.
Catherine CREVINSE - 1-1; 0-0-1-1.
Baptiste BRAZEAW - 0-1-1-0-1; 0-0-0-1.
J. B. LABOUSINE - 2-0-2-0-1; 2-3-1-0-1.
Ann McCRACKEN - 1; 0-1.
James FARRIES - 1-1-0-1; 2-2-0-1.
James QUARL - 0-0-1-0-1; 0-0-1-0-1.
Moses HEMPSTEAD - 0-2-0-1; 1-0-0-1.
Haskins RANDELL - 1-1-0-1; 3-1-0-1.
Ross DAVIS - 0-0-2; 0-0-0-0-1.
Eliza TYLER - 0; 0-0-1.
Samuel STOKES - 0-1-0-1; 0-0-0-0-1.
Wm. ENGLESON - 1-0-2; 0-3-0-1.
Bartlett COLLINS - 0-0-0-0-1; 0-0-0-0-1.
Louis CHARLEVILLE - 2-1-1-1; 0-1-1-0-1.
Celeste CHEVALIER - 0-1-2; 0-1-0-0-1.
Chas. DANGER - 0-0-0-0-1; 0-0-1-0-1.
Michael WINDENEAN - 0-0-0-0-1.
Anthony RENDEN - 0-0-1.
Gye WALLACE - 0-0-0-4; 0-0-0-1.
Isaac JOHNSON - 0-0-0-1; 0-1.

Shelby County:
Theodrick - 0-1.
George BUCKNER - 1-0-0-1.
Tabitha, free colored - 2; 2-0-1.

Scott County:
Winston HUNT - 2-0-3; 0-2-0-1.
Elizabeth CARTER - 1-0-1; 1-0-1.

Van Buren (now Cass) County:
Joseph LEWIS - 1-2-2; 1-0-1.
Lewis BRUCHIER - 1-0-1; 0-0-1.
Richard FLAURNOY - 1-0-0-1; 0-1-0-1.
William S. CALLAWAY - 0-0-0-0-1.

Washington County:
Cloway, free colored - 4; 1-1-1.

Nancy VAUM - 2; 0-1.
Sam RAY - 2-0-0-1; 3-1-1.
Larry MADDEN - 0-0-0-0-1; 0-0-0-0-1.
Edward, free colored - 0-1-0-0-2; 0-0-0-0-1.
Peter, free colored - 0-0-0-0-1; 0-0-0-0-1.
Jas. H. JOHNSON - 2-0-1; 1-0-1.

Wayne County:
Jordon HARRIS - 1-2-1.
Ruben KELLY - 0-0-0-1; 0-0-0-0-1.
Daniel OVERTON - 0-0-0-1; 0-0-0-0-1.

Clay County Registry of Free Negroes.
Spencer SEALS, Thomas ESTES, Silvia, a free woman of color, and Joseph COLLET and his wife were all granted a license to stay in the state of Missouri on February 8, 1836.

Ambrose SCOT, a free man of color, was granted a license to remain in the state on February 20, 1836.

On October 2, 1837, David MORTON was licensed to remain in the state.

Harry and Elijah, both free men of color, were granted a license on September 2, 1854, to live in MIssouri.

William LLOYD obtained his license to remain in the state on January 7, 1856.

Emancipations and Manumissions.
Warren County - This indenture made the 25th day of July 1837, between Alexander McKINNEY and Bill, his slave, age 60...in consideration of $250 paid to McKINNEY by Bill, does hereby emancipate Bill for life.
Pike County - Maria, alias Maria GALE, a free person of color vs Johnson SACY. The court ruled Maria was entitled to her freedom, and ordered she be released from service on June 23, 1843.
Warren County - Frederick, a man of color vs

Lewis NUNN. The court ruled Frederick had been held illegally after February 7, 1838.

Pike County - Circuit Court, Book D, page 315. Henry HAGOOD acknowledged a deed of emancipation from him to a negro boy slave named Joe.

Warren County - Sidney and Mary, both women of color, appeared in Circuit Court alleging they had been illegally held as slaves by Lewis Nunn since February of 1838. The court ordered their immediate emancipation.

Platte County - On October 9, 1845, Mary McAdam produced a deed of emancipation for her slave, Nancy.

Platte County - John W. SNODDY produced a deed of emancipation for his slave, Jack, on April 9, 1846.

Callaway County - Martha, a woman of color, received a deed of emancipation from Samuel RILEY. Book B, page 401, Circuit Court record.

St. Charles County - A deed of emancipation was filed by Jonas M. TEBBETTS freeing William HARRIS, age 28, on Sep 29, 1863.

Free Black Marriages.

Felix ST. CROIX Du RICHEVE married Clarisse REYNAL, a former slave of Anthony RENAL Sr. on Aug 15, 1827, St. Charles County.

Esther RAMOX, negro wife of Jean RAMOX, a spaniard, died Dec 4, 1818, and was buried at St. Mary's Catholic Church, Ste. Genevieve.

George PIPER and Mary Jane, both free people of color, were married Apr 27, 1848, in Monroe County. The groom was from Marion County.

Henri ST. GEMME and Marie Nanette LA PORTE were married in Ste. Genevieve, date not recorded.

Joseph SMOOT and Silvy, a mulatto were married in Marion County on Sep 15, 1850.

Acts passed by the Thirteenth General Assembly.

Any court of this state...hereby authorized to grant to Clarissa WILLIAMS, a free woman of color, license to remain in the state, as if she had been born here. Approved Mar 24, 1845.

The county court of Daviess, is hereby authorized to grant a license to William Henry HARRISON, a free person of color...Approved Mar 24, 1845.

Runaway notices from the *Jeffersonian Republican*.

Feb 6, 1836, 9:43. Ranaway - Near Jackson, on Sep 7, 1835, a negro boy named Squire, about 30 years of age, rather brown complexion, a scar on his left temple. The said boy was purchased from Henry DIXON, near Jefferson City, had been hired out at Massey's Iron Works, and it is possible he will make for one of those places. Anyone taking up said boy, notify Samuel L. SLOAN, Jackson County. James C. ESSELLMAN.

Feb 2, 1839, 12:539. Reward - On the night of the 12th of November, my negro man Bill, left a neighbor's house to go to another, about a mile and a half distant, and I have never heard from him since. I first believed he had lost his way and frozen, but after considerable search, I am induced to believe he was kidnapped. Said negro is about 30 years of age, rather tall and spare made, bends forward when walking, turns his toes out, has lost the first joint of one of his thumbs, has a fine and screaching voice. Drury PULLIAM, Old Jefferson, Saline County, Dec 22, 1838.

May 30, 1840, 13:635. Ranaway from 12 miles south of Boonville, a negro man named Wash, 5' 9", 22 years of age, a smart and intelligent, purchased in New Orleans. Harriet, is very black, had on a huge calico dress. Isom MASTON, May 22, 1840.

May 30, 1840, 13:63. Ranaway or Stolen - From the county of Cole, 20 miles from the City of Jefferson, a negro man about 23 years of age, slender made, rather yellow complexion, broad teeth a far apart, a scar on his cheek, the ball of his eye is yellow. Ranaway with a sorral horse, two hind feet are white. John McKENZIE, Apr 25, 1840.

St. Louis Emancipations, Powers Museum Collection.
In August of 1838, Nelson KERR, a free man of color, emancipated his wife, Rhoda, age 32, whom he had purchased from Franklin L. REDLEY.

Jefferson CLARK emancipated Delph, age 33, a mulatto female he had purchased from Stephen C. DORRISS earlier that year, on November 19, 1839.

On January 20, 1853, Lucian CARR emancipated Andrew YOUNG age 9.

Sylvestre LABBADIE freed Celestin, a male slave, age 29, on Dec 13, 1836.

On Dec 4, 1855, George KIBBY, a free man of color, made the final payment for his wife Susan a 25 year old mulatto, from Henry C. and Elizabeth HART.

St. Louis Runaway
A runaway warrent was issued by the court for four slaves owned by Richard GRAHAM on Sep 4, 1854. Govenor was described as being about 40 years of age, stout made, and a red mulatto with straight hair, 5' 8" in height. Nelson, about age 22, copper in color, 5' 6", thick set, active and intelligent. Henry, a pale mulatto, age 22, 5' 6", reddish looking whiskers, large dull eyes, and long hair to his shoulders. The fourth was Washington, 5' 8", with very bushy hair.

1830 Census Extractions.
Washington County
Judeth VAUGHAN - 4-0-0-0-1.
Abraham MARSHALL - 0-0-0-1; 0-0-1.
David L. JOHNSON - 0-0-1; 1-0-0-1.
Primos WAMMACK - 0-0-1.
Nace - 2-0-0-1; 2-0-0-1.
George CALVERD - 0-0-1.

Jefferson County
John, a free man - 0-0-0-0-2; 0-0-0-0-1.

Franklin County
Lewis ROGERS - 4-1-0-1; 0-0-1.
Nathan SAPPINGTON - 3-0-0-1; 0-0-0-1.

St. Charles County
May (illegible) - 2-1; 2-0-0-1.

St. Louis County
Benjamin BANNISTER - 0-0-1; 0-1-0-0-1.
Charles BLACKMAN - 0-0-0-0-1; 0-0-0-0-1.
Baptiste VANSAW - 0-0-0-0-1.
Judy - 0-0-0-1; 0-0-1-0-2.
Katherine - 0; 1-0-1-1.
William SMITH - 0-1-0-1; 1-1-0-1.
John SMITH - 0-0-0-1; 1-0-0-1.
Andre - 0-0-1; 0-1-0-1.
Nelson LUCUS - 0; 0-0-0-1.
Francis LABCHE - 0-0-1; 2-0-1.
Pear AUBESHON - 0-4; 1-1-0-1.
John BERDAU - 0-0-1; 2-0-1.
Winny - 1; 1-1-0-0-1.
Jinny - 0; 1-0-1.
Susan MATURA - 0-0-1; 0-2-1-1.
Lucinda - 0; 0-0-1.
Lavina BANNISTER - 2; 0-2.
Mary - 0-1; 1-1-0-1.
Ellen - 0; 0-0-0-1.
Jefferson CAMP - illegible.
Matilda - illegible.
Louis RAMIS - 1; 0-1-0-1.
Rachel - 1-1; 0-0-0-1.
Elisha RICHERSON - 0-0-11.
Bartlett - 0-0-0-1; 1-0-0-1.
Daniel KIVAN - 0-1-0-1; 1-0-1-1.
Baptiste - 0-0-1; 2-0-1.
Jerry DUNCAN - 0-0-1.
Nancy - 0-0-1; 0-0-1.
Lavina TILUS - 0; 0-1.
William JOHNSON - 1-0-1-0-1; 0-0-1-0-1.
Levi HANDY - 0-0-1; 0-0-1.
Deseara - 0; 0-0-1.
Liza S. RAUL - 1; 1-1.
Joseph LEE - 0-0-0-1; 0-1.
George BROWN - 1-0-0-1; 0-1.
Ann RANDOLPH - 0; 2-1.
Matilda - 0; 0-0-0-1.

Manuel LOGAN - 2-2-0-1; 1-3-0-1.
Sofa - 0; 2-1-0-1.
Louize - 0-0-0-1; 0-0-0-1.
Sarah TOBEN - 1; 1-0-0-1.
Mary - 0; 1-0-1.
Harriet - 0; 1-0-1.
Mary - 0; 0-0-1.

Ste. Genevieve County
James WILLIAMS - 0-0-0-1; 1-1-0-0-1.
Mrs. LOUISON - 0-2-1; 0-1-0-1.
Michael BADEN - 5-0-0-1; 0-0-0-1.
Rachel BURK - 0-1; 0-0-0-1.
Bastean - 0-0-0-1; 1-0-0-1-1.
Antoine BECAHAL (sic) - 0-1-0-1-1; 0-0-1.
Mary - 0; 0-0-0-1.
Jenny - 0; 0-1-0-0-1.
Mrs. PORTERIQUEL - 0-1-1; 0-0-1-0-0-1.
Aaron - 1; 0-0-0-0-1.
James MORITOU (slaves)* - 0-0-0-1; 2-0-0-1.
Jacques OBUCHON - 0-0-0-1; 0-0-0-0-1.
Valeo - 0-0-0-1; 0-0-1.
Mrs. MOLLIE - 0-1-1; 0-1-0-1.

St. Francois County
Margaret MASCRAL - 1; 2-3-0-1.
Will BLACKWELL - 0-0-0-1; 1-1.

New Madrid County
Beverly MATHEWS - 0-0-1; 1-0-1.

Howard County
David Johnson - 1-0-0-0-1; 1-0-0-1.
Susan, a free girl - 1; 1-0-0-1.
Suzier, free colored man - 3-0-0-1; 3-0-0-1.

Saline County
John TRETTSON - 0-0-1; 1-0-1.
Joseph BLACKABEE - 0-1-0-1; 0-1-0-1.
Robert PRICE - 1-1-2; 1-0-1.
Philip SHIRKEE - 0-0-1; 0-1-0-1.
Ginger REAVIS - 0-1-0-1; 0-0-0-1.

*This is the only slave family listed on any Missouri census.

Clay County
Joseph COTTEL - 0-1;2-1.
Ambrose SCOTT - 0-0-0-1.
Franceis CEIL - 0-1.
Thomas ESTES - 0-1; 0-1.

Madison County
Robert ISOM - 0-0-1.
Baptiste TESERRAU - 0-0-0-1.
Eve REVELL - 3-3; 2-1-0-1.

Washington County, Records of the County Court.
Last will and testament of John JOHNSON, Sr., written on Apr 11, 1834, and filed in May of the same year, freed two of his slaves, James and Celia.

Last will and testament of Upshaw R. MASSEY, was entered into record in May of 1834, and left the slaves belonging to this estate to MASSEY's widow, Susannah. She was to keep a woman named Moses, Aaron, Robertson, Thomas, Milly, Johnny, Jack, and Soakey for here own use, but after her death, the slaves were to be freed.

Last will and testament of Joseph HOLT, written Jan 15, 1835, and probated Jan 19th of the same year gave two slaves, Jude and her husband, John, to HOLT's widow Polly to use during her lifetime, but after Polly died, they were to be freed. It was also stipulated that when the other slaves belonging to the estate were sold, it could only as family units. Parents and children were to remain together.

Ste. Genevieve County Court Records.
Joseph D. GRAFTON filed emancipation papers for his slave, Susannah, in consideration of $1 paid to him by the slave. In this document, GRAFTON declared he had purchased Susannah from the estate of Augustine OUBUCHON and Maria Theresse OBUCHON, both deceased, on May 11, 1833. Susannah was over the age of 45 when she was freed.

Shelby County, Records of the County Court.
After being freed by the last will and testament of John FOWLER, Caleb FOWLER, a former slave, applied for and was granted a license to remain in the Missouri.

CHURCH RECORDS

<u>Catholic Baptisms, St. Louis, Missouri.</u> After each child's name is the date of baptism, followed by the parent's name.

Amanda ALLET, Oct 24, 1833, William and Agatha, slaves.
Marie Antoinette AMARANTHE, Dec 5, 1819, Amaranthe, a free colored.
Matilda BECKWARD, Dec 25, 1823, Eugene and Elizabeth, free colored.
Marie Therese BIZAT, Dec 4, 1819, BIZAT and Lise Lassus.
Edmund BODE, Oct 26, 1836, Jesse and Louise LAVIGNE.
Elizabeth BOUDON, Apr 21, 1829, Jean and Marie Louise ARGERAULT.
Simon CABANNE, Aug 8, 1829, Pierre and Therese.
Joseph DUMAINE, Aug 20, 1837, Rodehilla and Caroline.
Luce DUNKIN, Sep 6, 1829, DUNKLIN and Eliza.
Frederick FRANKLIN, ? 16, 1835, Frederick and Julie.
Pelagie GEORGE, age 18, Nov 24, 1834, George and Marie.
Mary LOUISE JOHNSON, age 3, Oct 9, 1837, George and Mary WILLIAMS.
Elisa JOSKEY, May 24, 1832, Therese ST. JEAN, metis.
Mary LABADIE, Nov 24, 1832, Joseph and Mary PRICE.
Louis LABEAUME, Mar 10, 1822, Louis, free colored and Henriette, a slave.
Thomas LESTAN, Mar 4, 1820, Erime and Genevieve LATOUCHE.
_____ MANDREVILLE, June 28, 1822, Thomas and Manette BRAZEAU.
Elizabeth WILLIAMS, July 3, 1825, William Samuel and Mary, free colored.
Edward ST. PIERRE, Mar 12, 1813, George, free colored and Therese.
Louise AUBUCHON, Sep 23, 1804, Adelaide, a free mulatto.
Margaret BARADA, Feb 6, 1822, Charlot and Polly.
Aurelie AUBUCHON, born Apr 10, 1826, Aurora

DATCHURUT AUBUCHON.
Pierre BLANCHET, Aug 20, 1773, Pierre.
Emilie DATCHURUT, Sep 28, 1804, Elizabeth DATCHURUT.
Marie Therese DATCHURUT, June 18, 1802, Elizabeth DATCHURUT.
Pierre Joseph DATCHURUT, born Apr 29, 1815, Pierre and Celeste Flore.
Ann FRANCES, age 6, Sep 6, 1838, Francis, a free woman.

Deceased Ministers of the Central West Conference, Methodist Church.
Spencer TAYLOR - d. Apr 22, 1870, Sedalia.
C. L. BROWN - d. 1874.
Scott McCORMACK - d. Oct 19, 1881, DeSoto.
W. R. LAWTON - d. Feb 12, 1886, Sedalia.
W. O. LYNCH - d. 1886, Louisiana.
Reuben SMITH - d. Mar 6, 1889, Kansas City.
Edgar PITTS - d. Apr 6, 1889, Springfield.
J. W. HILL - d. Jan 28, 1893, St. Louis.
A. BURTON - d. Sep 12, 1890, Mexico.
W. B. ASHBY - d. 1898, Dalton.
J. W. BROWN - d. May 13, 1900, Sedalia.
Benjamin STEELE - d. June, 1900, California.
Allen ABERNATHA - d. Dec, 1900, Kansas City.
Jeremiah WRIGHT - d. Jan, 1901, Lexington.
John JEFFERS - d. Sep, 1891, Troy.
J. G. DINSMORE - May, 1902, Sedalia.
Edward ANTHONY - d. Feb 9, 1904, Lexington.
G. W. PATTON - d. June, 1903, Moberly.
John TATE - d. Jan 7, 1904, Mexico.
James A. DORSEY - d. May 2, 1904, Sedalia.
Martin REED - d. Aug 27, 1905, Smithton.
John J. CLARK - d. Jan 13, 1906.
D. J. KENOLY - d. Mar 4, 1907, Windsor.
H. A. HENLEY - d. Aug 12, 1907, Sedalia.
Christopher TAYS - d. June 7, 1911, Holen.
J. M. SMALLEY - d. Jan 22, 1912, Clarksville.
B. D. DIXON - d. Aug 25, 1913, Fredericktown.
T. W. FUGHEM - d. Nov, 1913, Elsberry.
William WHEELER - d. 1913.
Henson BAKER - d. 1913, Warrensburg.
G. B. ABBOT - d. Aug 23, 1914, Sedalia.
Wm. McCUTCHEN - d. 1914, Joplin.
Alexander HUBBARD - d. 1914, Louisiana.

J. W. PAYNE - d. 1914, Waverly.
S. H. NOLAND - d. Aug 12, 1915, Kinloch Park.
George GRADY - d. Mar, 1915, DeSoto.
F. H. SMALL - d. June 17, 1916, St. Louis.
A. COLEMAN - d. July 2, 1917, Lebanon.
O. E. WHALEY - d. Nov 16, 1917, Bowling Green.
R. E. GILLUM - d. Dec 22, 1917, Foristell.
R. H. SMITH - d. 1918, Slater.
T. L. FRANCIS - d. Apr 16, 1918, Moberly.
W. H. H. BROWN - d. June, 1919, DeSoto.
Richard DAVIS - d. Jan 10, 1920, Kansas City.
Isaac CATO - d. Aug, 1920, Fulton.
Poriah McCAIN - d. Sep 8, 1920, Warrensburg.
W. R. RIVERE - d. Aug 26, 1921, St. Louis.
J. D. EVANS - d. 1921, Butler.
Wm. DIVERS - d. June 10, 1923, Holden.
John L. BROOKS - d. July 1, 1924, Sedalia.
J. Will JACKSON - d. Oct 16, 1924, Sedalia.
Geo. W. REEVES - d. Nov 28, 1924, St. Louis.
B. F. BATEMAN - d. Jan 30, 1926, Springfield.
O. A. JOHNSON - d. Feb 11, 1926, Kansas City.
Wm. A. BOHANNON - d. Feb 17, 1926, Fulton.
W. J. DEBOE - d. Aug 31, 1926, St. Louis.
T. H. LOCKWOOD - d. Mar 18, 1927, Slater.
R. G. WILLIAMS - d. May 26, 1927, St. Louis.
F. D. AVIANT - d. May 30, 1928, Armstrong.
W. C. ELLIS - d. Aug 14, 1928, Sedalia.
Robert WOODS - d. Oct 5, 1928, St. Louis.
T. J. JONES - d. Dec 2, 1928, Webster Groves.
L. C. DAWKINS - d. June 1, 1930, Blackburn.
E. W. HANNAH - Nov 5, 1930, Kansas City.

St. Charles Borromeo Church.
Cary, slave of Mr. KNOT, married to Nelsey, slave of Mr. La Fr. CHAUVIN in 1827, St. Louis County.
Paul NEGTO, slave of Mr. La Fr. CHAUVIN married to an unnamed woman in St. Louis County in 1826.
Spidel, slave of Jsai HELY to Charlotte, slave of B. LYNCH, married May 10, 1831.
Vedmond married Marie, people of color belonging to Michael KELLY, on Apr 21, 1832.
Baptiste, slave of Nicholas JANIS, married to Marie, a slave of Madame KNOTT on Oct 24, 1833.

Louis, son of Eugenie, a slave of Gabriel CERE, baptized Feb 12, 1794.

Francois Antoine, age 2, and Noel Francois, born May 30, 1799, both children of Ester, and slaves of Mr. DUROCHER, baptized June 2, 1799.

Charles, age 1, mulatto son of Rebecca, slaves of Jean COUNS, baptized Oct 6, 1799.

Nicholas, age 9 mo., 10 dy., son of Marie Louise, a free woman of color, baptized Nov 1, 1800. Nicholas' sister, Lucille, was named as godmother.

Eulalie, daughter of Pelagie, both slaves o Mr. REYNAT, baptized Nov 4, 1800.

Moyse, age 3 mo., daughter of Kisaer, slaves of Jean LONG, baptized Dec 1, 1800.

Elizabeth, 3½ mo., daughter of Maime, slaves of Jean LONG, baptized Dec 1, 1800.

Pierre, 6 yr., legitimate son of Sincop and Neley, slaves of Lorence LONG, baptized Dec 3, 1800. Pierre's sister, Ester, age 10 mo., was also baptized on the same day.

Noel ALBAN, born June 20, 1801, son of Ester, both slaves of Lorent DOROCHER, baptized June 21, 1801.

Vital, born Feb 11, 1813, son of Marie Louise, mulatto slave of Louis BARADA, and Amable KENELLE, baptized Oct 5, 1813.

Louis, 3 wks., son of Rebecca, slaves of Jean COUNS, baptized Sep 6, 1801.

Charles, born Mar 21, 1804, son of Pelagie, slaves of Mr. REYNAT, baptized Mar 25, 1804. His godfather was Charles, mulatto slave of Mr. BARADA, and his godmother as Sophia, a slave of Mr. LeCURE.

Marie Magdeleine, 2½ mo., daughter of Rebecca, slaves of Jean COUNS, baptized July 22, 1804. Godparents were Pierre, mulatto slave of Charles TAYON, and Pelegie, a slave of Mr. REYNAT.

Josephine, 6 yr., daughter of Emilie, slaves of Sir Antoine JANIS, baptized Oct 7, 1804. Godparents were Pierre, slave of JANIS, and Felicite, mulatto slave of Louis BARADA.

Julie, born Dec 27, 1805, baptised May 11, 1806, slave of Mr. REYNAT.

Antoine, born 1807, son of Marie Louise, mulatto slave of Louis BARRADA, abptized Nov 4, 1807.
Eulalie, born Sep, 1806, daughter of Marie Louise, free woman of color, baptized Nov 4, 1807.
Emilie, norn Dec 2, 1804, mulatto slave of Mackey WHERRY, baptized June 11, 1808.
Jean Bte., 8 mo., slave of Antoine JANIS, baptized June 11, 1808.
ESCLAVE, Marie, born Oct 14, 1808, daughter of Charles, a slave of Louis BARRADA, and Marie, an Osage Indian, baptized June 26, 1809.
Therese, born Oct 16, 1810, baptized Aug, 1811, daughter of Charlotte and Pierre, both slaves of Mr. JANIS.
Pierre, born Sept 23, 1812, baptized Sep 24, 1812. son of Felicite, mulatto slave of Louis BARADAS, and Antoine, a Spaniard.
Euphrasie, born Nov 10, 1812, baptized Dec 1, 1812, child of Suzanne, mulatto slave of Vital BAUVAIS of Ste. Genevieve and Antoine "a half-breed whose name we ignore".
Andrea, born Apr 21, 1812, baptized Oct 5, 1813, son of Clariste, mulatto slave of Mr. REYNAT, and Dick RITCHIE.
Marguerette, born May 9, 1831, baptized May 13, 1813, daughter of Pelagie, a slave of Antoine JANIS and Charles, a slave of Mr. MORRISON.
Elizabeth, 8 mo., baptized July 26, 1814, slave of Mrs. DODGE.
Daughter of Pelagie, slave of Antoine JANIS, and Charles, a slave of MORRISON, born May 9, 1813, baptized May 13, 1813.
Jean Bte., 5 mo., baptized Aug 23, 1814, son of a slave belonging to Joseph DES COTES SANS DESSEIN and Bte. Marichal.
Therese, 8 mo., baptized June 1, 1818, daughter of Raphael and Gegrier, slaves of James MORESSON.
Marie, Eleanore, Genevieve, and Louis, slaves of Antoine JANIS, baptized June 21, 1818.
Josette Marguerite, born July 15, 1818, baptized Sep 13, 1818, daughter of Pelagie, a slave of Antoine JANIS.
Sem, 7 mo., mulatto, baptized Sep 13, 1818, son

of Fanny, slaves of Sir RAINET.
Julie, born Apr 1, 1819, baptized May 9, 1819, son of Eulalie.
Antoine, born Sep 8, 1818, baptized Oct 18, 1818, son of Sophia, slave of Lady CHEVALIER.
Baptistine, 2 yr., daughter of Pierre and Pelagie, slaves of Mr. JANIS, baptized Sep 15, 1822.
Sara Anne, born Sep 14, 1825, baptized Aug 8, 1826, daughter of Marie, slave of Wallace KIRKPATRICK.
Jean, baptized May 14, 1826, son of Anne, slave of Mr. CORN.
Felicite, 6 yr., slave of Louis BARADA, baptized 1826.
Guillaume, born Jan of 1827, and Charles, born May 22, 1828, DIEUDONNE, mulatto children of Eulalie PETIT, also a mulatto.
ROCINE, Helene Anne, born Jan 12, 1829, baptized Feb 14, 1829, daughter of Pierre and Sara ROCINE, negroes.
Helene, baptized 1829, slave of Mr. MORRISON.
Leander, baptized Mar, 1829, slave of L. JANIS.
Mary, David, and George, slave children belonging to John MICHEL, baptized July 1829.
Joseph, William, and Felix, slave children of Wm. ROBERSON, baptized July of 1829.
Lewis, slave child of Mr. RICKES, baptized July of 1829.
Marie, 3 yr., baptized July 26, 1829, slave of Antoine JEANISSE.
Mary, a child of color, baptized Nov, 1829.
George and Mary, slave children of Charles COUGHLY, baptized Nov, 1829.
BLACK, Marie, 4 mo., and Caroline, 4 yr., baptized Jan 3, 1830, daughters of Jeanene, slaves of Lucille JANIS.
Le PUNEN, Alexander and William, slaves, baptized Apr 10, 1830.
LAVA, Louis, son of Francois, a slave of Hubert TAYON and Louise BOURU, baptized Apr 5, 1830.
Francis and William, slaves of Edward KEATH, baptized May of 1830. George, a slave of James ELLIOTT, Edmond, a slave of Ann CARTER, and Nancy, a slave of Daniel EMERSON were also baptized on this date.

Jane, born Aug 25, 1830, and baptized Oct 12th of the same year, was a slave of Joseph PRIMAUT.
Perry, age 6, a slave of Van PERRY, was baptized on Oct 16, 1830.
Claire Anne, age 2, a slave of Mr. DOQUETTE, was baptized on Nov 9, 1830.
Elizabeth, slave of Mr. Nutt, was baptized on Nov 22, 1830. Another slave, Elisa, was baptized on the same day.
Joseph, born Jan 4, 1831, baptized Jan 18, 1831, was a slave of Mr. JEANISSE.
Antoine, born Dec 26, 1830, baptized Mar 2, 1831, was a slave of Silvestre CHAUVIN.
Victoire, age 14, a slave of Louis Le BEAU, and Marguerite, born Mar, 1830, a slave of Antoine TIBAULT, were both baptized on May 1, 1831.
Therese Minerva, a slave of Joseph HAYDEN, was baptized in June of 1831.
Emilie, a slave of Mr. DOQUETTE, was baptized on Aug 9, 1831.
Mary, a slave of Edourd KEITH, baptized in Aug of 1831.
Jane, age 5, and Emilie, born Nov 12, 1830, both slaves of Mr. DOQUETTE, were both baptized on Aug 9, 1831.
Jane and Nancy, slaves of Mr. KIRKPATRICK, were baptized on Oct 22, 1831.
Rebecca, a slave of La Freneire CHAUVIN, baptized in the fall of 1831.
Pierre Jason, born Dec 19, 1831, baptized Dec 28, 1831, son of Sara, a slave of J. MORRISON.
Henry, 7 mo., slave of Mdm. BESSONETTE, baptized July 22, 1832.
Jean B., born June 2, 1832, baptized July 22, 1832, was a slave of Mr. KNOTT.
Guillaume, born in May of 1832, and baptized Aug 19, 1832, was a slave of Lafreniere CHAUVEN.
BLACK, Antoine, born Dec 26, 1820, and baptized Nov 4, 1832, was a slave of Sylvestre CHAUVIN.
Robert, age 2 mo., a slave of Lafreniere CHAUVEN, was baptized on Feb 3, 1833.
Maria, born 8 years earlier, was baptized on

Feb 3, 1833, and was a slave of Les TWGMAN.
James, born Jan 30, 1833, and baptized Mar 24th of the same year, and belonged to Col. Walsh.

The following individuals were among those baptized during the cholera epidemic of 1833: Maria Adaline, Margueritte Helen, Emilie Ann, Marie, and Catherine, all owned by Mr. WALSH. Another slave, Marie, owned by Mr. CHARLIEA, and Margueritte Ann, owned by Mr. ECKERT, were also baptized during this time.

Eddy Louise, 5 mo., baptized Aug 18, 1833, was a slave of Wallace KIRKPATRICK.
Phitistine, daughter of Therese, slaves of Antoine TIBAU, was baptized Sep 15, 1833.
Mary, a slave of HENRIEUS, was baptized in Sep of 1835.
John, born in Feb of 1835, and baptized April 19, 1834, was a son of Isaac and Elsy who were slaves of La Freniere CHAUVIN.
Brigitte, age 6 mo., child of Paul and Marie, and slaves of Sulvestre CHAUVIN, was baptized Apr 19, 1835.
Jean Baptiste, 18 mo., baptized in Aug of 1835, was a son of Henry and Marie, both slaves.
Eliza and Marie, both slaves, were baptized in Aug of 1835.
Stephen, a black child, was baptized July of 1836.
COTE, Mathieu, son of Pouponne, was baptized Mar 12, 1837, both were slaves of B. COTE.
CHEVALIER, Elise and Marie, black children, were baptized in Aug of 1837.
Emilie, 1 mo., slave of Charles McNOT, was baptized Oct 22, 1837.
Joseph, William Henry, Marie, and Henrietta, all slaves, were baptized in Mar of 1838.
Charles and Jane Minerva were baptized in Aug of 1838, and Virginia and Edward were baptized in Nov, 1838.
Pierre, a slave of Mr. MULHART, was born in Oct of 1838, and baptized Aug 4, 1839.
Jean B., a slave of Antoine TIBAUT, was born May 6, 1840, and baptized four days later.
Cyprien, son of Joseph and Nancy, was born Aug 22, 1841, and baptized Sep 26, 1841. They

were slaves of Mr. SAUCIER.

Alexander, a slave of Mrs. DOQUETTE, was baptized on Jan 16, 1842.

In May of 1840, a slave named Joseph A. was baptized. William H. and Sophia were baptized the following July, and Margaret in November. Marcus was baptized on Jan 17, 1842, Stephen, on Mar 12, 1842, and Joseph S. and Thomas in the fall of 1842. All were noted as slaves, but their owner's names were not included in the record.

Charles, a slave of Jean Bte. H. La CROIX, died Apr 6, 1799 at the age of 65.
Claude, a slave of Antoine REYNAT, died Sep 19, 1802, age 40.
Joseph, an Indian-Creole slave of Mr. TAYON, Sr., died Nov 7, 1802, age 45.
Francois, son of Celeste, died Nov 30, 1802. Noted as a half-breed slave of Widow CHEVALIER.
Angelique, Indian slave of Bazil HEBERT, died Mar 13, 1803, age 14.
Child slave of Mr. CHAUVIN, died Dec 26, 1805, age 7.
Charles, age 3 yr., 8 mo., died Nov 10, 1807, and Julie, aged about 2, died Dec 221, 1807. Both were children of Pelagie, a slave owned by Mr. REYNAT.
A female slave of M. B. TAYON, died Jan 31, 1808, at the age of 15 months.
A female slave, age 30, belonging to Mr. REYNAT, died Mar 23, 1808.
A female mulatto slave of Mr. TAYON, died Nov 9, 1808, at the age of 4.
Henri, a slave of CHAUVIN, died Jan 7, 1809, at the age of 80.
Marguerite, mulatto slave of Louis BARRADA, died May 28, 1810, age 18 months.
Female, age 50, slave of Mr. MORESSON, died July 27, 1810.
Female infant, slave of Mr. CHAUVIN, died Nov 20, 1811 at the age of 10 months.

Child slave of Francois DUQUET, died Mar 19, 1811.
Therese, slave of Louis BARADA, buried Sep 29, 1811, age 20.
Margueritte, mulatto slave of Louis BARADA, buried Mar 26, 1812.
Margueritte, slave of Joseph TAYON, buried May 19, 1812.
Joseph, slave of Joseph TAYON, died Oct 16, 1813, age 16.
Charles, mulatto slave of Francois DUQUETTE, died Apr 12, 1815, age 4 or 5.
Marguerite, daughter of Pelagie, died Apr 16, 1815 at the age of 2. Both were slaves of Antoine JANIS.
Suzanne, slave of Vitale ST. GEMME BEAVAIS, died Aug 11, 1815.
Male slave of Jacques CHONAIN, buried July of 1816.
POINT DE SABLE, Jean Bte. (founder of Chicago), died Aug 28, 1818.
St. Dominique, age 80, slave of Mr. REYNAT, buried June 2, 1819.
Female slave of Mrs. DUQUETTE, buried Sep 16, 1824 at the age of 80.
Male slave of F. D. CHAUVIN, died at age 10 or 11, buried Jan 11, year not noted.
Elizabeth, slave of Mr. KNOTT, buried Apr 13, 1830.
Female child, buried Dec 27, 1831, slave of Mrs. DUQUETTE.
Pathi, slave of Antoine JANIS, buried Nov 23, 1832.
Adelaide, slave of Petray PAPIN, buried Dec 19, 1832.
Diana, age 7, a slave of Widow CHARLIER, buried June 7, 1833, and Marie, buried July 2, 1833.
Child slave of La Freniere CHAUVIN, died June of 1834.
Marguerite, buried June of 1834, was a slave of James MORRISON.
Kitty, child slave of Mr. HOUSE, buried July 9, 1834.
Josette, slave of Mrs. BARADA, died at age 95, and was buried Sep of 1834.
Marie, slave of Mr. KIRKPATRICK, buried Aug of

1837.
Rosanna, a slave of Mr. DIAH, and a boy slave of Mr. DIAL were both buried on Apr 3, 1839.
Stephen, a slave of Mr. DOQUETTE, was buried on July 5, 1839.
Houston, a child slave of Bernard FILTEAU, was buried in Sep of 1840.
Marguerite, buried July 12, 1843, was a slave of Louis BARADA.
Nathaniel, slave of L. CHAUVIN, was buried on Sep 8, 1843.
Jeanne, daughter of Louise, was born Dec 11, 1844, and baptized Jan 25, 1845. Both were slaves of Joseph La Freniere CHAUVIN.
Marie Roselle, born June 22, 1845, and baptized on Aug 24, 1845, was the daughter of Paul, a free negro, and Marie, a slave belonging to Sylvestre CHAUVIN.

Prairie Point Baptist Church, Cooper County. Records from this predominantly white church are on file at the Western Manuscript Collection.
July 10, 1842 - A colored woman named Sucky joined by letter, and Kissiah, a slave of John CRAMER, was baptized.
Sep 10, 1842 - George, a slave belonging to Mr. HERENDON, came forward to be baptized.
Oct 8, 1842 - Joe, a slave of Jesse B. TURLEY, was received into fellowship.
Nov 13, 1842 - Phebe, a slave belonging to Mr. PHARIS was received into fellowship.
June 10, 1843 - A slave named Hettie, belonging to Mr. Pharis, came forward to be baptized.
July 8, 1843 - Elsey, slave of Joshua GALE, was received into fellowship.
Aug 13, 1843 - SMITH, a slave of Abraham BARNES, was received into fellowship.
Oct 15, 1843 - Benjamin, a slave belonging to James HICKERSON, Patrick, a slave of Joshua GALE, and Greene, slave of A. BARNS, all came forward to be baptized.
Nov 12, 1843 - Howard, a slave belonging to Shedrick BARNS, Thomas, a slave of Joshua GALE, and Lewis, slave of Sanders TOWNSON, were received in fellowship.

2nd Saturday in July, 1845 - Henny, a slave of Benjamin HERNDON, and Dolly, a slave belonging to Charles F. FOX, both came forward to be baptized.
2nd Saturday in June, 1848 - Thomas, the property of B. TURLEY, was excluded and barred from attending church.
2nd Saturday in June, 1852 - Sally, a slave of Samuel MORTON, was received in fellowship.
Sep 16, 1854 - Dangerfield, a slave belonging to Garriod (sic) STEPHENS came forward to be baptized.
Sep 17, 1854 - Kissiar, a slave of Eedmoney TYLER, and Elisa, a slave of Clay TURLEY, were both received into fellowship.
2nd Saturday in Aug, 1856 - A slave belonging to W. L. SCOT was received into fellowship.
2nd Saturday in May, 1858 - George, slave of James POINDEXTIR came forward to confess his transgressions in order to be baptized.

Minutes of the Bethel Church, Cape Girardeau County.
Oct 11, 1806 - A female slave of Mr. BYRD was baptized.
Mar 12, 1808 - Hannah, a slave of Mr. RUSSELL was received by experience.
July 9, 1808 - Bob and Rachael, slaves belonging to Mr. STRONG joined the church.
Sep 11, 1808 - Mr. ABERNATHY's slave, Hannah, was received into fellowship.
June 9, 1810 - Mary, a slave owned by Mr. NAILS, was received by letter.
Feb 8, 1812 - Moses, a negro, was received by letter.
May 13, 1812 - Billey, owned by Mr. SMITH, was received by letter.
Aug 8, 1812 - Simon, owned by Mr. TANNER, was dismissed by letter.
Nov 21, 1812 - Forest, owned by Mr. Mathews, was received by experience.
Oct 9, 1813 - Vicey, owned by Mr. BYRD, was excluded from the congregation for telling a false tale, and refusing to hear the church. Toney, owned by Mr. HITT, was excluded for unbecoming behavior.

June 18, 1814 - Violet, owned by the Widow McCARITES, was received by experience.
June 8, 1816 - Tony, owned by Mr. EWINS, was received into fellowship as a transient member.
Nov, 1817 - Sister Flora, a black sister, was told to give a satisfactory reason for shouting in public worship.
June 13, 1818 - A committee agreed the black members were to have pew behind the white males.
May 8, 1819 - Flora, an African sister, departed this life.
Aug 7, 1819 - Vicey, a slave of Mr. Byrd, came forward and asked to have her membership restored. Her request was denied.
Dec 12, 1819 - Nancy, a slave owned by Capt. J. JOHNSON, was received by letter.
Apr 8, 1820 - Wenson, another slave owned by JOHNSON, was received by experience.
July 8, 1820 - BYRD's slave, Vicey, again applied for restoration of membership, which was granted by the church.
Oct 7, 1820 - Gem, owned by Mr. WILSON, was dismissed by letter.
Aug 7, 1823 - Violet, owned by Mr. M. BIRD, died.
Aug 16, 1834 - Hannah, owned by Edward F. IRWIN, was received into fellowship by letter.
Aug, 1862 - Dick GREEN, a black man, died at the age of 103.

Business records of Heath's Creek Baptist Church, Saline County.
May 22, 1841 - Nathaniel BRIDGEWATER's slave, Saul, was received into fellowship by experience.
May 23, 1841 - Mary, a slave of T. A. ADAMS, was received by experience.
Sep 26, 1841 - David and Stephen, both slaves of Nathaniel BRIDGEWATER, were received by experience.
Jan 30, 1842 - Rose, a slave of N. BRIDGEWATER, was received into fellowship by experience.
Jan 31, 1842 - Dorcas and Eliza, both slaves of

Mrs. SOUTHERLAND, were received into fellowship through experience.

July 10, 1842 - Lewis, a slave of J. H. HOWE, was received into fellowship.

Apr 23, 1843 - Peter and Hannah, both slaves of William TAYLOR, was received into fellowship by letter.

Sep, 1843 - J. McMAHAN's slave, Isaac, was received by experience into the fellowship of the church.

June, 1844 - Job, a slave of George W. WALLACE, George, a slave of John REA, and Joseph, a slave of Rev. W. B. WEAR, were all received into fellowship by experience.

Oct, 1844 - Richard MARSHALL's slave, Mariah, was received into the church by experience, and Sarah, a woman of color, died.

Aug, 1845 - Overton, a slave belonging to N. BRIDGEWATER, had an offense forgiven

Nov, 1848 - Reed HUGH, owned by Judge NAPTON, was received into fellowship by experience.

Mar, 1849 - Fanny, a slave of Dr. ROTHWELL, was received by experience.

TERRITORIAL RECORDS

French and Spanish Archives

Jan 20, 1768 - A male slave was sold by Joseph DESNOYER to Seur LACLEDE.
1774 - Nicolas BARSALOU sold a male slave to PAPIN.
Feb 22, 1774 - Jean Marie PEPIN dit LA CHAMSE sold a male slave to Francois GUYON.
Apr 19, 1775 - A male slave belonging to Monseiur CERRE to Monseiur LACLEDE.
Feb 9, 1775 - M. CERRE sold a male slave to Louis BOISLEDUE.
1775 - A male slave, owned by Lefevre MOTAR, was sold to Etienne Canolle ENRIGIRTRE. The same year, Joseph RIBAR sold one female slave to Joseph MOTAR.
Sep 20, 1776 - Carlos BIZET sold a female slave to Joseph DUCHENE.
Apr 1, 1779 - Marie, wife of Joseph HERBERT, sold a slave to Seiur DEBREUIL.
Feb 22, 1779 - A mulatto slave belonging to Gasper ROUBIEU was sold to Mons. PERAULT.
Jan 14, 1782 - Margarita, a slave owned by Pedro ROY was sold to Nicolas BOGENEAU.
July 18, 1783 - Mariana, owned by Louis BARADA and Maria BEQUET was sold by Carlos HANRION.
Aug 11, 1784 - Francesco VISONET sold a female slave to a Widow, Mariana BOULIEUR.
July 27, 1784 - One male and one female slave were sold by Juan ALEGRE to Nicholas BOCHENAU.
Aug 6, 1784 - A mulatto slave belonging to Luiz ROBERT was sold to Agustin CHOTEAU.
Nov 16, 1785 - Santiago Clan MORGAN sold a male slave to Philip TENT.
Aug 18, 1785 - Francisco CAILHOL and Madalina DELOV sold a female slave to Silvestre SARPY.
Nov 16, 1785 - A male slave was sold by Juan Pedro RUA dit LAPANSE to Antonio REINAL.
July 30, 1785 - Four slaves were sold by Carlos SANQUINET to P. BERNARDO.
Oct 26, 1786 - Fancisco DORLAC sold a mulatto woman to Agustin CHOTEAU.
Oct 11, 1786 - Felipe TENT sold one slave to Carlos SANQUINET.

Aug 14, 1786 - Juan Baptista MAYER sold a male slave to an unnamed individual.
Jan 3, 1786 - Gaspard ROUBIEU sold a male slave to Madam CHOTEAU.
Sep 22, 1786 - A female slave was sold by a widow, Genoveva RUQUIE to Silvestre SARPY.
Dec 22, 1786 - Juan Pedro REY dit LAPANSE sold a female slave to Tasin SANSIN.
Sep 14, 1786 - A female slave and her son were sold by Silvestre SARPY to Louis BODUEN.
June 4, 1788 - Anna OLIVIER sold a female slave to Antonio REILHE.
June 3, 1787 - Juan DATCHUNUT sold one female to Joseph MOTAR.
Mar 3, 1787 - Carlos GRACIOT sold a male to Thomas Tyler.
Nov 22, 1788 - Juan ALBRAN sold a female to Thomas TELEN.
May 27, 1789 - A male slave was sold by Angela CHOVEN, widow of BOLIAU to Juan Bautista LORAN.
May 28, 1789 - Angela CHOVEN sold a male and female slave to Santiago CHOVEN.
May 23, 1789 - Angela CHOVEN sold a male slave to Antoinio REILHE.
July 10, 1789 - Three slaves belonging to Santiago Clan MORGAN were sold to Benito BAZQUEZ.
Dec 25, 1789 - Two slaves belonging to Santiago Clan MORGAN were sold to Thomas TILER.
July 8, 1789 - Louis DUBREVIL sold a slave to Santiago Clan MORGAN.
May 28, 1789 - Two slaves were sold by Juan Baptista LA CROIX and Catarina HUBUCHON, his woman to Santiago NOYSE dit LABE.
May 1, 1789 - Daniel McDUFF, from the village of Kaskaskia sold a slave to Louis DUBREVIL.
Oct, 1789 - A male slave belonging to Carlos SANQUINT was sold Carlos TALLON.
June 23, 1790 - Four slaves belonging to Luyi BODUEN were sold to Silvestre SARPY.
May 5, 1790 - Luyi BODUEN sold a male slave to Alexas MARIE.
Oct 13, 1790 - A female slave was sold by Santiago Clan MORGAN to Jacinto _____.
June 7, 1790 - Carlos CADRON sold a female

slave to Juan Baptista LORENT.
Dec 28, 1790 - Juan BAPTISTA DELILE and Ipolita DEGUIU, his wife from the town to San Fernando to Gabriel CERR.
Oct 8, 1790 - Silvester LABADIA and Pelagiao CHOTEAU exchanged two slaves.
Dec 13, 1790 - Two slaves adjudicated by Maria LANCHEVEQUE in favor of Gabriel CERRE.
July 18, 1790 - Adjudication of three slaves belonging to Danial McDUFF and Anna Marie, his wife, in favor of Agustin CHOTEAU.
June 28, 1790 - A male slave was sold by Silvester SARPY to Emiliano YOSTY.
May 31, 1791 - A mulatto slave was sold by Simon CUSOT to Luis DUBREVIL.
Jan 1, 1791 - Santiago Clan MORGAN sold a female slave to Nicholas Heber LECONTE.
June 6, 1791 - Gabriel LA CHANSE sold a female slave to Fabriel CERRE.
Feb 1, 1791 - A female slave belonging to Antonio REIHLE was sold to the Rev. Father Juan Antonio LEDRU.
Jan 25, 1791 - Tomas TILEN sold a female slave to Santiago Clan MORGAN.
1791 - A mulatto slave belonging to Charles GRATIOT was sold to Filippe FINE, and another mulatto was sold to John COUNS.
1792 - Antoino RILHE sold a female slave to Silvestre SARPY.
Dec, 1792 - A female slave was sold by Benito VASQUEZ to Joseph MIGUEL.
1793 - A male slave of ____ BESSONET to Jacques CLAMOREAN.
Sep 14, 1793 - Jacques Clan MORGAN sold a male slave to Joseph BRAZEAN.
Dec 18, 1793 - Mons. Jacques Clan MORGAN sold a male slave to Philipe BACANE.
No date - Jacques Clan MORGAN sold a male slave to Jacquet CHAUVIN.
Oct 5, 1792 - A male and female slave were sold by Laulent BUROCHER.
Mar, 1793 - Clan MORGAN sold a male slave.
Mar 26, 1793 - A mulatto and two negro slaves were sold by Charles GRATIOT to Mr. REILHE.
No date - Jacento ST. CIR sold a mulatto.
Aug 3, 1793 - Jacento ST. CIR sold a mulatto

to Mr. VINSANT.
Oct 6, 1795 - Mariane CALDERON sold a female slave to Victoire RICHELET.
No date - Louis brevil sold a female slave to Benito VASQUEZ.
Nov 13, 1795 - Mdm. ROBIDOU sold a female slave to Ventura COLLETT.
Feb 20, 1796 - Joseph BRAZEAU to sold a male slave to Antoine REIHLE.
June 20, 1796 - Gabriel CERRE sold a male slave to Mr. BARRERA.
Apr 2, 1796 - Mr. LABADIE sold a male slave to Jacque CLANMORGAN.
June, 1797 - Joseph Marie PAPIN sold a male slave.
No date - Charles GRATIOT sold a male slave to William MUSICK.
June 6, 1797 - Guillermo Hebert LE CONTE to Luis COGNARD, sold one female slave.
July 11, 1797 - A female slave was sold by William MUSICK to James ROGERS.
No date - Mauuel GARCIA sold a female slave to Joseph MIGUEL, Antoine MERIN sold a female to Carlos GRATIOT, and Louis ROBERT sold a slave to Antoine VINCENT.
Apr 6, 1797 - A female slave was sold by Julian ROY to Jacqui CLAMORGAN.
Sep 12, 1797 - James HUILLAM sold a female slave to Joseph HORTIZ.
Oct 16, 1798 - A female slave was sold by John COFFE to Guillermo HEBERT.
Oct 20, 1798 - John COFFEE sold a female slave to Manuel MORO.
July 17, 1798 - A female slave was sold by Joseph HORTTIZ to Juan Baptesta CRELLEY.
June 19, 1798 - A female mulatto was sold by Bernardo MOLINA to Pedro CHOUTEAY.
Mar 22, 1798 - Joseph Maria PAPIN sold a female mulatto to Bernardo Malina.
Nov 26, 1799 - Gabriel CERRE sold a mulatto to Antonio SOULARD.
Sep 23, 1799 - A number of slaves were bought by the Rev. Father Carlos Leandro LUSSON, priest of St. Charles, from Santiago Clan MORGAN.
Mar 8, 1800 - Paticio LEE purchased a female

mulatto from Juan COFFEE, who also sold other slaves to Antonio SOULARD on the same day.
Oct 16, 1799 - William MUSICK sold a male slave to August CHOUTEAU.
Feb 1, 1800 - Juan Baptista CRELLY sold a female slave to Francesco Maria BENOLT.
July 24, 1800 - Juan CARR sold a male slave to Augusto CHOUTEAU.
Aug 17, 1799 - A male slave was sold by Pelagia ANTALLA, widow of Antoinio MORIN, to Luis LABEAUME.
May 18, 1799 - Sargent GONZALEZ sold a male slave child to Patrico LEE.
Sep 13, 1800 - A female mulatto was sold by Esteban DERROUEN to Augustin CHOUTEAU.
Nov 26, 1799 - A females slave was sold by Maria PAYANT, widow of RIGAUCHE, to Santiago Clan MORGAN.
Aug 4, 1800 - Luis LABEAUME sold a female slave to Manuel DE LISA.
June 6, 1800 - Guillermo HEBERT dit LE COMPTE sold a slave to Pedro JANIN, parish priest of the Village of San Luis.
Nov 24, 1800 - Pedro, age 18, was sold by Joseph MOTARDY to Pedro FOURNAT dit LAJOYE.
Nov 14, 1800 - Antonio, age 70, was sold by Joseph MOTARDY to Agustin DODIER.
Aug 7, 1800 - Pedro MENARD sold his slave, Judy, age 15, to Fuillermo HEBERT dit LE COMPTE.
Apr 5, 1800 - Celeste, age 25, and a mulatto, age 45, were sold along with another female mulatto and her three sons by Philippe PHEINS to Josef BRAZAUX.
May 3, 1800 - Martin ROSE sold slaves to Augusto CHOUTEAU.
July 2, 1800 - Sarah, age 28, was sold by William RATCLIF to David ROHRER.
June 21, 1800 - Francisco CACASAT, age 50, was sold by Carlos TAYON to Francesco LIBERGE.
Aug 20, 1800 - Lucy, age 26, was sold by Hugh WHITE to Juan PEDRO CABANA.
Apr 8, 1801 - Juan Baptista DUPLASY sold a male slave to Agustin CHOUTEAU.
Feb 16, 1801 - Nancy, age 25, was sold by Patricio LEE to Juan Pedro CABANE.

Apr 15, 1801 - Angelica, age 25, was sold by Manuel DE LISA to Pedro CABANE.
Oct 12, 1801 - Joseph, age 40, and Angelica, age 25, were sold by Manuel DE LISA to Gregorio SARPY.
Feb 16, 1801 - Angelle, aged between 45 and 50, was sold by Luis LABEAUME to Luis BOYCE.
Mar 4, 1801 - Jacobo, age 6, and Andrew, age 4, were sold by James McDONEL to Juan Pedro CABANNE.
Nov 3, 1801 - Catalina, age 40, was sold by Isaac PACKARD to Patricio LEE.
Nov 30, 1801 - Anequiem, age 15, was sold by Fildem PRUET to Augustin CHOUTEAU.
Apr 2, 1801 - Julian ROY sold Luis, age 35, to Santiago CLAMORGAN.
Oct 13, 1801 - Agustin, age 11, was sold by Antonio REILHE to Manuel DE LISA.
Feb 24, 1801 - Fobe, age 25, was sold by Joseph ROBIDOU to Francesco Maria BENOIT.
Mar 20, 1801 - Onoxe, age 25, was sold by Jacento ST. CIX to Manuel DE LISA.
Apr 13, 1801 - Jacento ST. CIX sold Sophia, age 26, and a female mulatto and her child to Manuel DE LISA.
Feb 12, 1802 - Helena, age 25, was sold by Francesco BRAZEAX to Andres ANDERVILLE,
Aug 19, 1802 - Rhoebe, age 18, was sold by Agustin CHOULEAU to Juan PEDRO CABANNE.
Mar 4, 1802 - Jacobo, age 6, and Andres, age 5, were sold by Juan Pedro CABANNE to Manuel de LISA.
Aug 21, 1802 - Estera, age 23, was sold by Antonio CURIN to Joseph PERILLIOT.
May 14, 1802 - Samuel, age 25, was sold by Carlos DEHAULT DELASUS to Pedro CHOUTEAU.
Aug 26, 1802 - Salee, a slave of Andres ANDREVILLE was sold to Calvin ADAMS.
Aug 12, 1802 - Rachel, age 6, was sold by Patricio LEE to Joseph PERILLIOT.
Oct 19, 1802 - Antonio Mina, age 40, was sold by Joseph ROBIDOU to Carlos SANQUINET.
July 31, 1802 - Naneta, age 22, was sold by Susana SAINTOUSE to Joseph and Francesco PERILLIAT.
Aug 27, 1802 - Baptista, a mulatto, age 5, was

sold by Susana SANTOUSE to Joseph PERILLIATE.
May 8, 1802 - Louisa, age 26, was sold by Tomas WHITLEY to Manuel DE LISA.
June 11, 1803 - Luis, age 30, was sold by Santiago Clan MORGAN to Francesco CHAYE.
Nov 23, 1803 - Juan Baptista LORENZ exchanged his slave, Luis, age 19, for a slave named Simango, age 45, belonging to the Widow CHOUTEAU.
April 2, 1803 - Juan Baptista LORENZ sold his slave, Magdalena, age 23, to Juan Maria DURAND.
Jan 16, 1803 - Adudication of Pedro, age 25, slave of Joseph MOTARD, dec'd. to Gregorio SARPY.
July 9, 1803 - Teresa, age 12, was sold by Antonio ROY to Auguste CHOUTEAU.
Oct 13, 1803 - Manuel DE LISA sold a slave Pedro, reportedly 130 years of age.
Jan 14, 1803 - Emi, age 15 or 16, was sold by Gregorio SARPY to Manuel DE LISA.
May 5, 1803 - Cioce, age 30, a slave of Antonio Francesco SAVGRIN, was sold to Juan Baptista PRATTE.

Sep 17, 1799 - George, a free mulatto purchased a house from Enrrique DUCHOUQUET.
Jan 16, 1803 - An inventory of the goods in the estate of Juanita FORCHET, a free negress, made. Her will had been entered into probate on Jan 2nd of the same year.
Aug 24, 1790 - Obligation with a mortgage by Marie Juanita, a free negress, was found in favor of Carlos SANQUENET.
Oct 22, 1773 - An inventory of the estate of Valentine and Jeanette, both deceased, and free negroes, was made. A copy of their marriage contract was also filed on the same date.

Ste. Genevieve Archive Records.
Oct, 1794 - Francois DAGUET hired a slave named Marie Louise from Vital BEAUVAIS.
May 10, 1799 - Israel DODGE hired Tom, Ralfa, and two female slaves belonging to Jesse SCHELLY.

Dec, 1798 - William GRIFFIN Jr. mortgaged his slave Bartlett to Mr. CLANMORGAN.
1779 - Jacques BILLERON emancipated his slave, Marie Rene.
1838 - Michael, age 26, was emancipated by Michel BADEAU, who had purchased him two years earlier from Barthalemie ST. GEMME.
No date - Melanie CAILLOT was ordered by the court to free her slave, Juliet.
July 23, 1797 - A slave named Marianne was emancipated by Louis DELORIERS.
1779 - Jeanette, an indian slave, was freed by Louis De NOYON.
Oct 23, 1798 - Robert GREEN, of Randolph County (state not noted), emancipated his slave named Dick.
1833 - Allen W. KIMMEL freed Arthur LAPORTE, age 36, described as having large hands, a muscular build, and over six feet in height.
1778 - Jean Bte. LABASTILLE freed his slave, Marie, and another who's name was not noted in the record.
1779 - A slave belonging to the wife of J. BILLERON was freed.
1788 - Jasmine and Catherine, slaves belonging to Charles VALLE, were emancipated.
May 7, 1801 - Pierre VIVIAT emancipated his slave, Rodda Christie.
May 28, 1805 - Bates ORANGE, a slave belonging to Pierre VIVIAT was emancipated.
1787 - Francois CRUZAT and Charles VALLE exchanged two slave, both named Maria.
Dec 14, 1787 - Louise DESPIN offered property for a slave, Michel dit Diann.
May, 1793 - John DODGE exchanged his slave, Ferere, for one owned by Francois PERNID.
1777 - Slaves belonging to Antoine DUCLAC and Joseph Decella DUCLOC exchanged slaves.
1784 - Pirre CORRICO was freed by Jean Bte. VALLE.
Apr 12, 1781 - J. LAFFONT traded a slave for a boat owned by A. GENNEVOIS.
1788 - Charles CHARLEVILLE filed suit against Hugh HOWARD for a slave which had been mortgaged.
May 21, 1767 - Charles BEAUVAIS and Pierre

AUBUCHON filed a lawsuit against Andre VIGNON for selling liquer to their slaves.
1802 - Thomas RIARDON brought suit against Godfroie ISAAC for stealing his slave.
1797 - Hannah MUSGROVE brought suit against E. B. MUSGROVE for falsely claiming a slave as his.
1788 - Charles CHARLEVILLE lost a mortgaged slave to Nathan WILLIAMS.
1797 - Jeduthen KENDALL lost a mortgaged slave to William JAMES.
1798 - Joseph FENWICK lost possession of a slave he had mortgaged to William MORRISON. FENWICK, William MORRISON, and Israel DODGE lost another to John CLIFFORD.
May 18, 1782 - Joseph QUESNEL gave a slave to the Widow of J. B. LA CROIX as a gift.
Mar 18, 1773 - An investigation was held because an Indian slave, belonging to the Widow AUBUCHON had escaped with a man named CALEDON, who supposedly killed her later.
1766 - Joseph NIBERVILLE sold three slaves to Louis VIVAT. One slave belonging to Michel PLACET was also sold to Charles MAROIS the same year.
1767 - Frois. CHAUVIN dit JOVENEUSE bought one slave from Mr. ROBINET.
1768 - Antoine RENAUD sold one slave to Joseph SEGOND, and Simon HEBARDEAU sold a slave to Mr. POITOU.
1770 - Mrs. ALARY sold a slave to Francois VALLE. Daniel FAGOT sold a slave to Pre. GADOBERT.
1774 - Hanry CARPENTIER sold two slaves to Charles BEAUVAIS who also bought a slave from St. PIERRE that same year. Emanuel ESCALERA bought a slave from Mons. DUCHOUQUET.
1775 - Guillaume HEBERT dit LaCOMTE bought one slave from Philippe ROCHELAVE
1776 - Widow Louis TRUDEAU sold a slave to Trope RICARD, and Carlos VALLE sold his slave to Francois VALLE. Jean Baptiste MOTARD sold one slave to Emilien YOSTI, and Pierre Grammont sold his slave to Sylvestre LABBIE. The same year, Joseph ST. AUBIN bought a slave from Ant. DUCLOS and Jos. DESELLE.

Ste. Genevieve District Ordinances.

Slave-holders were taxed in 1795 to defray the expense of executing slaves in New Orleans who had been found guilty of sedation.

In 1796, slave-holders were ordered to keep their slaves at home owing to the critical condition of the country. No slave would be given passage across the river unless they showed a passport, and all slaves were to be in their cabins after a cannon was fired at night.

TRANSFERS, SALES, AND HIRES

Johnson County - In consideration of the sum of $8,500, paid by William M PHIPPS for nineteen slaves, to wit: Martin, a blacksmith, his wife Edy, and their three children, Tazwell, Julia, and Catherine; Hannah, and her two children, Lucy and Rachael; Tempe, and her three children, Lizzy, Edmund, and Judy; Polly, and her three boys, Gordon, Campbell, and Washington; Nancy and her child, Matilda; and a man named Philip. Agate HARVEY, Feb 29, 1836.

Callaway County - ...proceeded to hire slaves belonging to the estate of William R. BENSON, dec'd., in the town of Miame, Saline County on Dec 30, 1846. The result follows: Jordan, hired of $130; Pleasant, $129; and Rachel for $41. Those hiring said slaves were required to treat them humanely, and furnish them with two suits of summer clothes, and one suit for winter, also a blanket, and hat, or cap.

Lafayette County - We, A. J. READ and Evaline READ of Cooper County, and Joel H. EWING, Young EWING, and N. H. EWING of Lafayette County, in consideration of $1,950, paid by Elizabeth H. EWING, assign the following slaves, to wit: Abraham, age 30; Susan, age 28; Charity, age 28; and Maria, age 2. On the same day, N. C. EWING paid $1,650, for: Mathias, age 30; Caesar, age 13; and Henry, age 6. June 13, 1853.

Ste. Genevieve County - Last will and testiment of William JAMES...slaves to be freed are Eliza, Lewis, Tom, Sophy, Moses, and Mary Ann, with each to be given $400, so they may relocate to a free state, Canada, or Liberia, but if they decide to remain in the state of Missouri, they are to receive three hundred arpens of land for a home for them and their heirs, together with twelve cows and calves, three yoke of oxen, six horses, and all the farming utensils and kitchen furniture that belongs to me. Also, on the liberation of Eliza, her two youngest children, Maria, now age 4, and Richard, age 2, shall be delivered to her. Immediately on the emancipation of Lewis, and Sophy, their youngest child, Martin, age 5, shall be given to them. I direct the remaining part of my slaves: Sam, about age 18; Manuel, about age 16; and Eliza Ann, about age 15, are to be freed when they reach the age of 30, and are to receive half the proceeds of their labor that had accrued between the time of JAMES' death and their reaching age 30 so they could remove to a free state, or go to Liberia.

Callaway County - Inventory of the estate of Robert NEWSOM, taken in 1855. Lewis, a boy, was transferred to Harvey NEWSOM; George, first charged as an accessory in the murder of his owner, was sold in Saline County; Celia was hung after a jury found her quilty of murdering NEWSOM; Cine, age 3, and Jane, age 1½, infant children of Celia, were sold on August 19, 185?.

Boone County - Negroes hired and sold by Wm. LAMPTON, auctioneer. Hire of slaves of JOhn SHOCK, dec'd.: James to Dr. YANCY, Robert to R. H. SMITH, Squire to Thomas SINCLAIR, Davis to Robert H. SMITH, Elijah (boy) to R. G. LEONARD, Green (boy) to James H. WILLIAMS, Kirk (boy) to Samuel KELLY, Nat (boy) to Mary SHOCK. Hire of slaves belonging to Moran H____, dec'd.: Henry to James BRISON, Jr.; Susan, age 17, to Dr. YANCY: Harriet, age 12, to F. T. RUSSELL; and Nancy, age 10, to W. W. BRYAN. Sales from the estate of Lawrence BASS, dec'd.: Robert, over age 55 to R. T. SLATE; Preston to Edwin BASS; Minor to Joseph WILLIAMSON; Robert to Peter BASS; Henry to John Ellis; John to O. GUITAR; Absalom to J. GUITAR; Martha and two children to E. M. BASS; Zerelda and three children to G. E. BASS; Susan and one child to Samuel DUNCAN; Clara, age 17, to John W. ROLLINS; Emma, age 80, to Samuel DUNCAN: Maria and Jerry to J. S. STRODE; Harriet to John W.

ROLLINS; Ruth to W. A. HAMILTON; and Mollie to Reuben PULLIS. Sale of slaves belonging to Calvin _____, dec'd.: Robeson, age 22, to Dr. YANCY: William, age 15, to Robert McBAIN; Samuel, age 11, to R. H. GENTRY; James, age 9, to David STEPHENS. Sale of slaves belonging to H. B. HULETT, dec'd.: Henry, age 28, to Lawrence ROCHFORD Caroline, age 40, and Rebecca, age 2, to _____. Other slaves sold were: Emily, age 16, belonging to Jesse PATTON, sold to Delbert SLATE; Ellen, age 7, belonging to James TOALSON, sold to J. A. BOULTON; Edward, belonging to Mr. MELLEN, sold to G. COUNCE; and Charlotte, age 16, sold to Samuel DINWIDDIE.

Lafayette County - Division of the slaves belonging to William MOSBY, dec'd. To John S. MOSBY: Randall, valued at $400; Charles Anthony, $800; and Frances and her two children, $1,000. To Robert MOSBY: Edward, valued at $1,000; Joseph, $500; and Amanda, $650. To William MOSBY, Jr.: Charles, valued at $1,000, Lewis, $700; and Sallie, $600. To James MOSBY: Travis, valued at $800; Susan and her child, $800; and Sidney, $550. To Mary MOSBY FLOURNOY: Tom, valued at $800, and $300 to make her portion equal to the others.

Boone County - Slaves hired and sold by Wm. LAMPTON, auctioneer, in 1859. Slaves belonging to William SUTTON: Ellen, age 12, and Harrison, age 8; slaves of J. H. WILKERSON: Milly and her child, and Charlotte; slaves belonging to Morgan BRYANT, dec'd: Harriet, age 15; Henry, age 14; and Nancy, age 12. Slaves belonging to the estate of John Shock: James, age 24; Elijah, age 16; Green, age 15; Kirk, age 13; and Nat, age 11. Slaves belonging to the estate of Mary SHOCK: Mary and her child, and Peter. J. S. CLARKSON's slave Mary, age 23, sold to H. R. COWDEN, and Willis, sold to J. H. WAUGH; and Alex, belonging to the estate of Dr. HALL, was sold to F. BURNHAM. Slaves belonging to W. H. IRWIN, sold on credit were: Eliza and her child to T. C. PARKER: John, age 10, to

Robert LEMON: Mary, age 7, to W. D. TRUE; and Martha, age 7, to J. M. SAMUEL. J. F. BURNHAM sold Dave, age 9, to J. MADDOX, and A. SUBLETT sold a slave named Mary to H. R. C. COWDEN.

Callaway County - New Year's Day, 1861. Slaves belonging to the estate of John DYER, dec'd. were sold: Nancy, age 36, and her child; Betsy, age 32; Cinda, age 14; Judy, age 9; and Lizzie, age 5. Slaves sold belonging to the estate of Cassandra CARLTON: Jenny, age 36, and her child; Henderson, age 12; Adeline, age 6; and Peter, age 4.

Lafayette County Record of Inventories and Appraisements, Book A, 1850 - 1855.
Richmond TYREE, dec'd, inventory taken Sep 12, 1850: Eliza, valued at $500; Mary Jane, $100; Betsy, $375; Alexander, $225; Harrison, $275; Priscilla, $125; Charles, $150; Frances, $350; and Allen, $600.
John WALLACE, dec'd, inventory taken Sep 3, 1850: Mark, valued at $700; Dysy and her child, $630.
Wiley B. TEASWELL, dec'd, inventory taken Aug 24, 1850: Ann, valued at $250; Ben, $300; and William, $150.
John FLETCHER, dec'd, inventory taken Oct 18, 1850: Alech, age 17; Gill, age 16; Henry, age 40; Liza, age 35; Margaret, age 14; Harriet, age 12; Mary, age 10; and Patsy, age 60.
William D. BULLARD, dec'd, inventory taken Oct 1, 1850: Zerelda, age 18.
Robert CARLYLE, dec'd, inventory taken Nov 2, 1850: Ellen, Sarah, and Daniel.
Mary BANKS, dec'd, inventory taken Dec 23, 1850: Jenny, valued at $500.
William Y. HENDRICK, dec'd, inventory taken Nov 16, 1850: Dapney, aged between 25 and 30 years.
Thomas HAYS, dec'd, inventory taken Mar 3, 1851: Daphney and her two children.
Robert W. WILEY, dec'd, inventory taken May 23, 1851: Charlotte, Woodson, and Coleman.
Floval VISION, inventory taken in June of 1851: Daubbin, William, Charles, an unnamed woman,

and Dicy, all freed by the will; Fielding, valued at $600; Samuel, $700; James, $875; Britain, $850; Simon, $850; Henry, $850; David, $800; Patterson, $500; Caroline and two children, $950; Betty, $300; and Milly and her child, $625.

Aaron CAMPBELL, dec'd, inventory taken Aug 12, 1851: Caezar, Barnett, James, Wilson, Peter, Jesse, Abby, Lucinda and her children, Nancy and Elizabeth; Sally and her children, Sarah, Charles, Bowerges, and French.

David WARD, dec'd, inventory taken Dec 27, 1851: Sharp, Elizabeth, Henry, Darby, Hannah, Silva, and Ned.

John H. TAYLOR, dec'd, inventory taken Nov 1, 1851: Abraham, Thornton, Minda, Mat, and Alsy and her four children, Preston, George Ann, Martha, Louisa, and Mary Frances.

William W. SHROYER, dec'd, inventory taken Jan 6, 1852: Sally, age 30, Henry, age 15; Alexander, age 12; Eliza, age 8; Sarah, age 6; Elijah, age 4; Gabriel, age 2; Joanh, age 55. Henry was hired out to George W. HALL.

Givens L. ROBERTS, dec'd, inventory taken Jan 10, 1852: Henrietta, age 27; Phillip, age 51; Henry, age 11; Paulina, age 9; and Lucy, age 6.

Judge Thomas GORDON, dec'd, inventory taken Jan 7, 1852: Toney, age 30; Jacob, age 24; Levi, age 19; Josiah, age 18; Sam, age 3½; Sarah, age 28. Jack, age 40; Rebecca, age 50; Clarresa, age 14; and Wesley, age 14, were not inventoried with the rest of the estate because they were left to his wife, Elizabeth GORDON.

Daniel H. BROWN, dec'd, inventory taken Jan 29, 1852: Celia, age 8, and a little girl, age 1 year, 8 months were both in the care of a Mr. ARNOLD.

Nancy B. MOOREMAN, dec'd, inventory taken Dec 30, 1851: Eliza and her daughter, Betty, age 3; Susan, a mulatto, age 4½; Martha, age 9; James, a mulatto, age 11; Robin, a male mulatto, age 18; George, mulatto, age 12; Jerry, a mulatto, age 15; Tom Dyke, age 10; Violet, age 36, and her infant; Price, age 7;

Sarah, age 7; Nancy, age 4; and Indy, age 2.
William SKAGGS, dec'd, inventory taken Apr 20, 1852: Sam, age 37, a blacksmith by trade; Harriet, age 30; and Elizabeth, age 4.
Libbus COBB, dec'd, inventory taken Feb 14, 1852: a male slave, age 35.
Jonathan HICKLIN, dec'd, inventory taken May 8, 1852: George, age 46; Tom, age 19; Moses, age 10; Ance, age 40; Joshua, age 16; Joannah, age 12; Toby, his wife Lucy, and their children, Toby, age 5, and Eliza, age 3; Mark, age 21; Malan, age 15; Laura, age 15; Lucky, age 20, and her child; Matilda, age 48; Rebecca, age 21, and her child; Harriet, age 26, and her child Malinda, age 6; Elizabeth, age 26, and her two children, Marion, age 6, and Doniphan, age 4; Rosanna, age 25, and her child, Charlotte, age 2.
Manuel SHARP, dec'd, inventory taken Sep 1, 1852: one male slave, age 12.
Thomas Hopper, dec'd, inventory taken Sep 3, 1852: Lucy and John.
Andrew E. RENNECK, dec'd, inventory taken Oct 15, 1852: Joseph, James, Henry, Harriet and her four children (not named) Huldah, John, Thomas, Richard, and Martha Ann.
Dr. William WARD, dec'd, inventory taken Nov 3, 1852: Allen, age 24.
William SMITH, dec'd, inventory taken Feb 9, 1853: Mike, age 35; Tuck, age 19; Cenda, age 23; Beck, age 15; Andrew, age 23; George, age 18; Julia Ann, age 19; Harriet, age 13; Sally, age 12; Fanny, age 6; Adaline, age 3; Mary Eliza, age 3; Ellen, age 2; and an unnamed male infant, age 6 months.
Charles McCLUNE, dec'd, inventory taken Feb 25, 1853: One girl, not named.
William Y. C. EWING, dec'd, inventory taken Mar 16, 1853: Abner, Clary, Joseph, and Harriet.
Jackson LAUDY, dec'd, inventory taken Apr 6, 1853: Betsy, age 40; Jim, age 40; Pony, 25; Proctor, 24; Nuly, 24; Mary, 22; Henrietta, 22; Martha, 20; Emily, 16; David, 12; Hillary, 10, and seven other children who's ages were unknown.
Mary J. WALTON, dec'd, inventory taken Apr 15,

1853: Harrison, Charles, Mary Jane, Betsy, Frances, Alexander, and Priscilla.
Sampson BECK, dec'd, inventory taken Oct 8, 1853: Rachel and her two children, Sally and Edward, Mary, Bob, and Martha.
Jesse COUCH, dec'd, inventory taken July 29, 1853: Percy.
William Y. HENDRICK, dec'd, inventory taken Sep 10, 1853: A woman, Gracie Ann; a boy named Stokes, and a girl, Ann Elizabeth.
Estelle READ, dec'd, inventory taken Apr 1, 1853: Willie, Aaron, Ned, Harrison, Winney.
Christopher SLUSHER, dec'd, inventory taken Jan 28, 1854: Edmund, Jim VIVION, Tom, Jim, George, Moses, Dan, Charlotte, Jane, Fanny, Tempe, Kelly, Frank, Mary, and Laura.
London BATES, dec'd, inventory taken Dec 12, 1853: Sam, Enoch, Merry, Polly, Margaret, Reuben, Will, John, Panes, Jim, Liza, Ann, Maria, Elic, Nancy, Nelly, Horace, Tom, Lupie (sic), Fanny, Frank, Betsy, Mitch, Frances, Liddy, and George.
Christian HAND, dec'd, inventory taken Nov 26, 1853: Charles EVANS and David MILLON.
Jane BOOTON, dec'd, inventory taken Feb 6, 1854: Sam, age 46; Maria, age 44; Jane, 18, and her child, age 3; Jane, age 17; George, age 17; Jerry, age 8; and Paulina, age 12.
John RAMSEY, dec'd, inventory taken Jan 17, 1854; Henry, 30; Sarah, 52; Mariah, 18; and Harriet, 5 weeks.
George CALLAWAY, dec'd, inventory taken July 13, 1854: Dandridge, aged between 40 and 45; Lucy, age 40; David, age 9; Eliza, age 6; and Lucy, age not given.
Richard M. B. CHICHISLER, dec'd, inventory taken Sep 11, 1854: John and Sims.
Dr. John PERRIE, dec'd, inventory taken Aug 19, 1854: Barel, age 40; Alfred, age 35; William, age 32; Charles, age 28; Frank, age 25; Jno., age 18; Maria, age 40; Sarena, age 16; Susan, age 12; Sarah, age 8; Joanna, age 5; Daniel, age 24; Nicholas, age 18; Columbus, age 14; David, age 12; William, age 12; Tobias, age 10; Charles, age 10; Henry, age 6; Colvin, age 2; Sarah, age 45; Nellie, age 38; Eve-

line, age 30; Valinda, age 28; Polly, age 14; Elenor, age 12; Annice, age 11; Frances, age 10; and Mary, age 2.

John V. WEBB Jr., dec'd, inventory taken May 7, 1855: Silus, age 19; Andrew, age 19; Joe, age 30; Henry, age 27; Abraham, age 16; Edmund, age 45; Winny, age 45; Elvira, age 16; Cela, age 19; Parker, age 45; Harriet, age 33; Milton, age 3; Margaret, age 9 months; John, age 8; Sarah, age 10; Meria, age 12; Caroline, age 14; Thornton, age 16; William, age 6; Ibby, age 50; Tom, age 28; George, age 14; Sidney, age 9; Albert, age 5; Isaac, age 3; Priscilla, age 12; Ben, age 14; Hardin, age 23; Ann, age 8; Jim, age 28; Matilda, age 22; Allen, age 14; Ellen, age 23; Jenny, age 30; William, age 3; Walker, age 4; Jake, age 9.

Mary D. FORT, minor heir of George W. FORT, dec'd, inventory taken Apr 2, 1853: Manuel, age 45; Nancy, age 45; Wyatte, age 18; George, age 6; Sam, age 15; Joshua, age 14; Elizabeth, age 5; Sally, age 3; and Jane, age 13.

Moniteau County, Inventories, Appraisements, and Sale Bills, 1855 - 1861.

Theodosia BRANCH, dec'd, inventory taken Nov 24, 1855: Eli, Amanda, and their child, Maria. All sold to J. H. C. BRANHAM for $1,980.

Stephen STINSON, dec'd, sold on Apr 12, 1856, by John H. STINSON, gaurdian of minor children: one slave and her children sold to Jonathan TODD; Burt, sold to Wm. G. HOWARD; Simon, sold to Sandy HILL; Tom, sold to H. C. MARTIN.

Minor heirs of Mary WHITE, dec'd, sold on Apr 12, 1856: Jane, and her child, to Isaac HILL, and Green was sold to John B. FISHER.

Malory Ann FREEMAN, minor heir of Jonathan FREEMAN, dec'd, inventory taken Sep 9, 1855: Jane, appraised for $600.

James ANDERSON, dec'd, slaves sold Jan 1, 1857, by E. H. DOGGETT, administrator: Sidney and a girl named Alley to M. M. PARSONS.

Griffen SIMMONS, dec'd, inventory taken July 18, 1857: Simon, age 46; Charles, age 9; and Henry, age 11.

Stephen HOWARDS, dec'd, inventory taken Mar 12, 1858: George, Tom, Narcis, and her children, Mary, age 3, and Rachael, age 14 months.

Richard BRUCE, dec'd, inventory taken Apr 15, 1858: Louisa, age 25; Roy HARRISON, age 20; Edy, age 7, and George, age 3.

Rebecca DEARING, inventory taken June 4, 1858: a woman and her child, and a girl, age 15.

John D. MILLER, dec'd, inventory taken Aug 5, 1858: Old Bob, Young Bob, Rhodes, Mose, Cavil, Jim, Clif, Paulina, Viney, William, Peter, David, and Greenberry.

Richard BRUCE, dec'd, slaves sold Jan 1, 1859: Roy HARRISON, sold to W. J. STEPHENS: Edy, sold to L. L. WOOD; Louisa and her child, George, sold to J. P. H. GRAY.

John DEFOE, appraised Jan 5, 1860: Henry, Frank, Jacob, Harry, George, and Mary and her child, Caroline. With the exception of Henry, they were all sold to William ROBERTSON in a private sale.

Stephen HOWARD, dec'd, slaves sold Jan, 1860: George, age 28; Tom, age 20; Narcis, age 28, and her three children, Mary, age 5; Rachel, age 3; and an infant, age 10 months.

Slaves belonging to William T. LANCASTER and Marcella A. LANCASTER, minor heirs of Thomas G. LANCASTER, inventory taken June 11, 1860: Nelson, age 35; Ann, age 26; Judd (female), age 59; Frederick, age 9; Mary Ann, age 8; Amanda, age 6; William, age 4; Jack, age 2; and George, age 4 months.

Lincoln County, Inventories, Appraisements, and Sale Bills, Book A, 1855 - 1858.

Robert McMAHILL, dec'd, inventory taken Jan. 1855: Henry, Warton, Marion who was hired out to Whitson COX; Jasper, hired out to Arthur McMAHILL; Angeline, hired out to William COONCE: Harry, hired out for one month to Calib CHILES; and Jeremiah, hired out to Drury SITTON.

John Allen WOOLFOLK, dec'd, slaves hired out

Feb 22, 1855: Clara, age 57; Milly, age 35; Burrill, age 27; Barton, age 23; Lucretia, age 21; Anderson, age 19; Henry, age 16; Sarah, age 15; William, age 14; Benton, age 11; Juin (sic), age 11; Rilla, age 9; Tom, age 7; Andrew, age 7; Jackson, age 5; Bailey, age 3; Harriet, age 3; Joseph, age 6 months; and Matilda, age 4 months. Arch, age 27, was owned in partnership with James H. BRITTON, and one-fourth the value of Rachel and her three children who were part of the estate of Ruben SMILEY's estate.

Elizabeth LEWIS, dec'd, inventory taken Sep 15, 1855: Thomas, Charles, Henry, Thomas, William, age 30; Addeson, Bill, Betsey, Mariah, and her child, Elisa, Nick, Ameda, Quintus, Sally, age 9, an infant, Lucy, Franklin, age 4; Martha, Irene, and Ellen, age 25, and her three children.

Thomas TILLER, dec'd, inventory appraised Oct 8, 1855: Charlotte, age 29; Jerry, age 2½; and a male infant.

James T. MOORE, dec'd, slaves appraised and hired out Sep 11, 1855: Ruben, age 64, hired to Jas. L. WILSON; Peachy, age 43, hired to Q. MOORE; Lewis, age 26, hired to Elizabeth MOORE; Lewis, age 23, hired to J. ROHN; Rose and her child, hired to John JAMESON; Amy and her child, hired to F. ROHN; Harriet, age 13, hired to Jos. NELSON; Eliza, age 11, hired to Robert POOR; Larkin, age 9, to Thomas WELLS; George, age 8, hired to George PALMER; Nelly, age 35, and five children, Luke, age 6; Patrick, age 4; Sarah, age 3; Henry, age 2; and Lucy, age 3, were hired out to Elizabeth MOORE.

James P. GUTHRIE, dec'd, inventory and appraisement made Sep 25, 1855. He owned one-ninth of the slaves belonging to the estate of Samuel GUTHRIE: Heathy, age 50; Henry, age 30; Paten, age 18; Benjamin, age 10; and Anderson, age 8.

Edwin JACKSON, dec'd, appraised Sep 24, 1855: Ester and her child, and Silas and John.

Jas. CLARK, dec'd, sale of slaves was Jan 1, 1856: Anderson, bought by A. H. BUCKNER,

Old William, sold to Wm. HARDING: William, sold to C. D. McQUEEN; Bob and Nancy, sold to Chas. A. CLARK; Isaac, sold to A. H. BUCKNER: Phill, sold to Jas. A. CLARK; Julianna and Betsy, sold to A. COCKRAN; Lucy and her child, sold to F. J. ELGIN; and Mary was sold to Austin BEASLEY; Braxton was privately sold later.

John S. WYATT, dec'd: Clark was sold to Elias B. MARTIN on Jan 12, 1855; Alfred was sold to Francis WYATT on June 1, 1855, and George was hired out to Elias NORTON on Dec 25, 1855. For the distribution of assets, slaves sold on Jan 1, 1856, were: Miranda and Lucy STONE, sold to Rebecca M. and James R. WYATT; Ann and Fanny Fern were sold to Francis WYATT; George was sold to Thomas GRAVES; and Jenny Lind was sold to Elias NORTON. Miranda was later hired out to Mary F. WYATT, and Ann was hired out to Jordan S. SALLEE.

William SYDNON, appraised Mar 11, 1856: Cloe, age 48; Anthony, age 44; Charles, age 44; Brance, age 42; William, age 28; James, age 27; Christina, age 30; Nat, age 19; Billy, age 17; John, age 13; Benton, age 14; Sophronia, age 22; Ned, age 13; Celia, age 13; Angeline, age 12; Sylvia, age 14; Nancy, age 9; Victoria, age 6; Missouri, age 5; Zackery, age 8; Mary, age 6; Tamar, age 2; Philis, age 2; Winnie, age 1; Colby, age 3; and Ben, age 4. Charles was hired out to Alex WILLSON, and Anthony was hired out to Alex BUCHANAN.

Charles O. VANCE, dec'd, inventory taken Feb 20, 1856: Margaret, John, George, Reuben, and Henry.

Morgan WRIGHT, dec'd, slaves sold Jan, 1856: Ben, sold to John WRIGHT, and Theresa and her child, sold to Josephine and John WRIGHT.

Daniel DRAPPER, dec'd appraised June 24, 1856: Andrew, age 55, valued at $240; Rene, age 57, valued at $95; and Jane, age 79, no value.

John RAY, dec'd, appraised Aug 18, 1856: George, Hannibal, Harrison, Susan, Columbus, and Mary.

Mary Ann McCORMICK, appraised Jan 10, 1857:

John.

Daniel WALKER, dec'd, appraised Mar 23, 1857: Sam, age 28; Sarah, age 8; Harriet, age 6; Amanda, age 3. The administrator hired Sam out to Harvey ERVIN, and Sarah was hired out to Ruben GENTRY until Dec 25, 1857.

Nicholas H. MERIWETHER, dec'd, slaves appraised Apr 7, 1857: Tom, age 26; Mary Ann, age 18.

Joseph W. GIBSON, dec'd, inventory taken June 11, 1857: Henry, age 41; Lawrence, age 17; Fisher, age 17; Peter, age 16; and Carter, age 5.

John O. WELLS, inventory taken Sep 23, 1857: a male slave, age 28, and a girl, age 13.

James F. MOORE, inventory taken Nov 13, 1857, at Louisville: Emanuel, Clarisa and her child Susan, Violet and her child, Charles; Bland, William, John, James, Willy, Mary, Sally, Margaret, and Isabella.

George M. McGRIGGER, dec'd, inventory taken Feb 1, 1858: Andrew, age 34; Jacob, age 30; Bob, age 21; Louisa, 27; Charles, aged a few months.

Sale bill of the slaves belonging to Caleb McFARLAND, dec'd, sold Dec 22, 1857: Emanuel, bought by Hugh B. McFARLAND; Violet and Isabella, bought by David STEWART, who also purchased John ESTON; Hannah, James, William and Charles were purchased by Caleb W. PRARR (sic); Clarissa, Sarah, Susan and her child, sold to James H. McFARLAND: James, Bland, Mary, and William were bought by John B. McFARLAND; and the others, John Mitchel, and Margaret, were sold to Marcus McFARLAND.

Samuel CANNON, inventory taken Jan 11, 1858: Stephen.

Sale bill of the estate of William MATTHIAS, dec'd, sold at Millwood on Mar 27, 1857: Sarah, age 20, sold to J. L. MUDD.

Burton PALMER, dec'd, inventory taken Mar 20, 1858: Meredy, age 47; Ben, age 44; Lucinda, age 50.

John W. GILLUM, dec'd, inventory taken Apr 28, 1858: Fountain, age 48; Cupid, age 34; Hannah, age 60; Jane, age 27; Burnet, age 11; Anderson, age 9; Maria, age 7; Henry, age 5;

Thurman, age 4; Sarah, age 3; and Mary, age 1.
John RAY, dec'd, inventory taken after his widow died, on Apr 8, 1858: George, Harrison, and Hannibal.
Orvil COTTLE, dec'd, inventory taken July 27, 1858: Minnie, age 57.
Barton WOOLFOLK, dec'd, inventory taken July 1, 1858: one-half interest in Lia, Rachel, and Robert.
Richard WRIGHT, dec'd, inventory taken Oct 7, 1858: Emanuel, age 35; Ambrose, age 38; David, age 51; Jack, age 50; George, age 15; Calvin, age 10; Levi, age 7; Ruben, age 4; Harvey, age 2; Jiles, age 6; Charity, age 35; Milly, age 50; Sallie, age 14; Candis, age 10; Jane, age 8; and Martha, age 5. On Apr 2, 1860, Jack was sold to Noncy M. TAYLOR. Milly, Charity, and Charity's daughter were sold to George W. ZIMMERMAN. Jane was sold to Christopher L. CARTER, and Daniel was sold to Judy WRIGHT.

Lincoln County, Inventories, Appraisements, and Sale Bills, Book B.
Solomon JENKINS, dec'd, inventory taken Nov 10, 1858, but the slaves were withheld from administration: Cato, age 25; Giles, age 35; Perry, age 18; George, age 10; Ben, age 5; Lewis, age 2; and Lucinda, age 38.
J. William GUILLUM, dec'd, inventory taken Dec 2, 1858: Iverson.
James ADMIRE, dec'd, inventory taken Dec 6, 1858: Priseler, age 40, and George Washington, age 9.
Joseph B. WELLS, dec'd, inventory taken Jan 31, 1859: Armstead, Moses, and Aaron.
Thomas J. CONNER, dec'd, inventory taken Feb 14, 1859: Eliza, age 30; Riley, age 13; and Harriet, age 10.
Simon THORNHILL, dec'd, inventory taken Jan 15, 1859: Mary and two boys, Jordan and Giles.
Silas D. REDISH, dec'd, inventory taken Mar 18, 1859: Betty, age 25; George, age 8; and Rachel, age 2.
Nathaniel WILLIAMS, dec'd, inventory taken May

5, 1859: Jesse, Sally, Mahala and her child, Mary, Peggy, Queen, Caroline, Martha, Silva and her child, Lucy, Charles, John, Rob, William, and Daniel. B. A. WILLIAMS bought Silva, her child and Lucy. William was purchased by W. WILLIAMS, and Elijah WILLIAMS bought Daniel.

Henry MARTIN, dec'd, inventory taken Aug 20, 1859, with the slaves hired out until Dec 25th: George to Mary A. MARTIN, Johnson to B. F. ROBERTSON, and Daniel to John A. PULLIAM.

Solomon JENKINS, dec'd, slaves sold on Jan 3, 1860: Cato and Giles to Joseph M. HEADY, Perry, Lucinda, George, Ben, America and her child, and Lewis were sold to Mrs. James (Jane) JENKINS.

Robert HOLLIDAY, dec'd, inventory taken Dec 1, 1859: Caroline, age 46; Phillip, age 23; Ned, age 19; Joseph, age 16; and Mag, age 9.

David CLARK, dec'd, inventory taken July 13, 1860: Peter.

Susannah MYERS, dec'd, inventory taken Feb 13, 1860: Sarah, age 62; Polly, age 20, and her child; Louisa, age 20; Jane and her child, age 2; Jefferson, age 18; Franky, age 32, and her child; Lewis, age 12; and Henry, age 9.

Isaac HOUSTON, dec'd, inventory taken Jan 2, 1860: Isaac, Loid, Oliver, Sarah and her child, Martha, age 5 months.

David BARTLEY, dec'd, inventory taken Mar 13, 1860: Nancy.

On May 8, 1834, Thomas M. HORINE, one of the heirs of Jacob HORINE, transferred his right to any further claim in the estate of Reuben SMITH in exchange for Bates, a slave valued at $500. Washington County Court Records.

The heirs of Andrew PERRY, dec'd, petitioned the County Court of Washington County to sell the following slaves: George, Jacob, Sally, Rachel, and Mariah.

Boon's Lick Times, Fayette, Howard County.
Jan 16, 1847. "To be sold on Jan 30, 1847,

at the home of Porter JACKMAN in Howard County, two men, Wat and George, three boys, Hardy, William, and David, two women, Judy and Lively, and Betty, Verlena, Minerva, Martha, and Lucy, all girls.

Dec 11, 1847. To be sold on Jan 1, 1847, in Fayette: Jim, age 35; Mary, age 22, Harriet, age 19, Mary, age 14; Manda, age 6; Booker, age 4; Owen, age 3, slaves belonging to the estate of John W. RAWLINGS, dec'd.. Phillis, age 30, and her child, 1 year of age, slaves belonging to the estate of Jesse CREWS, were also sold on that date.

Nov 11, 1848. The sale of York, age 27, was advertised by Sarshel BYNUM for a deed of trust made by Robert BROWN to Joseph COOPER.

Missouri Statesman, Columbia, Boone County.

Dec 29, 1848. To be sold on the first Monday in 1849 - Two women, one age 40, the other, 21 years of age. Two girls, ages 18 and 14 will also be sold, estate of Squire J. REDMAN. Also advertised was the sale of George who was 25 on May 11th, James, 25 on May 18th, and Eliza Jane, age 16 on Sep 1st, all held by the estate of John HICKAM.

Apr 12, 1850. To be sold on Apr 23rd, Mary, age 45, and her child, 4 months; William, age 7; and Robert, age 15, held by the estate of Samuel HANNA.

Dec 22, 1850. Sale to be held on Jan 1, 1851 at the Boone County Courthouse in Columbia, Amelia, age 23, and Rebecca, age 10, held by the estate of William Y. and Frances CROCKETT. Six slaves belonging to the estate of Jesse MELLON were also advertised: Jim, age 25; Abe, age 21; Peter, age 14; America, age 25, and America's two children, ages 4 and 5.

Salt River Journal, Bowling Green, Pike County.

John MACKEY, administrator for the estate of William S. MACKEY, dec'd, will sell on Jan 1, at Bowling Green, on credit of twelve months, to wit: two men and one woman, ages 18 to 23.

Feb 1, 1840. I will sell at the courthouse in Bowling Green, Pike County, on the 3rd of

February, all slaves belonging to the estate of Asa GUN, by Samuel Fielder, adm'r.. Also to be sold on that same date was a woman and child belonging to the estate of Joseph THOMAS by Hezekiah ODEN, adm'r., and one negro woman belonging to the estate of Daniel ADAMS by Thomas BLAND, adm'r..

CLAIMS FOR COMPENSATION
OF ENLISTED SLAVES

These records were extracted from the papers of Louis Benecke which are on file at the Western Historical Manuscript Collection, and Record Group 21, U. S. District Court of Kansas.

Joseph WILKERSON of St. Louis, made claim for Joe WILKERSON, who was inherited from the claimant's mother. Joe enlisted Feb, 1866, at Cape Girardeau, claim filed Nov, 1866.

Horace WINDSOR of Cooper County, made claim for three former slaves: Oscar L. COOK who enlisted Nov, 1863, at Boonville, David RUNNELS, born 1849, enlisted Mar, 1864 at Tipton, both born to claimant, and Taylor HAWKINS who also enlisted Mar, 1864, at Tipton. Claim filed Nov, 1866.

George STROTHER who enlisted Nov, 1863, at Boonville, was first owned by William SCOTT who died in 1855, then by SCOTT's widow, Louisa, who died in 1865. Compensation was claimed by R. F. WAYLAND, executor of Louisa's estate in Howard County in Nov, 1866.

Oscar R. WHITE of Howard County filed a claim for compensation in Nov, 1866, for two former slaves: Albert WHITE, who enlisted Jan, 1864, and John WHITE, who enlisted the next month.

George SLEMONS, born in 1847, at Jefferson County Virginia, enlisted Feb, 1864, at Platsburg, and Nat SLEMONS, purchased in 1843 or 1844 from John Randolph TUCKER of Jefferson County, Virginia, were both claimed by Montgomery SLEMONS of Clinton County in Nov, 1866.

Joe MURPHY enlisted Jan 1864, at Syracuse, was claimed by the estate of John MURPHY, dec'd., of Cooper County.

Elizabeth TURNER of Howard County, filed for compensation in Nov, 1866, for Nelson TURNER, who she claimed from the time of his birth in 1842.

Milton NANCE who enlisted Jan, 1866, at Tipton,

was claimed by Benjamin NANCE of Howard County. In his claim, Benjamin stated he had purchased Milton at age 14, in Nov, 1854, form W. HEDRICK in Charleston, Virginia.

Catherine RICHOMOND of Marion County, filed for compensation for Basil HAYDEN who enlisted in either the 54th, or 56th Massachusetts Regiment, claiming Basil had been born to a slave in her possession.

Horace KINGSBURY of Howard County, filed for compensation for Albert CAVANAUGH, who was 30 years old when he enlisted Jan, 1864, at Tipton, claiming he had purchased Albert from William H. TRIGG, agent for George WAIT, in 1851.

William P. MOORE filed for compensation for Simon GRAY, claiming he had received Simon from his father-in-law, James W. WADDELL of Lafayette County, in 1855.

Joseph GRISBY and George GRISBY, owned since birth by the claimant, and Hiram GRISBY, all enlisted Jan, 1864, at Tipton. These three were all claimed by Samuel T. HUGHES of Howard County in his claim filed in Nov, 1866.

Reuben HERNDON and Harrison SMALL, age 18, enlisted Nov, 1863, at Boonville. Both were former slaves of John HERNDON of Howard County, who filed for compensation in Nov, 1866.

James HAMILTON, alias Joseph HAMILTON, who served with the Colorado Cavalry, was claimed by James P. HAMILTON of Buchanan County. His former owner stated he had purchased the slave form James W. DAVIS of Hart County, Kentucky, in 1849.

William C. HALL of Lafayette County filed for compensation for Stephen SMITH in Nov, 1866. SMITH had been about 30 years of age when he was purchased from Elisa C. BRYCE of Bayou Rapide, Louisiana, in Nov, 1843.

Joseph M. GENTRY of Ralls County, filed for compensation for one slave, Richard GENTRY.

French GLASCOCK of Ralls County, filed a claim for compensation for Beverly BELTS, in Nov, 1866.

William PEMBERTON who had enlisted in Oct, 1864, was named as a former slave of William L. FRENCH, of Audrain County. French claimed he had been given the slave by his father, Pinkney FRENCH in 1852.
James R. ESHILL of Howard County, filed a claim for compensation for a slave he had purchased from W. H. BOWMAN. The former slave, Allen ESHILL, enlisted Jan, 1864, at Tipton.
Henry FRANKLIN enlisted Jan, 1864, at Tipton, was claimed as a former slave held by Ira C. DARBY, of Howard County, who had owned him since birth.
Samuel Cole of Cooper County, filed for compensation for his former slave, Harrison BATES, who was born in 1843.
Bennett C. CLARK of Cooper County, filed for compensation for a slave he had purchased from Thomas RUSSELL in 1843, named Edward "Ned" GATEWELL in Nov, 1866.
Joseph CLARK enlisted in Sep, 1862, at Sedalia. He was claimed by Moses CHAPMAN, administrator for the estate of Jackson PATRICK of Lafayette County. He was previously owned by Christopher MULKEY who sold Joseph in 1857.
William CHANCELLOR made claim for compensation for his former slave, Henry CHANCELLOR, who enlisted Nov, 1863, at Boonville, stating his wife, Jenny, had inherited Henry in 1851, from her father, James BLANKENBAKER.
Phillip BURRUS who enlisted Jan, 1864, at Tipton, was claimed by Thomas P. BURRUS of Howard County, who stated he had purchased the slave on Mar 1, 1855, from Thomas PASCHAL.
Jesse BROWN, of Clinton County, claimed he had purchased Simon BROWN on July 5, 1862, from James T. HUGHES of Holt County. Simon enlisted Feb, 1864, at Plattsburg.
Pink D. BOOKER, of Saline County, filed for compensation on Step BLAND, who he claimed to have held from 1842, when Step was born, to the outbreak of the war.
Lewis TURNER who enlisted in Jan, 1864, at Carrollton, had been held as a slave by Lewis

TRUNNEL, of Lafayette County, who sold TURNER to George W. BAKER in 1862. BAKER also filed for compensation for George BELL, who was bought from John N. CARTER in the same year.

John H. PEACOCK of Lafayette County, filed for compensation for two slaves in Dec, 1866. The slaves, Edmond MASON, alias Anton MASON, enlisted Aug, 1864, at Lexington, and Archer JOHNSTON, about 21 or 22 years of age when he was purchased from Stephen JOHNSTON in Oct, 1854.

John FRANKLIN, son of Hanah, was born in Stafford County, Virginia, enlisted in 1863, at Little Rock, Arkansas according to a claim for compensation filed by Lucretia C. PEYTON of Cooper County.

Miller PRICE was claimed by James D. PRICE, of Chariton County, who's wife inherited Milton from her uncle in Prince Edward County, Virginia.

Henry JOHNSON, enlisted Mar, 1864. He and his mother, Lavinda, were both held by Zachariah GRAVES before the war, and were later claimed by Wm. D. McHATTON, and William S. DRUMMOND, executors of the estate Malinda D. GRAVES.

William NEALE of Lafayette county, claimed compensation for George PATTON, son of Sally, owned since birth by the claimant, and Volney, inherited in 1850 from the estate of George NEALE, formerly of Wood County, Virginia.

Lewis HILL, alias Lewis JAY, and his mother, Dorcas, were both claimed by Harriett C. JAY, of Lafayette County.

Benjamin LAWLESS of Pettis County, filed for compensation for George, who enlisted in 1863, at Sedalia, and Lewis. George had previously been owned by David N. JONES.

Reuben SWOPE, enlisted in 1864, at Tipton. He had been inherited while still a child, form the estate of Giles EDWARD of Virginia, by Samuel S. SWOPE, of Howard County, who filed for compensation.

George C. FLETCHER, of Lafayette County, filed for compensation for Frank FLETCHER, alias Frank CONNER, son of Rachel, in Dec, 1866.

Anderson JONES who enlisted Oct, 1864, was owned from birth by Walter C. DRAKE, of Audrain County, who also claimed Sidney DRAKE, who enlisted at the same time. Sidney had been inherited by the claimant form his mother's estate in Jassamine County, Kentucky.

Hector A. CHINN of Lafayette County, filed a claim for a slave he purchased from William G. McCAUSLAND on Apr 15, 1862. The former slave, Reuben HERIFORD, enlisted Jan, 1864, at Glasgow.

Samuel DOXEY enlisted Jan, 1864, at Marshall. He was claimed by John DOXEY, who had inherited him in 1849, from John DOXEY, Sr..

Robert E. DAVIS of Marion County, filed for compensation for a slave he purchased from Charles M. DAVIS in 1859. The slave, Anthony DORSEY, enlisted in Pope's Division.

Sarah S. CORDER, administrator of John CORDER, Jr., dec'd., filed a compensation claim for Daniel PRICE, alias Daniel CORDER, who had been purchased from Nathaniel PRICE in 1856, Jack RECTOR, purchased from Mrs. MUNDY of Rappahannock County, Virginia in 1840, and Strother WARD, who was inherited from the claimant's father-in-law who died in Rappahannock County in 1849.

Henry LEWIS who enlisted Feb, 1864, at Carrollton, was later claimed by Martha A. BARKER, who had purchased him from Robert H. COURTZ, trustee for Mr. PATTERSON of St. Louis, in 1842.

Robert who enlisted at the age of 18, at Tipton, in 1864, had originally been held by Mr. DEXARD of Cooper County. A compensation claim was filed by George ANDERSON of Pettis County, administrator for the estate of S. B. SCOTTS.

Forest MAUPIN enlisted Dec, 1863, at the age of 21, at Brunswick. John M. DAVIS had purchased him from John M. and Jane E. (DAVIS) DUNCAN of Chariton County, on Aug 8, 1850.

Reese WYNN, age 17, enlisted Jan 4, 1864. A compensation claim was filed by James WYNN of

Livingston County, who had owned Reese from birth, as his parents', Floyd and Hetty, and sister, Ann, were slaves on James Wynn's farm.

Sanders TOWNSEND of Cooper County, filed a compensation claim for two former slaves, Stephen, son of Phillis, who was owned by the claimant from birth, and Lewis, who was 15 years old when he was purchased from Uriah BAILEY, of Howard County, in July of 1823.

Fleming STRADFORD, age 17 when he enlisted in Feb, 1864, at Sedalia, had been inherited from the estate of Powhatan WOOLDRIDGE, by his daughter, E. M. WOOLDRIDGE, of Pettis County, who filed for compensation Jan, 1867.

Mickey ANDERSON, born in 1842, and Benjamin TYLER, born in 1846, both enlisted in Mar, 1864, at Tipton. Both were former slaves of James QUARLES of Cooper County.

John RAMSY of Livingston County, claimed compensation for his former slave, Thomas JASPER, who enlisted in 1863, at St. Joseph.

Samuel CREEL enlisted Feb, 1864, at Lexington. He and his mother, Eliza, had been slaves of Richard H. CREEL, dec'd., of Lafayette County.

Charles W. FLEETWOOD, administrator for the estate of William FLEETWOOD, Sr., dec'd., filed a compensation claim for two slaves. These were: George FLEETWOOD, age 30, born Burtee County, North Carolina, who enlisted Dec 21, 1863, and Henry FLEETWOOD, age 35, born in Kentucky, and purchased from the estate of Abram LOCK, on Jan 1, 1847, who enlisted on the same day as George.

Robert WILLIAMS and Samuel WILLIAMS both enlisted on Jan 1, 1864, at Des Moines, Iowa, with the 63rd U. S. C. T. Inf., and Gilbert LANDERS, who enlisted on the same date with the 65th U. S. C. T. Inf., were all claimed by Thomas L. WILLIAMS, of Chariton County, who had received them as a gift from John M. WILLIAMS, of Amherst County, Virginia, in 1858. Thomas WILLIAMS returned to Virginia in Dec, 1866, from where he filed his claim for compensation in Jan, 1867.

Francis HAYES, alias Jarvis HAYES, and Daniel CARNEY enlisted Jan 2, 1864, in Co. K, and George WALLACE who enlisted in Co. D, on Jan 16, 1864, were all members of the 65th U. S. C. T.. These men were claimed by Daniel HAYES in a claim for compensation filed in Jan, 1867.

John SCOTT, age 26, born in Boone County, Kentucky, enlisted on Jan 5, 164. He had been purchased by Samuel JOHNSON, who filed for compensation from Chariton County from a sheriff's sale of property owned by William G. WILLIS.

James PAP of Chariton County, filed for compensation of his slave, Pap, who enlisted on July 4, 1864.

John CAMPBELL of Layfayette County, filed a claim for compensation of Jim, who he had purchased on Oct 16, 1850, when Jim was about 10 years old. Jim had originally been owned by William EARLY.

Stephen D. SHORES filed a claim for compensation for two of his slaves, Jefferson SHORES, and James SHORES, who both enlisted in Co. D, 67th U. S. C. T., on Feb, 1867.

James GLASCOCK, executor of the estate of Noah GLASCOCK, dec'd., of Ralls County, filed for compensation for five slaves. They were: Marshall THOMAS, age 16 when he enlisted in Sep, 1863, at Hannibal, born to claimant, Smith and Paul SHELTON, who had been owned by the claimant's wife, James MADISON, purchased in 1858, from Rosabella MADISON, and Washington, born in 1836.

Bemis BROWN filed for compensation for his slaves who had joined the service in Feb, 1867. The former slaves were listed as Simon, age 40; Horace, age 34; Stephen, age 23; Morgan, age 25; Jess, age 30; Martin, age 30; Dick, age 35; and Charles, age 40.

Mary C. GEORGE filed for compensation for a slave in Feb, 1867, known as Edgar GARDINER, alias Edgar GORDON, alias, Edgar GEORGE, alias, Edgar RED, alias Edgar RATCLIFFE.

Mary A. GIVENS of Chariton County, filed for compensation in Feb, 1867, for one slave,

Nelson GIVENS.

William G. W. CURRIN, of Grundy County, filed a claim for his former slave, Silas, in Feb, 1867. Silas enlisted in Co. D, 60th U. S. C. T. in Oct, 1864, when he was 37 years of age. He had been owned since birth by CURRIN, who had obtained title to Silas' mother, Rebecca, from CURRIN's father-in-law, Thomas PEERY.

RESOLUTION PASSED BY THE FIRST OF SESSION OF THE TENTH GENERAL ASSEMBLY

A resolution respecting Slavery:
1. Resolved that since the Constitution of the United States has no where deprived the states from regulating domestic slavery, that institution is therefore plainly and expressly left to the regulation and control of their domestic policy and forms one among the most important features of their reserved rights.
2. Resolved that the interference with such institutions, on the part of the citizens of other portions of the Union where it does not exist, is in direct contravention of the United States and the solemn compact subsisting between the members of this confederacy, derogatory from the dignity of the slave holding States, grossly insulting to their sovereignty and ultimately tending to destroy the union, peace and happiness of these confederated States.
3. Resolved that we approve the course of our Representatives in the Congress of the United States, for their able and manly defence of the domestic institutions of the Southern and Southwestern States, and for their uncompromising opposition to the wanton encroachments now attempting to be made upon them.
4. Resolved that we view the active agents in this country in their nefarious schemes to subvert the fundamental principles of this government, in no other light than as the mere tools of a set on arch machinators, who envy the prosperity of these confedrated States, and desire to effect by management, what they can not do through force of arms - the destruction of our domestic peace and the reign of equal laws.
5. Resolved that we can see in these numerous acts of aggression and interference with the domestic institutions of the southern and southwestern States, nothing but wanton invasion of their rights, and contemptuous insult to their dignity as sovereign and inde-

pendent States; and that they have no other safe alternative left them but to adopt some efficient policy by which their domestic institutions may be protected and their peace, happiness and prosperity secured.

6. Resolved that copies of this preamble and these resolutions be printed, and that the Governor be requested to transmit a copy of them to the governor of each of the States of this Union, and one to each of the members in the Congress of the United States. Approved, Feb 12, 1839.